CRITICAL PRAISE FOR THE FUTUI

"Virginia Postrel is stirring it up...arousing praise and criticism across the country."
—Arthur Hirsch, *The Baltimore Sun*

"Postrel's aim is to provide a defense of adventurous, optimistic attitudes to social and technological change. That she has done very admirably, with passion and vigor."
—John Derbyshire, *National Review*

"The strength of *The Future and Its Enemies* lies in the author's passionate belief in the inherent virtue in creativity, innovation, and competition."
—Anthony Day, *Los Angeles Times*

"It is a fervent partisan statement, an unabashedly dynamist work. Postrel's conviction displays itself not just in the content of the book, but in the style she has developed to explain it. Postrel writes like a dynamo."
—James W. Ceaser, *The Weekly Standard*

"In industrial America, centralized bureaucracies believed they could identify and impose what 1910's management expert F. W. Taylor called 'the one best way.' In post-industrial America, Virginia Postrel argues in her insightful book *The Future and Its Enemies*, it makes better sense to set out simple rules, allow flexibility and accountability."
—Michael Barone, *U.S. News & World Report*

"If there's a better book published during the past few years, I don't know of it. With this book, Virginia Postrel takes her place along side Rose Wilder Lane, Isabel Paterson, and Ayn Rand as the 20th century's greatest heroines of liberty... Like the philosophy she advocates, her book is dynamic."
—Don Boudreaux, President of the Foundation for Economic Education

"Her message is a bracing one."
—David Boldt, *The Philadelphia Inquirer*

"Read this superb book."
—George C. Leef, *The Detroit News*

"A thought-provoking look at an important subject."
—*Library Journal*

"Virginia Postrel smashes conventional political boundaries in this libertarian manifesto...*The Future and Its Enemies* is at once intellectually sweeping and reader-friendly; it has the potential to join a pantheon of books about freedom that include works by Friedrich Hayek and Milton Friedman."
—John J. Miller, Amazon.com

"Virginia Postrel, the brilliant editor of *Reason* magazine... does an excellent job of cutting through some of the most troublesome aspects of liberal-conservative conflict."

—Joseph J. Jacobs, *Los Angeles Daily News*

"Postrel provides some important food for thought for those seeking to encourage creativity and innovation in their workplace."

—Teresa McUsic, *The San Diego-Union Tribune*

"A terrific book...Keep your eyes and Amazon.com account open for *The Future and Its Enemies.*"

—Richard Karlgaard, *Forbes*

"Virginia Postrel has launched a national debate over how to face the next millenium."

—Hank Hoffman, *New Haven Advocate*

"Postrel's book breaks ground with a piercing analysis...[she] offers an impassioned case for dynamism."

—Steven Greenhut, *The Orange County Register*

"Thought provoking... Postrel's arguments have special relevance in dynamic Silicon Valley, a garden of capitalist creativity and creative destruction."

—Joanne Jacobs, *San Jose Mercury News*

"Challenging and entertaining... Postrel... lyrically invok[es] her vision."

—Phil Leggiere, *Upside*

"Astute"

—Mark Williams, *The Red Herring Magazine*

"Provocative... [a] defense of the free society, the free market, and even the free person."

—*Kirkus Reviews*

"This is Postrel's dynamist manifesto...An offbeat treatise for serious politicos."

—Gilbert Taylor, *Booklist*

"Postrel [is] the talented and provocative editor of *Reason* magazine."

—*Fast Company*

"A reasoned and passionate argument."

—Jeffrey L. Seglin, *Inc.*

"Virginia Postrel [is] one of America's true original thinkers."

—Larry Cohen, *Hartford Courant*

"There's a lot of provocative material in Postrel's book."

—David Futrelle, *Newsday*

"A powerful new book that will define the next decade as George Gilder's *Wealth and Poverty* defined the 1980s."

—Grover Norquist, *SpinTech*

"An excellent book...clearly written, well argued, and broadly sourced."

—Neal Lipschutz, *BookPage*

"I highly recommend {*The Future and Its Enemies*}....Postrel explains much of today's conflict in the evolution of culture—The Culture War—with a new dichotomy....Stasists want us to decide centrally....Dynamists want a thousand flowers to bloom and freedom to choose. The Internet is, I gather, for dynamists , like me."

—Bob Metcalfe, *Infoworld*

"Virginia Postrel's book is going to be widely read and then widely discussed and debated. I know I bought a copy for my CEO.'

—Fred Nickols, *Journal of Management Consulting*

"Read this wonderful book! Like no other author of social and political commentary, Virginia Postrel celebrates the texture of modern life and shows us how to love the unknowable future."

—James K. Glassman, columnist for *The Washington Post*

"What to say? Magisterial! Encompassing! Crystal clear, plain English! The best damn nonfiction I've read in years! Uncategorizable...which is the point. I have been liberated by this book, and my hands literally shook as I read— word for word—every page! Few will not be offended by something Ms. Postrel has to say...to which I say, 'Hurrah!'"

—Tom Peters, co-author of *In Search of Excellence*

"In this bold and compelling book, Virginia Postrel uses a breathtaking range of examples, from music to software to hairstyling, to argue that progress comes not from a master plan but from courage, experiment...and even playfulness. She makes you look again at what you thought you already knew."

—Esther Dyson, Chairman of EDventure Holdings and author of *Release 2.0*

"Virginia Postrel has a radically old-fashioned view of the future. She believes in progress. She thinks that the world we are building, you and I, is a decidedly messy place, that nonetheless is turning out pretty nice. Go ahead. Imagine that."

—Joel Garreau, author of *Edge City: Life on the New Frontier* and *The Nine Nations of North America*

THE
FUTURE
AND
ITS ENEMIES

The Growing Conflict over
Creativity, Enterprise, and Progress

Virginia Postrel

A TOUCHSTONE BOOK
PUBLISHED BY SIMON & SCHUSTER

To Steven

TOUCHSTONE
Rockefeller Center
1230 Avenue of the Americas
New York, NY 10020

First Touchstone Edition 1999

TOUCHSTONE and colophon are trademarks of Simon & Schuster Inc.

Manufactured in the United States of America

10 9 8 7 6 5

Library of Congress Cataloging-in-publication Data

Postrel, Virginia I.
The Future and its enemies : the growing conflict over creativity,
enterprise, and progress / Virginia Postrel
p. cm.
Includes bibliographical references and index.
1. Social prediction. 2 Quality of life—Forecasting.
3. Technological forecasting. 4. Creative ability. I. Title.
HN25.P67 1998
303.49—dc21   98-34090

ISBN 978-0-684-86269-9

CONTENTS

Acknowledgments

This book could not have been completed without the enormous dedication, talent, and support of the *Reason* editorial staff, who made it possible for a hands-on magazine editor to find the time for extended research, thinking, and writing. My undying gratitude goes to my current colleagues, Barb Burch, Chuck Freund, Nick Gillespie, Rick Henderson, Robert Honrado, Michael Lynch, Jacob Sullum, Brian Taylor, and Mary Toledo, and to our former colleagues Ed Carson and Brian Doherty. Thanks also to my boss, Bob Poole; to Lynn Scarlett, Bryan Snyder, and Mike Alissi; and to the trustees of the Reason Foundation.

In developing the ideas in this book, I've benefited greatly from writing for other editors, in particular Jodie Allen and Chuck Freund at *The Washington Post*, who worked with me on the 1990 article that got it all started; Spencer Reiss at *Wired*; and Rich Karlgaard at *Forbes ASAP*.

To track down source materials, I was fortunate to have two energetic research assistants: Leigh Creighton, who applied her determination and near-infinite borrowing privileges to every library on the UCLA campus and who shared her ethnomusicology expertise when her own discipline finally arose; and Nick Schulz, whose pinch-hitting was a lifesaver. Ed Carson, Marc Levin, Jessica Melugin, Lisa Snell, Brian Taylor, and Cosmo Wenman also helped gather materials. Sara Baase, Ron Bailey, Stewart Brand, Chris DeMuth, Richard Epstein, Jim Glassman, Mike Godwin, Rick Henderson, Keating Holland, Mike McMenamin, Mark Miller, Joel Mokyr, Chris Nippert-Eng, John Nye, Charles Oliver, Walter Olson, Jack Pitney, Jonathan Rauch, Lynn Scarlett, and Sam Staley answered questions about references and examples. And Gene Miller went above and beyond the call of duty to ferret out an obscure document from the University of Georgia archives.

ACKNOWLEDGMENTS

Greg Benford, Chris DeMuth, Chuck Freund, Nick Gillespie, Jim Glassman, Steve Hayward, Grant McCracken, Walter Olson, John Nye, Bob Poole, David Post, and Lynn Scarlett read and commented on some or all of the manuscript. Barb Burch, Abe Crystal, Brian Doherty, Jennifer George, and Brian Taylor helped proof the galleys. Early on, Richard Epstein gave me invaluable advice about how to organize and manage the process.

My thanks to my agents, Lynn Chu and Glen Hartley, for believing in my sketchy proposal enough to sell it; to Adam Bellow for buying it; and to my editor, Paul Golob, for seeing the book through to completion and living up to his reputation as a terrific editor.

Finally, my greatest debt is, as always, to Steven Postrel, my beloved partner in life and work, with whom I spent countless hours discussing this book. He was tough, thorough, insightful, and endlessly patient in reading and critiquing the manuscript through what seemed like hundreds of drafts. He also wrote the title.

THE SEARCH
FOR TOMORROW

In May 1998, for the third time in its history, Disneyland opened a revamped Tomorrowland. It didn't just add an attraction or two. It reimagined the future. Gone is the impersonal chrome and steel of the old buildings, along with the Mission to Mars ride, the PeopleMover, and the Circle-Vision theater. In their place is a kinder, gentler tomorrow where the buildings are decorated in lush jewel tones and the gardens are filled with fruit trees and edible plants. Tomorrowland still has spaceships aplenty—the new Rocket Rods ride is the fastest in the park—but it hasn't shut out things that grow.

Nor has it jettisoned the past to make way for the future. Just as the food plants connect human beings with nature, the new attractions connect yesterday and tomorrow. The area's design draws on the long-ago visions of Jules Verne and Leonardo da Vinci, and Tomorrowland has restored some of its own history. Its new restaurant is decorated with posters of 1960s rides, and Disney has rebuilt the classic Buck Rogers–style Moonliner rocket it once dumped as out-of-date.

"What we're saying here is that the future has a place for you in it," says Tony Baxter, a senior vice president at Walt Disney Imagineering and the chief spokesman for the project. People can love technology, Disney is betting, and also want a human-centered world of rich texture, warm colors, and sweet-smelling plants. Rather than prescribing a single ideal, the "one best way" to progress, the park offers a "culture of futures" that celebrates many different visions, both historical and contemporary. The goal, says Baxter, "is to get your dream machine working in your mind, rather than turning you off by creating a clinically sterile future."[1]

The old modernist ideal was indeed too sterile for most tastes. Real people don't want to live in generic high-rise apartments and walk their dogs on treadmills, à la *The Jetsons*. Real people want some connection to the past and to the natural world. And Disneyland is in the business of catering to real people. It can't force customers to embrace its favorite future. All the park can do is propose possible futures and test them against the public's own dreams. When those dreams change, or the present becomes too much like "the future," Tomorrowland has to change too. "It is always right when you do it," says Bruce Gordon, who headed construction of the new Tomorrowland. "The question is, How long will it last?"[2]

To many observers, however, Tomorrowland's most recent adaptations represent not normal evolution but failure and broken promises. These social critics see the revisions as proof that the future is scary, progress a fantasy, and technology suspect. To them, a good future must be static: either the product of detailed, technocratic blueprints or the return to an idealized, stable past. The new Tomorrowland, says popular-culture scholar Norman Klein, is "no longer about planning in the long run, or about social imagineering."[3] To reject planning, in this view, is to reject progress. Writes the cultural critic Tim Appelo:

> A '60s kid could cherish the illusion of evolution as progress, especially if he was watching Tomorrowland's all-robot drama the Carousel of Progress. . . . Now, however, everybody thinks the jig is up for apes like us. . . . The Imagineers know we're scared of the future, and they've booted the scary old-fashioned Tomorrowland machines from their garden. . . . The old Disney dream of erecting a futuristic techno-paradise is dead.

Appelo quotes Judith Adams, the author of a book on the meaning and history of amusement parks, who claims that we have come to see technology as "a killing thing." It is, she says, something used "to destroy your peers, so you can be more successful yourself. You're never caught up with technology. You're never safe."[4] The new Tomorrowland, in this assessment, proves technology is bad. After all, it's always changing.

The idea that to be good the future must be finite and "safe" is a common one. Disneyland itself once promised that sort of carefully controlled future. When the park was new in the late 1950s, many people saw it as a model of perfection not just for amusement parks but for the rest of life. City planning was in its heyday, and observers as varied as Vice President Richard Nixon and science-fiction writer Ray Bradbury praised Disney's meticulously designed world as the way all of society ought to be: a contrast to the spontaneous sprawl of southern California and the untidiness of eastern cities. Bradbury even suggested that Walt Disney run for mayor of Los Angeles, so he could impose his vision on that city.

But Tomorrowland undercut this static ideal. Its revisions in the 1950s and mid-1960s, writes historian John Findlay, "dramatized Disneyland's lack of control over the future. The success of the theme park was predicated on complete mastery of its world, but the future refused to cooperate, and thus it compelled the theme park to make constant adjustments."[5] Even the hypercontrolled world of the park was always changing, for two reasons. First, Disneyland was a competitive business. It could not afford to insist on a "tomorrow" that failed to attract customers, whether because of changing tastes, new inventions, or better rides elsewhere. When Tomorrowland added the Star Tours flight simulator in 1987, for instance, Disney wasn't revising the future. It was conceding the popularity of George Lucas's space opera; *Star Wars* wasn't even a Disney movie.

Second, the park's managers were always learning. Disneyland itself was a technology you could never catch up with. Not just Tomorrowland but all of the park continuously evolved. True, Disneyland started from scratch; the company bulldozed and reshaped every bit of the original landscape. Once established, however, Disneyland took on a life of its own, adapting through trial and error: The Autopia ride, which Walt Disney imagined as a great way for kids to learn the rules of the road, unexpectedly turned into a demolition derby, as wild-eyed children smashed all but six of the original thirty-six cars; the ride was remodeled to keep the miniature cars in their lanes. Another Walt favorite, the live circus, was eliminated after animals kept escaping; llamas stampeded through the streets and once, during a parade, a tiger and a panther smashed through the barrier separating them and began tearing each other apart.

Not every lesson was so dramatic or embarrassing. Over time, the park replaced individual-ride tickets with ticket books and later with all-day, one-fee passes. It added whole new "lands," such as Toontown and New Orleans Square, and updated old ones. Disneyland was dedicated to what Walt Disney called "plussing": continuous improvement through both new ideas and changes to existing attractions. Control freak that he was, Disney loved the revisions the theme park allowed. Its open-endedness appealed to his desire for perfection. "If there's something I don't like at Disneyland, I can correct it," he once said. "I can always change it [here], but not in the films." The great thing about the park was that it "will never be finished. . . . It's alive."[6]

Outside Disneyland's walls, too, the future is alive. Like the present, the future is not a single, uniform state but an ongoing process that reflects the plenitude of human life. There is in fact no single future; "the" future encompasses the many microfutures of individuals and their associations. It includes all the things we learn about ourselves and the world, all the incremental improvements we discover, all our new ideas, and all the new ways we express and recombine them. As a system, the future is natural, out of anyone's control, though it is driven by the artificial: by individual attempts (including Disneyland) to fashion realms of personal control. This open-ended future can't be contained in the vision of a single person or organization. And, as Judith Adams says of technology, it is something we can never be caught up with.

How we feel about the evolving future tells us who we are as individuals and as a civilization: Do we search for *stasis*—a regulated, engineered world? Or do we embrace *dynamism*—a world of constant creation, discovery, and competition? Do we value stability and control, or evolution and learning? Do we declare with Appelo that "we're scared of the future" and join Adams in decrying technology as "a killing thing"? Or do we see technology as an expression of human creativity and the future as inviting? Do we think that progress requires a central blueprint, or do we see it as a decentralized, evolutionary process? Do we consider mistakes permanent disasters, or the correctable by-products of experimentation? Do we crave predictability, or relish surprise? These two poles, stasis and dynamism, increasingly define our political, intellectual, and cultural landscape. The central question of our time is what to do about the future. And that question creates a deep divide.

"I think there's a personality that goes with this kind of thing," says economist Brian Arthur about the emerging science of complexity, which studies dynamic systems. "It's people who like process and pattern, as opposed to people who are comfortable with stasis. . . . I know that every time in my life that I've run across simple rules giving rise to emergent, complex messiness, I've just said, 'Ah', isn't that lovely!' And I think that sometimes, when other people run across it, they recoil."[7]

The future we face at the dawn of the twenty-first century is, like all futures left to themselves, "emergent, complex messiness." Its "messiness" lies not in disorder, but in an order that is unpredictable, spontaneous, and ever shifting, a pattern created by millions of uncoordinated, independent decisions. That pattern contains not just a few high-tech gizmos, but all the variegated aspects of life. As people create and sell products or services, adopt new fashions of speech or dress, form families and choose home towns, make medical decisions and seek spiritual insights, investigate the universe and invent new forms of art, these actions shape a future no one can see, a future that is dynamic and inherently unstable.

That instability, or our awareness of it, is heightened by the fluidity of contemporary life: by the ease with which ideas and messages, goods and people, cross borders; by technologies that seek to surpass the quickness of the human mind and overcome the constraints of the human body; by the "universal solvents" of commerce and popular culture;[8] by the dissolution or reformation of established institutions, particularly large corporations, and the rise of new ones; by the synthesis of East and West, of ancient and modern—by the combination and recombination of seemingly every artifact of human culture. Ours is a magnificently creative era. But that creativity produces change, and that change attracts enemies, philosophical as well as self-interested.

With some exceptions, the enemies of the future aim their attacks not at creativity itself but at the dynamic processes through which it is carried. In our post–Cold War era, for instance, free markets are recognized as powerful forces for social, cultural, and technological change—liberating in the eyes of some, threatening to others. The same is true for markets in ideas: for free speech and worldwide communication; for what John Stuart Mill called "experiments in living"; for scientific research, artistic expression, and technological innovation. All of these processes are shaping an unknown, and unknowable, future. Some people look at such diverse, decentralized, choice-driven systems and rejoice, even when they don't like particular choices. Others recoil. In pursuit of stability and control, they seek to eliminate or curb these unruly, too-creative forces.

Stasists and dynamists are thus divided not just by simple, short-term policy issues but by fundamental disagreements about the way the world works. They clash over the nature of progress and over its desirability: Does it require a plan to reach a specified goal? Or is it an unbounded process of exploration and discovery? Does the quest for improvement express destructive, nihilistic discontent, or the highest human qualities? Does progress depend on puritanical repression or a playful spirit?

Stasists and dynamists disagree about the limits and use of knowledge. Stasists demand that knowledge be articulated and easily shared. Dynamists, by contrast, appreciate dispersed, often tacit knowledge. They recognize the limits of human minds even as they celebrate learning.

Those conflicts lead to very different beliefs about good institutions and rules: Stasists seek specifics to govern each new situation and keep things under control. Dynamists want to limit universal rule making to broadly applicable and rarely changed principles, within which people can create and test countless combinations. Stasists want their detailed rules to apply to everyone; dynamists prefer competing, nested rule sets. (Disneyland's rules may be good for the park, but that doesn't make them the right rules for everyone else.) Such disagreements have political ramifications that go much deeper than the short-term business of campaigns and legislation. They affect our governing assumptions about how political, economic, social, intellectual, and cultural systems work; what those systems should value; and what they mean.

These are not the comfortable old Cold War divisions of hawks and doves, egalitarians and individualists, left and right. Nor are they the one-dimensional labels of technophile and technophobe, optimist and pessimist, or libertarian and statist that pundits sometimes grab to replace the old categories. They contain elements of those simpler classifications, but they are much richer, encompassing more aspects of life—more aspects of the emergent, complex future.

This book examines the clash between stasis and dynamism and explores those contrasting views. It starts by recognizing that the distinction between dynamism and stasis is a real and important one that explains much that otherwise appears puzzling in our intellectual and political life. Beyond that recognition, it explores what dynamism is and how it works: What are the processes through which human creativity produces progress, prosperity, happiness, and freedom? What are the characteristics of a dynamic civilization, and how do they differ from the ways in which we usually hear our world described?

An unabashedly dynamist work, *The Future and Its Enemies* devotes most of its pages to limning the dynamic vision, which has rarely been articulated in full. It does not pretend to invent that vision from scratch or claim to discover new truths for a new age. In true dynamist fashion, it builds on the knowledge and experience of the past to better understand how dynamic systems work in general—and how, therefore, they work in our own particular time, place, and circumstances. It unites the work of scholars from many different fields and relates them to the textures of life in an evolving world, past, present, and future.

As a result, the book's rhetorical choices break the conventions of serious nonfiction: Why talk about political philosophy and hairstyling, economics and computer games, environmental policy and contact lenses, legal theory and doughnut shops, bioethics and Post-it notes in the same work? Why mix the high and the low, the masculine and the feminine, the exalted and the mundane, the abstract and the concrete? Why not stick to a single, static genre? It would make the book so much easier to sell.

The question, of course, answers itself. Static visions depend on hiding the connections between disparate aspects of life. My purpose is to expose them. Stasists gain credibility by treating dynamism as a shallow fad. My aim is to reveal its rich heritage. Stasists thrive by issuing prescriptions that ignore the details of life, believing that details are unimportant, the stuff of anonymous specialists, and can safely be ignored. My goal is to encourage respect for those details, even when they can only be evoked in passing. Piling up widely divergent examples, reflecting a tiny sample of the plenitude of life, is one way to do that.

Stasist social criticism—which is to say essentially all current social criticism—brings up the specifics of life only to sneer at or bash them. Critics assume that readers will share their attitudes and will see contemporary life as a problem demanding immediate action by the powerful and wise. This relentlessly hostile view of how we live, and how we may come to live, is distorted and dangerous. It overvalues the tastes of an articulate elite, compares the real world of trade-offs to fantasies of utopia, omits important details and connections, and confuses temporary growing pains with permanent catastrophes. It demoralizes and devalues the creative minds on whom our future depends. And it encourages the coercive use of political power to wipe out choice, forbid experimentation, short-circuit feedback, and trammel progress.

Along the way, therefore, *The Future and Its Enemies* tries to capture some of the wonders we take for granted. It celebrates the complexities and surprises of the contemporary world, and of the world to come. I hope that instinctive dynamists will see themselves in that world, and will work to protect the systems that make it possible. The evolving future is for humans, just as Tony Baxter says. But sometimes we need a reminder that it's not confined to Disneyland.

A word about terminology: *Stasis* and *dynamism* are ordinary words, and I use them in a fairly ordinary way, to represent stable or evolving states. The only variation from the conventional meaning is that I use *dynamism* more precisely, meaning not just change but evolution through variation, feedback, and adaptation. Stasis and dynamism may be actual or envisioned states; their qualities, in either case, are described as *static* or *dynamic*. The coined words *stasist* and *dynamist*—which, like *feminist* or *socialist,* may be either nouns or adjectives—refer to intellectual positions and the people who hold them. A dynamist is one who supports dynamism.

For readers who would like more information about the ideas in this book, I have established a Web site at www.dynamist.com.

THE FUTURE
AND
ITS ENEMIES

CHAPTER ONE

THE ONE BEST WAY

One of the most common rituals in American political life is the television debate between right and left. Producers round up conservative and liberal representatives and set them to arguing with each other: about the federal budget, campaign finance, gun control, or whatever other issue is hot that particular day. Since the purpose is as much to entertain as to inform, and since many shows like to feature politicians, these debates tend to be predictable. They rehash familiar arguments, repeat familiar sound bites, and confirm traditional views of the political landscape.

Nowhere is the ritual more established than on CNN's *Crossfire*. The hosts and their guests are stuffed into familiar boxes—even positioned on the right or left of the TV screen according to political convention—and are expected to behave predictably.

Which is why the first *Crossfire* of 1995 was so remarkable.

For starters, the subject was an unusual one for a Washington show: the future. Not the future of the new Republican-led Congress or of welfare reform or of Bill Clinton's political career, but the future in general. The guests were Jeremy Rifkin, the well-known antitechnology activist, and Ed Cornish, the president of the World Future Society. Rifkin sat on the left, aligned with Michael Kinsley; Cornish on the right, aligned with Pat Buchanan.

Or at least that was how the producers planned it. That was how conventional politics prescribed it. Rifkin, the former antiwar protester and darling of environmentalists, clearly belongs to the left. Cornish, a technophile, becomes a right-winger by default. And hosts Kinsley and Buchanan were, of course, hired for their political positions.

But as soon as the discussion began, the entire format broke down.

1

Buchanan and Rifkin turned out to be soulmates. Rifkin answered Buchanan's opening question with a fearful description of "this new global high-tech economy" as a cruel destroyer of jobs. "You sound like a Pat Buchanan column," replied his interrogator. "I agree."

Both men were deeply pessimistic about the future, upset about changes in the world of work, and desperate to find government policies to restore the good old days. Both spoke resentfully of the "knowledge sector." Neither had anything good to say about new technologies. Neither could imagine how ordinary people could possibly cope with economic changes. "There are many, many Americans who are not equipped to do this kind of work. They're the ones losing their jobs," said Buchanan. Responded Rifkin: "Let me say I find myself in a position of agreeing with Pat once again, which gives me alarm, but I really do agree with you on this one."[1]

It was surely a bad day for the *Crossfire* bookers. They had managed to call the show's entire premise into question. How could such a thing happen? How could *Crossfire* become a love-in between Jeremy Rifkin and Pat Buchanan?

The problem lay not in the bookers' Rolodexes but in the conventional categories. Like a geographical territory, our political, cultural, and intellectual landscape can be divided many different ways. The features may be fairly stable, but the boundary lines change. A defining question in one era—whether to nationalize the railroads, give women the vote, outlaw racial segregation, or abolish the draft—may be settled, and therefore meaningless, in another. Or questions may be important to individuals without creating meaningful political divisions: Nowadays, "conservatives" may support careers for women, and "liberals" may back the death penalty; not since Walter Mondale's disastrous presidential bid have Democrats made raising taxes a defining "liberal" position. Similarly, the economic issues that have divided the American political landscape matter little in Israel, where defense and foreign policy dominate the debate.

Once upon a time, before the Berlin Wall came down, Buchanan and Rifkin did indeed belong on opposite sides of the *Crossfire* table. Whatever agreements they might have had about the evils of corporate restructuring, the dangers of new technologies, or the rigidity of job skills paled in comparison to their fundamental disagreements about how to deal with the Soviet Union. That defining issue has now vanished, and others have faded. Government spending is no longer seen, even by most liberals who support it, as a simple solution to the problems of poverty. Nor do conservatives all agree that expansive military spending and vigorous engagement abroad are the best approach to American defense. There are plenty of practical policy differences over such issues, but they no longer define clear ideological camps. People can change their minds without changing their political identities.

Meanwhile, seemingly strange alliances have popped up on subjects no one paid much attention to until recently. Treaties to loosen trade restrictions, once uncontroversial beyond a few protection-seeking industries, draw fierce opposition from a left-right coalition that includes both Rifkin and Buchanan. Indeed, the subtitle of Buchanan's latest book is *How American Sovereignty and Social Justice Are Being Sacrificed to the Gods of the Global Economy,* a bid to woo both "conservatives" (worried about "sovereignty") and "liberals" (concerned about "social justice").[2] In its lobbying efforts, the antitrade alliance emphasizes its apparent breadth; it has described itself as "a strikingly broad cross-section" and the "broadest range of [the] American political spectrum ever to jointly petition a president." In 1994, for example, a motley collection of activists—including not only Buchanan and Rifkin but consumerist Ralph Nader and New Right organizer Paul Weyrich, feminist Gloria Steinem and antifeminist Phyllis Schlafly—all signed a letter opposing the General Agreement on Tariffs and Trade.[3]

Immigration attracts similar left-right opposition. In 1998, many leftists were shocked when the Sierra Club held a membership vote on whether to take an official stance supporting "an end to U.S. population growth . . . through reduction in net immigration," essentially an immigration moratorium. "Zealots Target Sierra Club," read a headline in the left-leaning *L.A. Weekly.* "The specter of xenophobic anti-immigrant sentiment now threatens to swallow the Green movement whole," said the article.[4] (The measure was defeated, 60 percent to 40 percent.) The movement to drastically curtail U.S. legal immigration levels has vocal conservative supporters, including Buchanan, former *National Review* senior editor Peter Brimelow, and Reagan administration immigration commissioner Alan Nelson. But the Sierra Club measure was supported by such leading environmentalists as Worldwatch Institute head Lester Brown, Earth Day founder Gaylord Nelson, former Interior Secretary Stewart Udall, and Earth First! founder

Dave Foreman. The foremost anti-immigration group, the Federation for American Immigration Reform, was founded by population-control advocates from the green movement. And many smaller anti-immigration groups, such as the Carrying Capacity Network, draw almost entirely from the environmentalist left.[5]

We have also seen increasing numbers of "conservatives" and "liberals" uniting in opposition to new technologies. Thus Neil Postman, the left-wing media and technology critic, writes in the neoconservative magazine *First Things* that "our technological ingenuity transformed information into a form of garbage, and ourselves into garbage collectors. . . . Information is now a commodity that is bought and sold."[6] To oppose genetic patents, Rifkin, in 1995, rallied nearly two hundred religious leaders, prominently including representatives of the conservative Southern Baptist Convention.[7] Self-styled neo-Luddite Kirkpatrick Sale, a well-known environmentalist, concludes antitechnology speeches by smashing computers with a sledgehammer;[8] the cover of the conservative *Weekly Standard* magazine features a sledgehammer crashing into a computer screen, with the headline "Smash the Internet."[9]

Economic and cultural dynamism get similar treatment. The *Standard* praises cultural critic Tom Frank, an anticommerce leftist, for promoting the idea that "both free speech and a free market did much to democratize values and attitudes that previous generations would have largely dismissed as pernicious or infantile."[10] Attacking management guru Tom Peters for his emphasis on change, flexibility, and innovation, Frank himself waxes conservative. He denounces markets for disrupting the social order: "Capitalism is no longer said [by management thinkers] to be a matter of enforcing order, but of destroying it. This new commercial ethos, not a few movies and rap albums, is the root cause of the unease many Americans feel about the culture around them."[11] Former Clinton aide William Galston praises Republican Bill Bennett for his attacks on market-driven popular culture: "The invisible hand," says Galston, "no more reliably produces a sound cultural environment than it does a sound natural environment."[12]

What all these left-right alliances have in common is a sense of anguish over the open-ended future: a future that no Galston, Bennett, Frank, or Buchanan can control or predict, a future too diverse and fluid for critics to comprehend. Their anguish is not always coherent, nor is it expected to be. If stasist criticisms are impossibly vague, they seem all the more profound. What matters is the general message: The world has gone terribly wrong, and someone needs to take control and make things right.

"The task of finding true meaning in a hyper-technologized and increasingly pointless society becomes ever more difficult. A gnawing feeling of hopelessness grows from the sense that living as a hero, or heroine, in one's own life is no longer possible," writes Gary Chapman, the former executive director of Computer Professionals for Social Responsibility and now a technology critic. "The all-pervasive 'system' we've created closes off both the value of ordinary virtue and any escape routes. . . . How do we smash this particular system and build an alternative we can be proud of?"[13]

A mere three decades ago, "the system" looked very different. Technology, its critics believed, was oppressive; even its supporters said it demanded predictability and order. Back then, what young leftists like Chapman wanted to smash was not the dynamic, out-of-control future but the static, hypercontrolled present. Technocracy and repression, not dynamism and creativity, were the enemy embodied in technology. Conventional wisdom had declared the market an obsolete myth, too fragmented and unpredictable to manage or produce advanced technology. Bigness, stability, and planning ruled the imagination of sophisticates.

To see how dramatically attitudes have changed, consider the following 1974 news report on the Nixon administration's plans to deal with energy shortages:

> What happens when spring's heavy driving begins depends on when word can be passed to U.S. refineries to start cutting back on production of heating oil and increasing output of gasoline. . . . That decision, which could come at any time, is up to Federal Energy Office chief William E. Simon. One of his aides says:
>
> "It's absolutely critical. If we decide to trigger the switch to gasoline and a long cold wave hits, heating-oil stocks might not last to spring. Heaven help us if we're wrong."
>
> Meanwhile Simon and his staff are putting final touches on the Administration's gasoline-rationing plan. . . .

5

The number of gallons a driver would be allotted is to depend on where he lives. Those in rural areas, or in urban communities of less than 100,000 people, would get the most. Drivers in large cities with good mass transit would get the least.

Present estimates by the Federal Energy Office show a gasoline shortage of 1.2 million barrels a day, or about 20 per cent below normal demand. At that rate, officials say the maximum ration per driver would be 41 gallons a month. Residents of cities with fair mass-transit facilities would get 37 gallons, while those in areas with good mass transit would get 33 gallons.[14]

As a description of the U.S. government at work—under a Republican administration, no less—this perfectly routine news story reads like science fiction. Only a quarter-century ago, however, it was an obvious truth that central bureaucrats could efficiently decide when refineries should switch from heating oil to gasoline and could wisely allocate gasoline supplies, carefully differentiating between drivers who needed thirty-seven gallons a month and those who required forty-one. Such technocratic manipulations were not limited to Soviet-style planning.

"The enemies of the market are . . . not the socialists," wrote the economist John Kenneth Galbraith in his influential 1967 book, *The New Industrial State.* "It is advanced technology and the specialization of men and process that this requires and the resulting commitment of time and capital. These make the market work badly when the need is for greatly enhanced reliability—when planning is essential." We lived, critics and supporters agreed, in what Galbraith called "the techno-structure," an oligopolistic industrial state where the future was carefully planned in advance, either through government or private bureaucracy. "With the rise of the modern corporation," wrote Galbraith, "the emergence of the organization required by modern technology and planning and the divorce of the owner of the capital from control of the enterprise, the entrepreneur no longer exists as an individual person in the mature industrial enterprise."[15]

In the era of Bill Gates, Ted Turner, and Andy Grove, no one much believes that any more. The efficient capital markets and entrepreneurship that Galbraith consigned to the crazed imagination of free-market ideologues are all too real and disruptive. Contrary to his confident claims, technology generates change, not predictability, and corporations cherish flexibility, leanness, and just-in-time management. The small and adaptable flourish. And the quest for freedom and authenticity that once inspired many of Chapman's friends on the left has mutated into the cultural—and business—dynamism that today disconcerts stasists from Pat Buchanan and Bill Bennett to Jeremy Rifkin and Tom Frank.

Our new awareness of how dynamic the world really is has united two types of stasists who would have once been bitter enemies: *reactionaries,* whose central value is stability, and *technocrats,* whose central value is control.[16] Reactionaries seek to reverse change, restoring the literal or imagined past and holding it in place. A few decades ago, they aimed their criticism at Galbraithean technocracy. Today they attack dynamism, often in alliance with their former adversaries. Technocrats, for their part, promise to manage change, centrally directing "progress" according to a predictable plan. (That plan may be informed by reactionary values, making the categories somewhat blurry; although they are more technocrats than true reactionaries, Bennett and Galston inhabit the border regions.) Despite their shared devotion to stasis, reactionaries and technocrats are sufficiently distinct that it makes sense to examine each category separately.

Buchanan expresses reactionary ideas when he yearns for "the kind of social stability, rootedness . . . we all used to know," the world in which his father lived in the same place and worked at the same job his whole life. International trade, he warns, disrupts that stability and should be controlled.[17] In his book *The Way,* the influential British green Edward Goldsmith similarly emphasizes stability, imagining a quiet and peaceful past in contrast to dynamic, progress-driven modernity: "It is the failure of modern man to observe the constraints necessary for maintaining the integrity and stability of the various social and ecological systems of which he is a part that is giving rise to their disintegration and destabilization, of which the increased incidence of discontinuities such as wars, massacres, droughts, floods, famines, epidemics and climatic change are but the symptoms."[18]

On a more violent note, the Unabomber echoes countless environmentalist tracts: "For primitive societies the natural world (which usually changes only slowly) provided a stable framework and therefore a sense of security. In the modern world it is human society that dominates nature rather than the other way around, and modern society changes very rapidly owing to technological change. Thus there is no stable framework. . . . The technophiles are taking us all on an utterly reckless ride into the unknown."[19]

Technocrats, by contrast, are less likely to emphasize the problem of social instability when they criticize the unruly vitality of contemporary life. They do not celebrate the primitive or traditional. Rather, they worry about the government's inability to control dynamism. Their nostalgia is for the era of Galbraithean certainties. In a 1997 essay for *Foreign Affairs*, the historian Arthur Schlesinger, Jr., condemns the "onrush of capitalism" for its "disruptive consequences." While the economist Joseph Schumpeter depicted the "creative destruction" of the market as a strength, emphasizing its creativity, Schlesinger sees it as a horror. He warns of dire results from the dynamism of global trade and new technologies:

> The computer turns the untrammeled market into a global juggernaut crashing across frontiers, enfeebling national powers of taxation and regulation, undercutting national management of interest rates and exchange rates, widening disparities of wealth both within and between nations, dragging down labor standards, degrading the environment, denying nations the shaping of their own economic destiny, accountable to no one, creating a world economy without a world polity.[20]

Across the Atlantic, the French bureaucrat-turned-consultant Jacques Attali warns that "the market economy today is more dynamic than democracy" and that its dynamism is dangerous. Abetted by the decentralizing power of the Internet and the mobility of "high-tech nomads," he argues, the dynamic marketplace erodes the ability of political elites to enforce collective decisions—a power he equates with "democracy": "Under such circumstances, Western civilization is bound to collapse."[21] What terrifies technocrats is not that the future will depart from a traditional ideal but that it will be unpredictable and beyond the control of professional wise men.

The characteristic values of reactionaries are continuity, rootedness, and geographically defined community. They are generally anticosmopolitan, antitechnology, anticommercial, antispecialization, and antimobility. They draw on a powerful romantic tradition that gives their politics a poetic, emotional appeal, especially to people with literary sensibilities. With some exceptions, they oppose not only the future but the present and the recent past, the industrial as well as the postindustrial era. The reactionary vision is one of peasant virtues, of the imagined harmonies and, above all, the imagined predictability of traditional life. It idealizes life without movement: In the reactionary ideal, people know and keep their places, geographically as well as socially, and tradition is undisturbed by ambition or invention. "The central concept of wisdom is permanence," wrote E. F. Schumacher, the environmentalist guru, in *Small Is Beautiful.*[22]

In part because they do not fit neatly into left-right categories, reactionary thinkers are rarely acknowledged in conventional discussions. But their ideas regularly turn up in books from major publishers, in influential magazines such as *Harper's* and *The Atlantic Monthly*, and on the opinion pages of leading newspapers. Their work shapes the worldview of the yuppie-green consumers of the *Utne Reader* and of the trade-hawk followers of Pat Buchanan. The most hackneyed speech about "sustainable development," "national sovereignty," or "preserving community" is but one or two footnotes away from the work of reactionary intellectuals such as Schumacher.

Although they represent a minority position, reactionary ideas have tremendous cultural vitality. Reactionaries speak directly to the most salient aspects of contemporary life: technological change, commercial fluidity, biological transformation, changing social roles, cultural mixing, international trade, and instant communication. They see these changes as critically important, and, as the old *National Review* motto had it, they are determined to "stand athwart history, yelling, 'Stop!'" Merely by acknowledging the dynamism of contemporary life, reactionaries win points for insight. And in the eyes of more conventional thinkers, denouncing change makes them seem wise.

By personal history or political background, many reactionaries are classified as leftists. Whether cultural critics or environmentalists, however, that label fits them awkwardly. Their tradition-bound views of the good life make them true conservatives. And they frequently voice disappointment that their views aren't shared by mainstream Republicans. The late social critic Christopher Lasch, a scourge of the left from which he came, complained, "A movement calling itself conservative might have been expected to associate itself with the demand for limits not only on economic growth but on the conquest of space, the technological conquest of the environment, and the ungodly ambition to acquire godlike powers over nature. Reaganites, however, condemned the demand for limits as another counsel of doom."[23]

As Buchanan's political career suggests, however, there is indeed a strong reactionary strain among elements of the Cold War right. Fred Iklé, the undersecretary of defense for policy in the very Reagan administration Lasch denounces, now attacks as "Jacobins" those conservatives who support "the philosophy of perpetual growth" and scorns as "xenophilia" the notion that individuals should ideally be free to trade across national borders.[24] He laments that "the intellectuals' jubilation throughout the world about our ever-expanding, homogenizing, perpetually-GNP-increasing global market creates a sense of inevitability even among the wisest of conservative thinkers."[25] Another conservative defense intellectual, Edward N. Luttwak, calls for "re-regulation and other measures to stabilize the economy, thus favoring *Gemeinschaft* over efficient *Gesellschaft*"—traditional, geographically settled life over cosmopolitan choice and fluidity.[26] He endorses the Unabomber's critique of conservatives as "fools [who] whine about the decay of traditional values, yet they enthusiastically support technological progress and economic growth."[27]

Similarly, the journalist Charlotte Allen excoriates fellow conservatives who support the "creative destruction" of market processes. She writes in the liberal *Washington Monthly:*

> Most of today's conservatives refuse to support the traditional social and economic arrangements—small towns, extended families, generational roots, secure livelihoods, and respect for the land—that create the stability in which a sense of duty to others thrives. Instead, conservatives function as shills for big business and, as if America weren't already the most prosperous country on Earth, "growth"—a perpetual frenzy of economic development designed to make life ever more expensive and transform people into slaves of consumption.

By "support" traditional arrangements, Allen does not mean simply "favor" or "adhere to" but rather "enforce through political action." Among her prescriptions: "Conservatives should work to destroy agribusiness" and "don't let Wal Mart wreck *your* downtown."[28] Both issues have in fact catalyzed coalitions of reactionaries from the "left" and the "right."

Intellectually, the roots of many conservative reactionaries lie in the antimodern writings of traditionalists such as Russell Kirk and the Southern Agrarians of the 1920s and 1930s, who anticipated many green arguments against the open-ended future: "The tempo of the industrial life is fast, but that is not the worst of it; it is accelerating," complained the Agrarians in their 1930 manifesto, *I'll Take My Stand.* "The ideal is not merely some set form of industrialism, with so many stable industries, but industrial progress, or an incessant extension of industrialization. *It never proposes a specific goal; it initiates the infinite series*" (emphasis added).[29]

This reactionary fear of the "infinite series" produces a conservatism more familiar to Europeans than to Americans. Unlike the striving descendants of American pioneers, wrote John Crowe Ransom in *I'll Take My Stand,* Europeans "have elected to live their comparatively easy and routine lives in accordance with the tradition which they inherited, and they have consequently enjoyed a leisure, a security, and an intellectual freedom that were never the portion of pioneers. The pioneering life is not the normal life, whatever some Americans may suppose."[30] (Such "comparatively easy and routine lives" are, of course, the privilege of a static upper class, while the "pioneering life" assumes upward mobility.)

Stasist reactionaries have in fact made greater inroads among British and European conservatives than among Americans. Before his death in 1997, the Anglo-French billionaire Sir James Goldsmith—known in the 1980s as a swashbuckling takeover artist and political Tory—had become a prominent opponent of international trade, immigration, and Third World development, arguing that such dynamic forces are too disruptive of traditional societies.[31] His manifesto *Le Piège (The Trap)* was a best-seller in France. "Families are broken, the countryside is deserted and social stability in towns is destroyed" when modern agriculture increases crop yields, he wrote.[32] Goldsmith's brother Edward, the author of *The Way* and founder of *The Ecologist* magazine, shares Sir James's antitrade, antitechnology views but not his conservative political associations. On a more scholarly note, the Oxford philosopher John Gray, whom James Goldsmith thanks as one of his advisers and who in turn praises Edward Goldsmith's *The Way* for its attack on progress, has called for an alliance between greens and conservatives.[33]

Such ideas are indeed influential among environmentalists, who include most of the reactionaries of the "left." (Some leftist reactionaries, such as Rifkin, actually engage a broad range of issues, but are often called "environmentalists" for lack of a better term.) Most green theorists, as opposed to garden-variety Sierra Club members or Washington-based lobbyists and regulators, are reactionaries. Their ruling metaphor for the ideal society is that of an ecosystem that has reached an unchanging "climax" stage where its flora and fauna remain constant. Environmental historian Donald Worster thus idealizes "a stable, enduring rural society in equilibrium with the processes of nature" and deplores the "constant innovation, constant change, constant adjustment [that] have become the normal experience of this culture."[34]

Green reactionaries celebrate premodern and, in some cases, prehistoric life. "Back to the Pleistocene!" is a popular, semiserious slogan among radical greens. Edward Goldsmith writes romantically of hunter-gatherer societies with "no history" and, he presumes, with no "wars, invasions, massacres, revolutions, assassinations, and intrigues." He marvels at the stability of these cultures: "During the old stone age, for instance, flint-chipping techniques did not change for some 200,000 years."[35] In his many books, the sledgehammer-wielding Kirkpatrick Sale praises various prehistoric cultures, including "the Paleolithic hunter-gatherers of prehistory—the 'cavemen.' "[36]

"The darkness is all around us: It is called industrial civilization," says Sale.[37] In his 1980 book *Human Scale,* Sale proposed the ideal of self-sufficient towns of five thousand to ten thousand residents, arguing that self-sufficiency—the absence of any trade with the outside world—helps a community "to create stability and balance and predictability."[38] Rifkin, a moderate by comparison, envisions cities that "once again return to their preindustrial size of 50,000 to 100,000 citizens," and an autarkic economy. In his ideal world, if a product "cannot be made locally by the community, using readily available resources and technology, then it is most likely unnecessary that it be produced at all."[39]

The friendly, popular version of this ideal is the "radical localism" espoused by Sierra Club president Adam Werbach, a self-described former "Valley boy" who calls for "self-sufficiency" without sacrifice. He wouldn't ban wheat from Cape Cod or much of anything from Los Angeles, but, he writes, "We should demand that the Safeway in Idaho carry only native potatoes. And we should draw the line when department stores bottom out prices, muscle out local businesses, and eradicate local culture." Once transformed into a platform bland enough for yuppie consumption, the stability of self-sufficiency becomes the stability of economic protectionism. The goal is to eliminate price-cutting competition, tacky merchandise, and international trade. Along these lines, Werbach zealously attacks Wal-Mart, which sells, he says, "row upon row of imported, low-quality junk—anything you might need for your work, home, or pleasure."

Even in Werbach's suburbanized vision, however, the ideal remains the static peasant village, where "whatever is produced in the village must be used, first and foremost, by the members of the village."[40] This peasant ideal—the good life imagined as hand-spinning and subsistence farming—runs through much green thought. Drawn originally from the writings of Mohandas Gandhi, it was popularized by one of the most influential environmentalist works ever, *Small Is Beautiful*. In that book, E. F. Schumacher praises peasant societies, singling out Burma in particular, for having less "pressure and strain of living" than developed countries. He sharply criticizes modern transportation and communications for making people "footloose":

> Everything in this world has to have a *structure*, otherwise it is chaos. Before the advent of mass transport and mass communications, the structure was simply there, because people were relatively immobile. . . . Now a great deal of structure has collapsed, and a country is like a big cargo ship in which the load is in no way secured. It tilts, and all the load slips over, and the ship founders. . . . Everything and everybody has become mobile. All structures are threatened, and all structures are *vulnerable* to an extent that they have never been before.[41]

Lurking in the background, such reactionary attitudes exercise a powerful, though sometimes indirect, influence on most discussions of environmental policy. And they help explain trends that have puzzled observers who see environmentalism as simply a "left-wing" phenomenon. A cultural–political movement opposed to mobility and change will, over time, come to support restrictions on immigration, technology, and trade, regardless of what its leftist allies think.

It may even come to extol values and people "the left" has traditionally scorned. The Marxist historian Eugene Genovese, once a supporter of Soviet socialism, now praises the southern conservative tradition represented by the Agrarians as the "most impressive native-born critique of our national development, of liberalism, and of the more disquieting features of the modern world." Among its other virtues, he notes, southern traditionalism has been "critical of capitalism's cash-nexus, recognizing it as a revolutionary solvent of social relations."[42]

Looking at a different traditionalist model, Lasch wrote fondly of the parochialism of urban ethnic neighborhoods:

> Lower-middle-class culture, now as in the past, is organized around the family, church, and neighborhood. It values the community's continuity more highly than individual advancement, solidarity more highly than social mobility. Conventional ideals of success play a less important part in lower-middle-class life than the maintenance of existing ways. . . . [Anthony] Lukas [in his chronicle of the Boston busing battles] contrasted the "Charlestown ethic of getting by" with the "American imperative to get ahead." The people of Charlestown, deserted by the migration of more ambitious neighbors to the suburbs, had renounced "opportunity, advancement, adventure" for the "reassurance of community, solidarity, and camaraderie."[43]

Buchanan's stump speeches and columns similarly invoke the stability of such neighborhoods and of industrial work—the Washington parish of his childhood, the steel mills of western Pennsylvania, the forges and factories of the industrial heartland. And Buchanan inspires disconcerted praise on the left: "I've been waiting my whole life for someone running for president to talk about the Fortune 500 as the enemy," *Village Voice* writer Tom Carson told him, "and when I finally get my wish, it turns out to be you."[44]

As Buchanan illustrates, in practical political terms the craving for stability translates most prominently into reactionary alliances against freer international trade—a stasist cause that neatly aligns the nationalism of Buchananites with the anticommerce instincts of greens. (It also draws ordinary interest-group support from unions and protection-seeking industries.) Analyzing the 1997 defeat of a bill to extend the president's "fast track" authority to negotiate trade agreements, *New Republic* writer Peter Beinart found many seemingly strange currents:

> I interviewed Congressman Cliff Stearns, a hard right, anti–fast track Florida Republican who last year held a press conference with Pat

Buchanan to oppose the Mexican bailout. "The administration cannot make the argument that the North American Free Trade Agreement [NAFTA] has been a winner," he said. "Public Citizen says 500,000 jobs have been lost." I wasn't sure that I had heard him correctly. "You're quoting Public Citizen, Ralph Nader's group?" I asked. "Oh," he replied, "let's not use that." Then, 30 seconds later, he noted that "the Economic Policy Institute says 11,300 jobs have been lost in Florida [as a result of NAFTA]." The Economic Policy Institute is a liberal think tank heavily funded by unions.

The exchange points to the most peculiar aspect of the nationalist transformation. In myriad small ways, the boundaries between right-wing anti–free traders and left-wing anti–free traders are blurring. . . . Last year, Pat Choate [a leading trade critic and Ross Perot's running mate in 1996] convinced the United Auto Workers to put up money for the United Broadcasting Network (UBN). The network, which now reaches 200 markets, boasts shows hosted by [Pat's sister] Bay Buchanan; nationalist San Diego Republican Duncan Hunter; Representative Marcy Kaptur; a passionate anti–fast track Democrat from Toledo; and populist Jim Hightower, the former Democratic Agriculture Commissioner of Texas.[45]

Despite intense lobbying by both the Clinton administration and the Republican congressional leadership, fast track went down to a shocking defeat, beaten by a reactionary coalition that defied the old categories.

Such victories are relatively rare, because the full reactionary package is a tough sell in contemporary America. Even trade protection, which enjoys support from interest groups that stand to benefit, has proven a consistent loser in presidential campaigns. And few people want to smash their computers, give up off-season fruits and vegetables, turn their backs on modern medicine, move in with their cousins and in-laws, or forgo higher incomes. Even fewer resonate to slogans like "Back to the Pleistocene!" But if, like Allen and Werbach, you want to stifle agribusiness and shut down Wal-Mart; if, like Schumacher and Sale, you want to make people less footloose and limit the size of cities; if, like Rifkin, you want to ban genetic engineering or, like Buchanan, you want to keep out foreign people and foreign goods; if, like Frank and Bennett, you want to rein in advertising and control popular culture, you can find powerful allies—and a friendly political system. If exhortation and polemics aren't enough to rally the public to voluntarily adopt your favored form of stasis, government help is available. Ever since the Progressive Era, when Theodore Roosevelt defined the mission of public officials as "to look ahead and plan out the right kind of civilization," technocrats have dominated American politics.[46] And technocrats know how to stop things.

Running for reelection in 1996, Bill Clinton and Al Gore promised again and again to build a "bridge to the twenty-first century." The slogan cast them as youthful builders and doers, the sort of people with whom forward-looking voters would identify. It contrasted nicely with Bob Dole's nostalgic convention pledge to build a bridge to a better past.

But a bridge to the future is not just a feel-good cliché. It symbolizes technocracy. Regardless of its destination, a bridge is a quintessentially static structure. It goes from known point A to known point B. Its construction requires big budgets and teams of experts, careful planning and blueprints. Once completed, it cannot be moved. "A bridge to the twenty-first century" declares that the future must be brought under control, managed and planned by experts. It should not simply evolve. The future (and the present) must be predictable and uniform: We will go from point A to point B, with no deviations. Fall off that one bridge—let alone jump—and you're doomed.

Technocrats are "for the future," but only if someone is in charge of making it turn out according to plan. They greet every new idea with a "yes, but," followed by legislation, regulation, and litigation. Like Schlesinger and Attali, they get very nervous at the suggestion that the future might develop spontaneously. It is, they assume, too important and too dangerous to be left to undirected evolution. "To conceive of a better American future as a consummation which will take care of itself—as the necessary result of our customary conditions, institutions, and ideas—persistence in such a conception is admirably designed to deprive American life of any promise at all," wrote Herbert Croly, among the most influential Progressive Era thinkers, in *The Promise of American Life,* published in 1909.[47]

Technocracy is the ideology of the "one best way," an idea that spread from Frederick Taylor's "scientific management" techniques to encompass the regulation of economic and social life. Turn-of-the-century technocrats, notes the historian John M. Jordan, used images of engineering to promise efficiency and order amid social and economic change: "In an era when the term *progressive* connoted a steady, teleological, restrained pace of improvement, *efficiency* implied change while at the same time suggesting security. The smoothly humming social machine envisioned by these reformers promised harmonious eradication of social problems. . . . This peculiarly American paradox of kinetic change made stable appears to have contributed to the ubiquity of efficiency claims in this era."[48] By design, technocrats pick winners, establish standards, and impose a single set of values on the future. Only through such uniform plans can they hope to deliver "kinetic change made stable."

Consider this statement from a CNN interview: "As the president said, we need a comprehensive system, one that's been worked out, that's affordable and has national standards."[49] Is this a legislator discussing national health insurance? A governor promoting education reform? An environmentalist proposing recycling mandates? The speaker is, in fact, a magazine editor talking about child care, but the prescription would fit just about any subject. To technocrats, institutional forms must be uniform and "comprehensive"; goals must be established once and for all; behavior must be molded to the proper pattern. In his 1998 State of the Union address, for instance, Bill Clinton denounced "untargeted tax cuts," which would reduce rates regardless of how taxpayers choose to spend their money, and he bragged about the complex "targeted tax cuts" passed the previous year.[50]

Accustomed to technocratic governance, we take for granted that each new development, from the contents of popular entertainment to the latest in medical equipment, deserves not only public discussion but government scrutiny. Every new idea seems to spark a campaign to ban or control it: breast implants and mobile phones, aseptic juice boxes and surrogate mothers, Japanese cars and bovine growth hormone, video games and genetic engineering, quality circles and no-haggle car pricing, telecommuting and MRIs, data encryption and book superstores—the list goes on forever.

Most political arguments thus take place between competing technocratic schemes. Should there be a mandatory "family viewing" hour on TV, or ratings and a V-chip? Should the tax code favor families with children, or people attending college? Should a national health insurance program enroll everyone in managed care, or should we regulate health maintenance organizations so they act more like fee-for-service doctors? The issue isn't *whether* the future should be molded to fit one static ideal. It's what that static ideal should be. There must be a single blueprint for everyone.

Technocracy declares that if automobile air bags are a good idea for some people, they must be required for everyone. If they turn out to injure children and small adults, planners may make an exception, but only if given a "good reason." Safety regulators "can't even consider a letter from somebody who says, 'Well, I'm scared, and I want to disconnect the air bag,'" a spokesman told *The New York Times*. "We've had somebody who said, 'I have claustrophobia, and I'm afraid.' That's not a medical condition that would require an air bag disconnection."[51]

The ill-fated Clinton health care plan, with its complicated price controls and monopoly health alliances, was a model of technocratic governance. It combined a role for private providers with extensive regulation of what could be sold, at what price, to and by whom, and in what quantities. It set up an appointed National Health Board, with subsidiary advisory committees, and local boards to govern the alliances. It fixed the form of health care delivery, down to the ratio of specialists to primary care physicians, leaving little room for evolution or experimentation. It assumed that health care institutions would not and should not change significantly over time. It expressed egalitarian values by opposing a "tiered system." And it was called, not coincidentally, the Health Security Plan.[52]

Comprehensive, neutrally administered plans are the technocratic dream. William Henry Smyth, who coined the term *technocracy* based on his experience with World War I planning, described it this way: "We became, for the time being, a real Industrial Nation. This we did by organizing and coordinating the Scientific Knowledge, the Technical Talent, and the Practical Skill of the entire Community; focussed them in the National Government, and applied this Unified National Force to the accomplishment of a Unified National Purpose." Smyth wanted technocracy to continue in peacetime, to "organize our scientists, our technologists, our exceptionally skilled."[53]

While reactionaries often denigrate learning and mock experts (witness Iklé's scorn for "intellectuals"), technocrats celebrate their own knowledge and hoard their expertise. They are social engineers, tin-

kerers who seek "rational solutions" to public problems. Those rational solutions are supposed to be above politics and ideology, the pure
results of science. Hence the multiplication of appointed boards and
independent agencies. If the ideal of reactionaries is the self-sufficient
family farm or the urban ethnic enclave, the ideal of technocrats is the
regulated monopoly or the independent administrative agency—a
rule-bound entity run by experts.

True to its Progressive Era origins, the pure technocratic vision combines the frisson of futurism—a combination of excitement and fear—
with the reassurance that some authority will make everything turn out
right. In 1984, amid the personal computer revolution, Newt Gingrich marveled at its creativity, but he worried that such uncoordinated enterprise lacked the focus necessary for national greatness.
"These developments are individually striking," he wrote. "Taken
together, they form a kaleidoscope that is difficult to develop into a coherent picture. Yet it is by sweeping dreams that societies shape themselves."

For technocrats, a kaleidoscope of trial-and-error innovation is not
enough; decentralized experiments lack coherence. "Today, we have an
opportunity *to shape technology,*" wrote Gingrich in classic technocratic
style (emphasis added).[54] His message was that computer technology is
too important to be left to hackers, hobbyists, entrepreneurs, venture
capitalists, and computer buyers. "We" must shape it into a "coherent
picture." That is the technocratic notion of progress: Decide on the
one best way, make a plan, and stick to it. Looking for a model, Gingrich had kind words for the French Minitel system of terminals run
by the state phone company—a centrally administered system whose
rigidity has stifled Internet development in France.[55]

In recent years, Gingrich has become more skeptical—and so has the
rest of the country. In 1984, he expressed his enthusiasm for space
exploration in demands for new heroic technocratic programs like the
moon landing. By 1995, he was musing about the great things that could
happen "if we got the government out of the business of designing space
shuttles and space stations. . . . The challenge for us is to get government
and bureaucracy out of the way and put scientists, engineers, entrepreneurs, and adventurers back into the business of exploration and discovery."[56] Far from creating a promising future, technocracy had stifled
its spontaneous evolution.

*   *   *

Today technocrats retain enormous power, but they lack intellectual or cultural vigor. "Got a problem, get a program" is still a deeply ingrained habit, but enthusiasm for technocratic schemes died in a gas line sometime during the Carter administration. From urban renewal in the 1950s to the savings-and-loan crisis of the 1980s, technocracy has not made good on its promises. In many cases, it has made things worse. Rather than the smooth-running engine promised by turn-of-the-century progressives, technocratic governance has been a Rube Goldberg device at best and, more often, a misfitting hodgepodge that grinds gears, shoots out sparks, and periodically breaks down entirely.

As government has grown and special interests have multiplied, bureaucracies that once seemed to function reasonably well have become decadent, rigid, and insulated. The U.S. Postal Service is both high-handed and frequently incompetent. NASA is sluggish. The public schools seem dedicated to mediocrity, when they aren't outright failures. Power corrupts, and monopoly power corrupts absolutely. No wonder the public was so easily rallied to oppose the Clinton health care plan, whose promises of security came at the expense of competition and choice.

Even technocracy's remaining true believers have become cynical, if not about their ideals, then about the people who administer them. Consider Ross Perot, the purest technocrat in recent American politics. With his desire to get the best experts, put aside differences of politics and ideology, and just work things out, Perot sounds like William Henry Smyth. And his political movement has been driven by disappointed technocrats, who, like their leader, believe that society can be rationally managed through effective leadership and expertise. They are both discomfited by dynamism and suspicious of the system that promised to control it.

These disappointed technocrats crave predictability and order—not the ancient stability of peasant villages but the apparent efficiency of Galbraithean big business. They idealize not the self-sufficient agrarian but the old-time Organization Man, the clean-cut manager with a clear career path. "Our real problem," Perot told ABC's Barbara Walters in 1992, "is our giant companies, like IBM, are downsizing. General Motors is downsizing. We want them growing."[57] If they aren't—if America's future isn't as a "real Industrial Nation" but as "emergent, complex messiness"—then something is wrong. The leaders entrusted with managing the nation's affairs have failed the people. They are either incompetent or, more likely, corrupt.

Disillusioned technocrats, angry at the broken promises of kinetic change made stable, turn to procedural reforms—term limits, restrictions on lobbying, more controls on campaign contributions—to both punish and more tightly supervise the politicians who have failed them. They also embrace reactionary causes. Gathering for a United We Stand America convention in mid-1995, Perot's supporters enthusiastically cheered the reactionary nationalism of Buchanan and protectionist Representative Marcy Kaptur.[58] The California chapter of United We Stand America led grassroots anti-immigration efforts in that state.[59] And Perot himself is among the most outspoken opponents of international trade. The two forms of stasis merge.

Just as disillusioned technocrats adopt reactionary dreams, so pragmatic reactionaries inevitably turn to technocratic regulations. The 1960s counterculture originally rebelled against the technocratic rule of "the best and the brightest," but many of its activists soon realized the power of independent agencies to enforce their own static visions of the one best way. The 1970s brought a host of new social regulations, notably safety and environmental laws, that could serve to limit technological development and achieve some of the goals of countercultural reactionaries.

The ostensibly antitechnocratic ideal of "participatory democracy" became in fact a new form of technocracy. This result, while counterintuitive, isn't really surprising. The New Left's founding document, *The Port Huron Statement,* demanded "that decision-making of basic social consequence be carried on by public groupings" and, more specifically, declared "that the economy itself is of such social importance that its major resources and means of production should be open to democratic participation and subject to democratic social regulation."[60] Both positions flatly reject the idea that social or economic evolution should proceed through decentralized trial and error. Both demand central control. Unlike traditional technocracy, however, they locate that control in vaguely defined "public groupings" and "democratic participation" rather than in agencies and experts. In practice, however, such forms of "democracy" require the time to sit in meetings and the attention to master specialized issues. They recreate bureaucratic governance by giving self-appointed activists the power to veto other people's experiments.

Whatever its form, technocratic governance by its very nature slows dynamic processes. It transfers to deliberate, centralized authorities decisions that would otherwise be made nimbly, through competition and feedback in dispersed, evolving markets, not only for goods and services but also for ideas. Technocrats therefore supply the machinery that reactionaries need to work their will.

So, for instance, antitechnology activists Richard Sclove and Jeffrey Scheuer call for "no innovation without evaluation," "no innovation without regulation," and "no innovation without participation"—lots of ostensibly technocratic panels and boards to discourage potentially disruptive information technology and preserve traditional forms.[61] Gary Chapman, the technology critic who sometimes collaborates with Sclove, campaigns for "democratizing decisionmaking about new scientific and technological priorities" in pursuit of "community stability," among other goals.[62] He works to redirect government science funding to create forums for "public participation" that will control research and slow innovation.[63] Edward Luttwak, the defense intellectual, laments the end of the regulated telephone monopoly, a classic technocratic structure. To his chagrin, deregulation permits "turbo-charged capitalism—namely accelerated change," which disrupts settled patterns of life even as it fosters new ideas and spreads new technologies.[64]

Technocracy does not allow such turbulence. It is centralized and inflexible. It asks people with new ideas to justify them to boards and commissions. It establishes rules, from broadcasting regulations to laws against working at home, that assume that neither technologies nor tastes will change. It allocates tax breaks, subsidies, and licenses to established lobbies. It rewards the articulate and the politically savvy, punishing those who lack smoothness, connections, or the time, patience, and legal counsel to endure endless meetings.

Such a system, whose goal is control, provides numerous opportunities for resourceful reactionaries: urban planning and endangered species laws to keep out Wal-Mart and block new housing; environmental impact statements to limit business development and, if used by someone as clever as Rifkin, to bar genetic engineering; Food and Drug Administration reviews to deter high-tech medical products; immigration quotas (a Progressive Era idea) to manipulate the racial stock; recycling mandates to attack new materials; antitrust laws to harass retail innovators; mass transit subsidies and car-pool mandates to fight the automobile; broadcasting licenses to control popular culture, and on and on. The original technocrats simply wanted to manage change. But the apparatus they created provides a million ways to stop it altogether.

The story of silicone-gel breast implants illustrates how technocracy can be captured to achieve reactionary ends. Breast implants offend every reactionary impulse. There is nothing traditional about enlarging one's breasts; the very act defies fate, asserts individual will. Implants are highly artificial—overt attempts to overthrow nature, to use the mind to reshape the body, to alter genetic destiny without giving a good reason. They serve no social purpose or "vital need." They would not exist without the pursuit of profit, the ambition of technology, and the instinct for self-improvement. And they portend an unknown future, filled with even stranger biological manipulations.

But the scientific evidence that implants cause serious health problems is nonexistent. For policymakers devoted to pure science, that would end the discussion. Nonetheless, in 1992 the FDA imposed a moratorium on the sale of most silicone-gel breast implants, essentially limiting their use to postmastectomy reconstruction, and only then if patients agreed to participate in long-term clinical studies. The moratorium was driven partly by the bureaucratic ambition to exercise greater control over medical devices. But it also represented the culmination of a campaign by feminists and antitechnology activists, notably Sidney Wolfe of the Health Research Group, who did not approve of the devices and who promoted the notion that they posed serious dangers. The moratorium's result was devastating. By feeding litigation against their manufacturers, it guaranteed that the implants would thenceforth be too risky to sell in the United States.[65]

Writing in the *New England Journal of Medicine*, FDA commissioner David Kessler justified his decision on technocratic grounds: "The legal standard is not that devices must be proved unsafe before the FDA can protect patients against their use. Rather, the law requires a positive demonstration of safety." By not banning the implants outright, however, the agency had "preserve[d] the option of access to silicone breast implants for patients whose need was greatest. . . . The FDA has judged that, for these patients, the risk-benefit ratio permits the use of the implant under carefully controlled conditions."

With its determination of "need" and its risk-benefit calculations, the agency's decision had a scientific aura. Kessler scornfully dismissed critics, including the journal's executive editor, Marcia Angell, who criticized the FDA as paternalist, even sexist, for implicitly assuming no benefit to breast augmentation. "If members of our society were empowered to make their own decisions about the entire range of products for which the FDA has responsibility . . . then the whole rationale for the agency would cease to exist," wrote Kessler. "These restrictions on the use of silicone gel implants are not based on any judgment about values," he said.[66] But, of course, they were. Otherwise, why differentiate between beneficial reconstructive surgery and frivolous augmentation? As Angell later noted, "In waving aside the benefits of breast implants for most women who had them, Kessler appeared to be introducing an impossibly high standard for the devices: since there were no benefits, there should be no risks."[67] Wearing the mantle of neutral, technocratic science, Kessler imposed reactionary values.

Technocrats' governing assumptions, while sometimes disinterested, can never be neutral. "Efficiency" implies objectives, values to be optimized. The optimization problem is a technical question. The values are not. The FDA's product approval process, while usually scientifically rigorous, is strongly biased against risk taking. The Consumer Products Safety Commission similarly considers only safety, not fun, in evaluating toys. The federal Corporate Average Fuel Economy (CAFE) standards, on the other hand, weigh only miles per gallon, ignoring auto safety. Old-style telephone regulation emphasized "universal access" at the expense of variety and product innovation.

Such values may change over time. Urban planners once wiped out neighborhoods to promote "renewal"; today, they are more likely to oppose new construction and building renovation to preserve "quality of life." Zoning once segregated businesses, apartments, and single-family homes, regardless of their occupants' preferences; today, the "new urbanism" does precisely the opposite. The Army Corps of Engineers once built subsidized dams in the name of progress; now it blocks private development to preserve wetlands. The power of reactionaries lies in their ability to alter the values enforced through technocratic structures, or to create new technocratic agencies devoted to reactionary purposes. They turn the tools of technocracy toward their own vision of the one best way.

We can see the synergy of technocratic means and reactionary ends in many political figures, pressure groups, and government agencies—even in those who occasionally pay lip-service to the value of dynamism. Consider Vice President Al Gore, the would-be builder of a bridge to the future. From computer encryption to rock lyrics, from energy use to biotechnology, Gore throughout his career has met dynamism and diversity with technocratic policy and often reactionary rhetoric. When he speaks the language of technology, he inevitably combines it with a desire for central control—a federally managed "information superhighway" to be laid over the all-too-spontaneous Internet, for instance.

In a typically technocratic appeal for a commission on genetic engineering, Gore, then a senator, declared in 1986, "We are at the present time woefully unprepared to grapple with the serious ethical choices with which the new technology will confront us. The very power to bring about so much good will also open the door to serious potential problems. If we are not careful, we may well cross the line separating the two."[68] Accustomed to technocratic governance, it is easy not to notice the assumptions buried in this statement: the belief that "we" collectively (or, a nice ambiguity, perhaps "we, the members of Congress") must come to a single conclusion about how to apply new technologies; the conviction that the way to prepare for moral choices is to solicit advice from a commission of experts; and, of course, the instinct that a new technology's "good" is merely an enticement to "serious potential problems." Nowhere is there any tolerance for diversity or for decentralized trial and error. And the call comes from a senator who had praised Jeremy Rifkin's anti-biotech book *Algeny* as "an insightful critique," lauding it for "giving us a framework for critical consideration of future technological advances."[69] With his talk of commissions, frameworks, and "critical consideration," Gore plays the technocrat, but he serves a reactionary cause.

He is not always so subtle. His most striking vision of the one best way is his 1992 book, *Earth in the Balance*. There, Gore writes that "we must make the rescue of the environment the central organizing principle for civilization," a moral equivalent of war that subordinates every other goal to that purpose: "Minor shifts in policy, marginal adjustments in ongoing programs, moderate improvements in laws and regulations, rhetoric offered in lieu of genuine change—these are all forms of appeasement, designed to satisfy the public's desire to

ware, their evolution frozen once the company deems them suited to the task. Dowe shows the audience a trial run. Tiny, green "bug" blips swarm the screen in search of either pink or blue food, dying out if they settle too far from the food, flourishing if they locate the right type. Later, Dowe cranks up a more powerful machine and runs matches of handwritten Japanese *kanji*, of fingerprints, of wildly different photos—all through databases with tens of thousands of entries, all in a matter of minutes. It's an impressive demonstration: the programmer's art imitating life, producing better programs.

"These little digital organisms," says Dowe, "show that when you're trying to solve a very complex problem, you don't always have to have a plan. . . . The solution *emerges* from the interaction of all the individuals."[1]

The solution emerges. You don't have to have a plan.

Dowe is offering, as a practical answer to difficult problems, the "infinite series" of Agrarian dread, the Unabomber's "reckless ride into the unknown," a world absent Schumacher's static "structure" and yet absent chaos. He is challenging as impractical, even irrational, the technocrat's assumption that order requires design, that every solution demands an overarching plan. Instead of promising bridges to the future, Dowe is selling *life:* fluidity, variety, competition, adaptation, learning, improvement, evolution, and spontaneously emerging order. And his audience—of hard-headed chip designers and self-actualizing human resources consultants, school voucher advocates and ecology enthusiasts, hedge fund managers and new-media gurus— is buying.

Dowe's talk is part of a conference dedicated to the intersection of artifice and life, one of a series given annually by the Bionomics Institute. A tiny think tank in San Rafael, California, the institute spent five years spreading the notion of "economy as ecology," a diverse, dynamic web of relationships rather than a machine to be stoked and managed. Nitpickers justifiably criticized the institute for caricaturing the serious work of economists, who have drawn on biological metaphors since Adam Smith.[2] But the critics missed the point: Whatever the organizers' original intentions, the Bionomics conferences as they evolved weren't really about critiquing or reinventing economics. They were opportunities to explore a shared dynamist world view in areas ranging from education policy to software development. The conferences, which ended in 1997, created a rare self-aware community of dynamists. That itself was a remarkable accomplishment.

Dynamists don't generally think of themselves as a coalition, let alone a community. They share beliefs in spontaneous order, in experiments and feedback, in evolved solutions to complex problems, in the limits of centralized knowledge, and in the possibility of progress. They are excited by the textures of daily life, the ingenuity and variety found in every corner of the contemporary world. They support the open society and instinctively oppose those who would close it to new ideas—whether economic, social, cultural, or scientific. They care about protecting the processes that allow an open-ended future to unfold.

But they don't share an identity. Depending on their backgrounds and interests, they may view themselves as libertarian or progressive, liberal or conservative, playful postmodernists or tough-minded technologists. Their shared values and worldview don't yet translate into any single political, cultural, or intellectual identity. With no interest in fighting over competing technocratic schemes, many consider themselves apolitical.

Yet dynamist ideas are popping up all over: in discussions of the global economy, of postcommunist transition, of cultural processes; in management theory and literary studies, complexity theory and ecology. The California high-tech world is only part of the story. Dynamic visions of the world can be found even in establishment precincts formerly monopolized by technocrats, informing analysis of economics, politics, and science.

Here is Treasury Secretary Robert Rubin releasing a report that declares, "The goal of policy in the coming century should be to encourage rather than suppress competition and innovation in finance," protecting the soundness of the system without guaranteeing any particular institution or outcome.[3] There is David Ignatius, who directs business coverage for *The Washington Post*, describing the global economy as "a dynamic, complex adaptive system that is constantly adapting to changing circumstances."[4]

Reviewing William Greider's book *One World, Ready or Not*, an attack on the fluid international economy, *Newsweek*'s Michael Hirsh notes that Greider "frets that *someone* should be in charge: a juggernaut of global capitalism is loose and 'no one is at the wheel.' Yet this begs the question. Whom do we really want at the wheel of the world economy? Just having Alan Greenspan at the Fed is scary enough."[5] Feedback and response, Hirsh suggests, generate order without control. Centralizing power only makes mistakes more catastrophic.

Open *The Wall Street Journal,* and you find Walter McDougall, who won the Pulitzer Prize for his history of the space age, analyzing "the death of technocracy," defined as "centrally planned assaults on the future."[6] Turn to *Scientific American,* and you see physicist-turned-biologist Albert Libchaber musing over how life works, in contrast to engineering: "There is no planning, only evolution." Yet this trial-and-error process generates amazingly efficient cellular "machines," so sensitive they can detect a single molecule.[7]

Dynamists are often drawn to biological metaphors, symbols of unpredictable growth and change, of variety, and of experiment, feedback, and adaptation. Hence management writer Tom Peters uses images of pruning roses and fertilizing wildflowers to suggest dynamic approaches to corporate strategy;[8] Jane Jacobs describes cities as "problems in organized complexity, like the life sciences,"[9] while Joel Garreau talks about suburban "edge cities" as "nymphal, if not larval" creatures whose mature forms are unknown;[10] *Wired* executive editor Kevin Kelly writes of "neobiological civilization;"[11] anthropologist Grant McCracken explores "the sheer number and variety of social species;"[12] journalist Jonathan Rauch examines subjects as diverse as Japanese society, free speech, and interest-group politics through the lens of evolution;[13] while Stewart Brand writes about "evolutionary design" approaches to making buildings adaptable.[14]

"I like building things," says the technology pundit Esther Dyson, discussing her work with entrepreneurs in postcommunist Europe. "But I'd rather be a gardener than in construction. I'd rather go out and water the plants, and clear the path for the sun to shine, and have them grow themselves."[15] Dynamism represents, in the words of its most important theorist, the late economist and social philosopher Friedrich Hayek, "the party of life, the party that favors free growth and spontaneous evolution."[16]

It is a party that has no true political or intellectual home in America today, a party that barely recognizes itself as an entity. Its central value is *learning,* which unlike stability or control is an open-ended process. Dynamists do not expect, demand, or desire a world that holds still. As journalist Walter Truett Anderson writes of the famous "blue marble" photo of the earth from space: "While the photograph is a powerful piece of visual information, it is also misleading. It is after all, a *still* photograph. It doesn't show how the world is changing, and that is the really interesting part—the part without which no worldview is complete."[17] This fascination with change doesn't mean that dynamists think every innovation is desirable, or that they agree about which changes are good and which aren't. But they care about the process: about the way in which human beings learn by doing, by trying things, and even by failing. They find that process not only valuable, but "the really interesting part" of life.

And while stasists see nothing but trouble in the exuberant, unruly, kaleidoscopic, post–Cold War world—with its fluid international trade, border-leaping communications, and ever-more audacious scientific discoveries—dynamists are delighted. Trade lawyer Brink Lindsey talks about the two developments that rocked his world: his "never-ending shock" at the collapse of the Soviet Union and his own frequent business travels to the emerging economies of Southeast Asia, where he sees first-hand "the enormous protean energies being released." Lindsey exemplifies the culture of dynamists. He is thrilled at the possibilities unleashed by choice and competition and disgusted by the respect accorded reactionary sentiment. He says this of traveling in Asia:

> It was breathtaking and awesome to see this creation of a completely new lifestyle out of a civilization that had been more or less static for thousands of years. . . . People who had been peasants and who would be born, live, and die within five miles of their home are being exposed to the whole world and relieved from the misery of backbreaking toil and the tedium of farm life.

Like other dynamists, Lindsey is repelled by the "casual dismissal of technology as being superficial and banal":

> Either people haven't thought it through, or they have enormous contempt for the billions of people whose lives would just be *horrid* if it weren't for the liberation that this kind of change and growth and open-ended dynamism has created. . . . To just casually wave that off and consign the world's population to being yoked up behind a water buffalo in a rice paddy is profoundly anti-humanitarian.[18]

Although not all dynamists are as optimistic as Lindsey, they do in general emphasize the joys and possibilities of life, and the amazing progress that can happen when people are free to experiment and learn. They have utter contempt for the claim that the world's peasants should be content with their lot.

Dynamists are also willing to put up with experiments they think are lousy—not to avoid criticizing them, since criticism is itself an absolutely essential part of the dynamic process, but to let them proceed. A dynamist world has room for a wide range of enterprises: for both Promise Keepers and *Ms.*, for the macho culture of Intel and the zaniness of Southwest Airlines, for Web sites devoted to biblical exegesis and Web sites devoted to pornography, for punks and debutantes, Mozart and Madonna, *The Little Mermaid* and *Pulp Fiction*. Dynamists embrace such plenitude not because they're unwilling to make judgments but because they believe that we learn from choice, competition, and criticism. They expect that Madonna haters will mock her work; that some critics will zap Quentin Tarantino's movies for their violence and vulgar language; that feminists will condemn Promise Keepers' traditional model of marriage; that evangelicals will try to convert unbelievers; and that new ideas about corporate management will spring up as often as new products.

Although dynamists are in many ways heirs to John Stuart Mill's nineteenth-century liberalism, they are less concerned that society accept eccentricity without protest. Dynamists view both "eccentricity" (new ideas) and criticism as part of the process of trial-and-error learning. Unlike stasists, however, dynamists do not greet every voluntary new development with instant, reflexive revulsion. They are more likely to be intrigued and to want to know more, even if they eventually don't like what they learn. They let many different ideas compete and coexist. And they do not demand that every new product, service, fashion, institution, or idea justify itself to public officials.

As individuals, dynamists may have strong opinions about the best way to do things——from the best way to run companies or raise children to the best way to cut hair or make music. But they realize that they may be wrong, and that someone may come along with a better idea tomorrow. They understand that what seems like a great idea in theory may turn out to have terrible results in practice. And they accept that, in some cases, what is best for one person may not be best for another. Different musical styles resonate differently to different people. For some couples, a marriage of equals may be best, while other people may be happier with traditional sex roles; personalities differ and so do personal relations. Dynamists do not expect everyone to be exactly like them. They appreciate, and accept, the variety of human life.

The dynamist moral vision, then, emphasizes individual flourishing and individual responsibility. It sees human nature fulfilled in learning, creating, and adapting to the world. It understands that cultures, as well as individuals, learn from experience and that we are foolish when we try to reinvent the world from scratch. Dynamists want people to be happy, and they believe that we will find more opportunities for happiness if we are free to learn, to stretch ourselves, to try new things. Except perhaps in a few corners, a dynamist world is not a place of hedonistic lotus eaters but of continual striving—not simply to survive, "yoked up behind a water buffalo," but to improve. "We ride the greatest trend of all," wrote the late economist Julian Simon, "the drive to create a bit more than we use, and to leave the world a little better than we entered it."[19]

When they think about it at all, its critics tend to treat the dynamic vision as a goofy California phenomenon, unmoored from both history and any serious intellectual tradition. "The Californian Ideology," two British hypertechnocrats of the left have dubbed it, "a bizarre fusion of the cultural bohemianism of San Francisco with the hi-tech industries of Silicon Valley."[20] Certainly the cybersages who attract attention with their technological determinism, in-your-face attitude, and hyperbolic rhetoric about the Internet as "the most transforming technological event since the capture of fire" do little to dispel such charges.[21] But their rhetoric shouldn't be taken too seriously. As Tom Peters, who quotes such philosophers as Hayek and Karl Popper amid sentences studded with exclamation points, says of his own sweeping statements, "It's called sales."[22] Mistaking sales for substance—and a cultural sliver for a broad phenomenon—creates an ignorant caricature.

Dynamist thought in fact draws on many intellectual traditions: classical-liberal philosophy and legal theory; several different strands of economics; the history of science and (a separate enterprise) of technology; ecology and evolutionary biology; the study of organizations and business strategy; even aspects of cognitive psychology and computer science. The growth of social history, with its emphasis on the textures of life and the many different sources of social change, has encouraged a dynamic understanding of the past. The same is true of postmodern cultural analysis and certain forms of anthropology. Although their pioneers and practitioners are by no means mostly dynamist, their work has exposed the complex processes of experiment and feedback that shape the evolution of culture.

In their dynamist manifestations, these varied endeavors share an interest in change over time—in evolution through variation, selection, and reproduction—and especially in the evolution of knowledge in all its forms. They are systemic, process-oriented approaches, suspicious of one-variable explanations. They discount claims of global knowledge and recognize the limits of conscious planning. And, as we will explore in future chapters, they appreciate how simple units and simple rules can form complex orders and countless combinations.

On top of these intellectual trends, the contemporary economy—competitive, global, and self-consciously entrepreneurial—has created a broad-based business culture that is essentially dynamist. It simply no longer sounds plausible to describe the market as a static conspiracy of a few faceless, unchangeable corporate monoliths; the Galbraithean conventional wisdom of a generation ago sounds like nonsense in a world where upstarts can threaten even Sears and IBM. The same loss of certainty that disturbs Ross Perot and Pat Buchanan has energized a cohort of mostly younger businesspeople, many of whom see their work as a way of influencing the world—as feedback in a dynamic economic and cultural system. "I needed a business and I wanted to do something culturally transforming," says Jim Belcher, the thirty-two-year-old cofounder of Renaissance Skateboarding Co., as though starting a company to sell skateboards adorned with uplifting art were an obvious thing for a newly minted philosophy Ph.D. to do.[23]

"There's been a change in the myths that talented people in this generation guide their lives by, and an entrepreneurial, rather than corporate, connection is a strong part of that mythology," says Ross Webber, chairman of the management department at the Wharton School. More than security, says a corporate recruiter, young businesspeople "want growth, variety, challenge," the characteristics of a dynamic system.[24]

Daniel Pink, who quit his job as the chief speechwriter for Vice President Gore to become a freelance writer, chronicles the rise of "free agents"—people like him who have abandoned formal organizations to work for themselves. Their numbers are staggering. Counting the 14 million self-employed Americans, the 8.3 million independent contractors, and the 2.3 million temps, Pink comes up with a total of 25 million, or one in six workers, "who move from project to project and who work on their own, sometimes for months, sometimes for days."

When he began his research, Pink assumed that free agency was driven by "the inexorable forces of capitalism, centrifugal forces in the new economy scattering people to the periphery," but he discovered no such thing. The people he interviewed hadn't been forced out of their jobs; they were choosing to "customize" their work, combining jobs from different "vendors" to suit their own financial, personal, and creative needs. Pink points to free agents as an example of the power of order without design. With no grand plan, they have spontaneously generated not only their own jobs but a complex infrastructure of support groups, buying cooperatives, placement agents, office supply vendors, and Kinko's shops. "There's no central authority," says Pink. "There's no headquarters. There's no boss. Nobody from the head office sent a memo and said, 'I want 25 million of you to become free agents.' "[25]

None of this means that such businesspeople are self-consciously or consistently dynamist in their worldview. Most aren't thinking in those terms. But the cultural background has changed. Work life itself is different from a generation ago—freer and more fluid, with greater risk and greater reward—and the general public is much more aware of the textures of how markets actually work. Introducing readers to Hayek's notion of the "extended order" that arises from trade under impersonal rules, Peters celebrates "the richness, messiness, and uncertainty of markets . . . the disorder, fun, and enthusiasm—and agony and despair—of markets."[26] That is not a vision traditional technocrats would recognize.

Stasists generally portray the market either as an impersonal machine crushing personal values or, quite the opposite, as a small cabal of powerful and greedy men who manipulate the rest of us for their own gain. Dynamists, by contrast, see the market as a *process*, a decentralized system for discovering and sharing knowledge, for trading and expressing value—"a web of value that holds people together," in the words of the poet and critic Frederick Turner.[27] There is nothing specifically Californian or high tech about this dynamist understanding of markets as discovery processes.

35

Undoubtedly, however, the growth of cyberspace—itself a complex "extended order"—has catalyzed both dynamist and stasist coalitions. Because its development defied technocratic assumptions, the Internet has become a symbol of dynamic, free evolution. The Net not only managed to become big and important before any would-be regulator noticed, it evolved both software rules and social norms without official direction. Its origins, as a Defense Department program are far less significant than its bottom-up growth and development. That development greatly upsets technocrats, who are forever trying to impose controls on what one critic, calling for "firm direction," decried as "an international computer web tying together about 30 million people [yet] governed by no one."[28]

As an interest group, Netizens have rallied to protect their domain from censorship and other forms of attack. But computer culture has done more than create a new lobby. It has reinforced dynamist assumptions. The intensely competitive, highly entrepreneurial culture of Silicon Valley has made "creative destruction" synonymous not only with wealth but with innovation, intellectual challenge, and, yes, fun. Progress by trial and error—even if the errors mean bankrupt companies, lost venture capital, and (temporarily) out-of-work employees—is not just a slogan but a lived experience.

Among software writers in particular, experience undercuts stasist aspirations to security and control. The computer has come to represent not omniscience and power but the inherent limits of complex systems. "One of the things that most people who are computer-oriented have learned already is the law of unintended consequences—there's always bugs," says Mike Godwin, the staff counsel for the Electronic Frontier Foundation, a civil liberties group that focuses on computer and communications issues. "And sometimes you find that every attempt to fix a bug creates new bugs. What it tells you is something about the limits of what designers can do, or to put it another way, the limits on what policymakers can do."

Rather than the civil engineer's confidence about design and construction—the confidence that lies behind technocratic governance—these technologists have developed an acute awareness of the limits of their own knowledge and, therefore, of anyone else's. Yet they also believe, in Godwin's words, that through decentralized experiments and feedback, "you can let collective wisdom form."[29] The Net has become a model of spontaneous order and dynamic, trial-and-error learning.

Although it gets the most attention, the Net is hardly the only such model. Scientifically inclined dynamists often talk about birds, who flock and seem to follow a leader at the head of a V. In fact, there is no leader. Each bird operates independently, adhering to simple rules, and the bird at the point of the V does not stay the same. The pattern emerges from the behavior of the individual birds. Such emergent patterns are characteristic of life, including human life.

"A bird flock is one of many phenomena organized without an organizer, coordinated without a coordinator," writes Mitchel Resnick, a researcher at the MIT Media Lab. "In ant colonies, trail patterns are determined not by the dictates of the queen ant but by local interactions among the worker ants, such as following a scent that their fellow ants emit when they find a source of food. In human societies, macroeconomic patterns arise from the haggling between millions of buyers and sellers in marketplaces and stock markets around the world. And in immune systems, armies of antibodies seek out bacteria in a systematic, coordinated attack—without any 'generals' organizing the overall battle plan."[30]

Dynamists see such undesigned order everywhere in human society, from the macrostructures of cities, capital markets, and languages to the microniches of subcultures and specialty products. These patterns are shaped not by a central plan but by decentralized action, feedback, and response. Our many choices and individual-level designs create a larger order whose specific outcomes are unknown. By shaping our individual lives, choosing among and arranging the things we do control, we form a larger pattern that is under no one's control, yet is complex and orderly.

This way of thinking is foreign to many people. It's not the way we expect the world to work. Herbert Simon—like Hayek, a heterodox Nobel laureate economist, but one whose intellectual roots are in public administration, not classical–liberal philosophy—explains it this way:

> We have become accustomed to the idea that a natural system like the human body or an ecosystem regulates itself. To explain the regulation,

37

we look for feedback loops rather than a central planning and directing body. But somehow our intuitions about self-regulation without central direction do not carry over to the artificial systems of human society. I retain vivid memories of the astonishment and disbelief always expressed by the architecture students to whom I taught urban land economics many years ago when I pointed to medieval cities as marvelously patterned systems that had mostly just "grown" in response to myriads of individual decisions. To my students a pattern implied a planner in whose mind it had been conceived and by whose fiat it had been implemented. The idea that a city could acquire its pattern as "naturally" as a snowflake was foreign to them. They reacted to it as many Christian fundamentalists responded to Darwin: no design without a Designer![31]

The dynamist insight that "sometimes unconscious evolution can come up with better solutions than our best engineers" is hard for many people to fathom. Confronted with such an undesigned order, stasists tend to personify it—to treat it as a single intelligence. So, for instance, Arthur Schlesinger talks about "the computer" and "the untrammeled market" as though technological and economic systems were unitary actors rather than complex, evolving processes driven by millions of individual choices.

While dynamists delight in order without control, technocrats see it as a threat, often acting to outlaw it or bring it under central direction. When Hurricane Andrew swept through Miami in 1992, residents spontaneously took to the streets to clear fallen trees and help neighbors. Some directed traffic at intersections where the lights were out. Floridians north of the stricken area loaded their cars with supplies and headed down to help. They were soon joined by private convoys from neighboring states, later augmented by volunteers from as far away as Canada. Such efforts, unplanned and uncoordinated, proved vital in reaching out-of-the-way towns missed by the Red Cross and government workers. Like ants following a scent without direction from the queen, charitably minded individuals found places that needed supplies and took care of them. Decentralized solutions worked even as centralized disaster authorities, specifically the head of Dade County's Emergency Management Office, were throwing tantrums on national television.

Soon, however, officials were telling the amateur traffic cops to stop—a county traffic-directing class was required—and asking Good Samaritans to stay away, lest relief be disorganized. When the immediate crisis was over and rebuilding began, Dade County ruled that out-of-county contractors couldn't do work unless they passed a licensing test, which it then failed to schedule. "We don't need 6,000 unemployed carpenters from Massachusetts clogging up Interstate 95 looking for a job," declared the executive director of the South Florida Builders' Association.[32] It was better to go without help, these technocrats reasoned, than to allow disorganized assistance—or competition.

The tension between technocratic control and spontaneous, productive order isn't limited to conflicts between public authorities and private action. Arian Ward sees the same phenomenon in large corporations that are trying to become more flexible. "The same polarized forces warring in Congress these days are at war in companies as well: control vs. freedom, order vs. chaos, hierarchy vs. empowerment," he writes. "I see this every day in my work here at Hughes [Space and Communications Company]. Example: as part of our Knowledge Highway vision, we are implementing an internal Web [electronic information system], just like so many other organizations. When I demo it to people around the company, there are invariably two distinct and opposing reactions: 'Wow! When can I get it? I can think of so many things I'd like to do with it,' and 'Wow! How do we control this? How do we kill this?' "[33]

As the company's "leader of learning and change," Ward works to get Hughes managers to see the advantages of "self-organization"—parallel, decentralized decision making driven not by detailed decrees but by shared goals. Although he often uses the word *chaos,* what Ward really seeks is order without design. He stresses that "self-organizing systems don't just self-organize around *nothing.* [They] get down to the most fundamental principles and continuously self-organize around those principles."[34] For Jim Dowe's digital organisms, that means seeking food to survive and reproduce. For posthurricane Miamians and their benefactors, it meant cleaning up, providing ice, food, and gasoline, and getting life back to normal. For managers, it means fulfilling the company's mission and goals. Such shared fundamentals provide a kind of control, but not a detailed design. The trick is to get beyond just posting vision statements on the wall, to turn goals into broad, simple, well-understood principles that genuinely allow people to make decisions without micromanagement. Managers must, in Esther Dyson's words, learn to do gardening rather than construction.

Even the most successful corporate models of dynamist management, however, do not carry over directly into the world of public policy. Employees who don't share the vision of a particular company have thousands of others to choose from—and even the option to start their own, possibly competing, firm. That's not the case for a whole society. To impose a specific "central organizing principle," à la Al Gore, on an entire country is to subordinate everyone's individual plans and purposes to the static vision of a powerful elite. A society or nation cannot have a single narrow mission or set of values without falling into totalitarianism. Rather, its underlying principles must be broader than even the most sweeping corporate vision statement. They must be general and stable enough to allow individuals to pursue their own ends, and to create their own artificial orders within the larger, naturally emergent order that is the society as a whole. Securing the rights of "life, liberty, and the pursuit of happiness" is such a broad "mission statement," which then generates a more specific rule of law. It does not, however, establish a single set of values or dictate an end state.

Along these lines, *Washington Post* columnist James K. Glassman suggests that congressional Republicans would have been more successful in 1995 if they had sold "a credo, not a contract"—a broad vision statement that trusted "in the imagination and intelligence of individual Americans, alone and in voluntary organizations," rather than a short-term list of programs and tax gimmicks. Such a credo, Glassman writes, would both inspire the public and give officeholders a way of checking specific bills against their broad goals. It would affirm "that 'rebuilding our country' and the like are not tasks for the government but the natural consequences of the play of free minds and free markets." But technocracy reigns in both parties. Republicans, writes Glassman, at heart "probably have as little taste as Democrats for change they can't oversee."[35]

The importance of letting the open-ended future evolve on its own, without political direction, is a common Glassman theme. "I think the government should set boundaries rather than promote anything in particular," he says. "I don't think it's the job of government to promote certain mile-per-gallon standards or whether people use insulation." This antitechnocratic attitude baffles friends who have long known Glassman as a "liberal"—he was an antiwar protestor at Harvard in the late 1960s and the publisher of the center-left *New Republic* in the early 1980s. They don't understand his dynamist perspective, especially when he writes positively about markets and the changes they generate. "People say, 'Hey, Glassman's gotten very conservative. What's happened here?' " he says. "But it seems to me this is not conservatism. It's the opposite of conservatism. There's nothing I'm trying to conserve at all. Except the rules," the basic legal background.[36]

Hayek, writing in 1960, at the apogee of technocratic politics, knew the problem. He was grappling with it when he wrote of "the party of life." Although he was widely considered a conservative, the label fit him no better than it fits Glassman. In a book dedicated "to the unknown civilization that is growing in America," he embraced a dynamic view of the future, titling his final chapter "Why I Am Not a Conservative":

> As has often been acknowledged by conservative writers, one of the fundamental traits of the conservative attitude is a fear of change, a timid distrust of the new as such, while the liberal position is based on courage and confidence, on a preparedness to let change run its course even if we cannot predict where it will lead. . . . Conservatives are inclined to use the powers of government to prevent change or to limit its rate to whatever appeals to the more timid mind. In looking forward, they lack the faith in the spontaneous forces of adjustment which makes the liberal accept changes without apprehension, even though he does not know how the necessary adaptations will be brought about.[37]

This faith in spontaneous adjustment, in adaptation and evolution, does indeed separate dynamists from their conservative fellows—left as well as right. Dynamists believe in the future, in the capacity of human beings gradually and voluntarily, by trial and error, to improve their lives. That dynamists cannot specify in advance exactly what that future will look like does not frighten them. Life is, after all, full of surprises.

In early 1996, about a year into the Republican takeover of Congress, I met with a Capitol Hill insider who tried to explain what had gone wrong, not just tactically but ideologically, with Newt Gingrich's "revolution." The problem, he said, was that most members of Congress— "revolutionary" Republicans included—couldn't really imagine

41

life without central, presumably governmental, direction. "They're good conservatives, so they want to reduce government," he said. "But they think of that as getting as close to the abyss as possible without falling off."

Life as the abyss. Such is the attitude that governs America, the technocratic spirit that seeks "kinetic change made stable" and responds to every problem with a politically administered program. Like Herbert Simon's students, it sees all order as emanating from centralized design. Stasis supporters, whether technocrats or reactionaries, expect specific outcomes, knowable in advance—not general patterns and an open future. Joel Garreau, the journalist who tracks the development of suburban "edge cities," tells of hearing a Frenchman ask "what the *ideal* of an Edge City was. What a wonderfully French question! Who *knows* what these things look like when they grow up?"[38] The "wonderfully French question" is, of course, what stasists always demand to know; France just happens to be the world capital of technocracy. Stasists crave not simply order but certainty, even if that certainty is an illusion, a promise that can never be fulfilled.

Conserving only the underlying stable rules, while letting individual decision making drive change, is a concept that a century of technocracy has made foreign to most people. It does not fit neatly into the comfortable old left–right dichotomy and does not line up with technocratic assumptions about the powers and uses of government. It has a hard time making its case, because it promises only general patterns of improvement—spontaneous order and discovery—not specific results. As the late political scientist Aaron Wildavsky noted, using *spontaneity* as his term for dynamism:

> Serendipity is the rationale of spontaneity. Incessant search by many minds, it is claimed, produces more (and more valuable) knowledge than the attempt to program the paths to discovery by a single one. . . . Not only do markets rely on spontaneity; science and democracy do as well. In all three arenas, proof is retrospective rather than prospective. Looking back over past performance, adherents of free science, politics, and markets argue that on average their results are better than alternatives, but they cannot say what these will be. . . . The strength of spontaneity, its ability to seek out serendipity, is also its shortcoming—exactly what it will do as well as precisely how it will do it cannot be specified in advance.[39]

ers work for the program, and may have invested their lives in it. Others simply benefit from its ongoing existence. Either way, they have a much stronger incentive to fight to preserve the status quo than the general public does to lobby for reform.

Over time, technocratic programs, insulated from competition and feedback, lose their own ability to adapt. Jonathan Rauch calls the problem "demosclerosis," noting in his book by that name:

> No one starting anew today would think to subsidize peanut farmers, banish banks from the mutual-fund business, forbid United Parcel Service to deliver letters, grant massive tax breaks for borrowing. Countless policies are on the books, not because they make sense today, but merely because they cannot be gotten rid of. They are like dinosaurs that will not die, anachronisms whose refusal to go away prevents newer, better-adapted rivals from thriving. In a Darwinian sense, the collectivity of federal policies is ceasing to evolve.

One advantage of dynamist approaches, then, is that they keep the underlying rules neutral and transparent—a flat tax, for instance, rather than "massive tax breaks for borrowing"—and they stigmatize changes designed to favor particular groups. Dynamist policies also try to maintain sources of competition and new ideas. "A good rule of thumb is this: where you see a government restraint on private competition, look for a way to get rid of it," writes Rauch. "And where you see a government agency sheltered from competition, look for a way to expose it. In every case, you will weaken interest groups and stimulate adaptation."[48] There is no way to avoid interest-group politics altogether. But dynamist approaches at least acknowledge the problem and try to avoid creating institutions that feed it.

Clearly, dynamists envision a much less obtrusive government than the technocratic status quo. But despite their dedication to competition and simple, limited rules, dynamists aren't just libertarians with a new name. While most libertarians do fall into the dynamist camp, so do people with a more expansive view of public goods. Godwin, for instance, is a big fan of increased spending on public education; to enhance competition and feedback, however, he would like to see many more independently managed charter schools. Some dynamists also support forms of paternalism, such as seat belt laws or antismoking regulations, that are anathema to libertarians. But the dynamist emphasis on local, often personal, knowledge limits the appeal of paternalism, which presumes to know what is in distant individuals' best interest better than they know themselves.

Many dynamists support a safety net for the poor. They would not, however, try to engineer the "right" distribution of income overall, since that goal both personifies and presumes to control the economy. And dynamists are wary of unintended consequences and perverse incentive effects, such as encouraging teenage motherhood or discouraging work—the sorts of effects that recent welfare reforms try to address, in part through trial-and-error experimentation at the state level.

Instead of rushing to address every new development with a grand plan or an ad hoc solution, dynamists have the patience to let trial and error—and well-established, well-understood rules—work. "It's easier to learn from history than it is to learn from the future," writes Godwin, counseling legal forbearance in the face of new communications technologies. Rather than try to address worst-case scenarios with technocratic schemes that will create legacies of their own, he urges an evolutionary, common law approach. "Almost always," he says, "the time-tested laws and legal principles we already have in place are more than adequate to address the new medium."[49]

Dynamism is about creating the future, but like the new Tomorrowland, it does not ignore the past from which the future evolves. It sees the past and future as inextricably connected and progress as incremental, made possible by what has come before. Knowledge is cumulative and so, in many ways, is experience. We seek to improve on the legacy of the past, but it is from that legacy that any improvement must start. This sense of continuity and time is essential to the many varieties of dynamist thought.

"To seek to look ahead into the future is to seek to understand the momentum of the past and the choices available to us in the present," writes the economist Thomas Sowell. "We live in a world of options constrained by decisions already made and actions already taken—many before we were born." By conventional standards, Sowell is a political, cultural, and temperamental conservative. But he has a dynamic vision. He wants "to allow systemic processes to generate material benefits and personal freedom. What is truly needed is not a blueprint to be imposed from on high but an understanding of what does and does not produce prosperity and freedom. History can be a valuable help in this. But we must never imagine that we can either recreate or atone for yesterday. What we can do is to make its experience the basis for a better today and a better tomorrow."[50]

The historian and philosopher of science Stephen Toulmin voices similar thoughts: "The dream of finding a scratch line, to serve as a starting point for any 'rational' philosophy is unfulfillable. *There is no scratch.*" Toulmin is a political liberal and a leading postmodernist—not the sort of company in which Sowell usually finds himself. Yet their dynamic understandings of the evolution of knowledge and society are not so different. "The belief that, by cutting ourselves off from the inherited ideas of our cultures, we can 'clean the slate' and make a fresh start," Toulmin writes, "is as illusory as the hope for a comprehensive system of theory that is capable of giving us timeless certainty and coherence. . . . All we can be called upon to do is to take a start *from where we are, at the time we are there.* . . . There is no way of cutting ourselves free of our conceptual inheritance: all we are required to do is use our experience critically and discriminatingly, *refining and improving* our inherited ideas, and determining more exactly the limits to their scope."[51]

To dynamists, there is no scratch. Starting from scratch, or staying there, is a static idea, a myth for technocrats who draft plans to redesign the world and reactionaries who dream of a return to Eden. Stasists imagine life out of time. Dynamists see time as the essential element of life, the key to its evolution. History matters. It provides the materials from which we create the future, the ideas and experiences we combine in new and sometimes surprising ways.

The textures of life that so fascinate dynamists are full of such historical surprises. Consider a strange fact about doughnut shops in California: More than 80 percent are owned by Cambodian immigrants. Doughnuts are not a Cambodian food; indeed, Cambodians don't even like them that much. But when Ted Ngoy fled to southern California in the 1970s and got a job in a doughnut store, he realized the possibilities. Here was a niche that matched his skills (or lack thereof) and had potential to grow. The business required hard work but little start-up capital and little English. Ngoy soon owned several doughnut shops. He hired and trained many other refugees, who then started their own stores, hiring and training still more immigrants. Over time, the community developed special expertise and suppliers, making it

nocrats often act as though the cultural changes of the 1960s sprang entirely from a handful of liberal intellectuals and left-wing activists, ignoring the broad dissatisfactions, and the economic and demographic trends, that began in the 1950s (or, in the case of women's roles, as early as the 1920s). Their liberal counterparts take a similar approach to the business culture of the 1980s, treating it as a Reaganite plot or a sudden, inexplicable spasm of decadence. A dynamic understanding of these cultural trends, by contrast, sees them as part of a decentralized, undirected process of experiment, feedback, and learning; cultural evolution is the outcome of individuals working to correct the excesses and mistakes of the past by trying new approaches.

Just as a flattened understanding of the past is essential to selling stasist prescriptions, so a textured sense of history helps illustrate how evolution takes place. It thus informs a dynamist understanding of present trends. A sense of history is also important because it allows us to make meaningful assessments of progress. While there is no scratch, any claim that an evolving future can be incrementally better than the past or present requires a basis of comparison. Using a false or nostalgic base can create great distortions.

Urban intellectuals, accustomed to an environment full of boutiques and family-owned ethnic restaurants, frequently and reflexively denounce the spread of chain restaurants and stores. While the chains may seem trivial in and of themselves, in much public discussion they have come to represent the evils of commercial evolution and, by implication, of dynamism in general. "America's the most boring country to tour already because everywhere looks like everywhere else," says *New York Times* columnist Thomas Friedman on the PBS *Charlie Rose Show.* "And what's sad to me, Charlie, is that the world is starting to look that way, you know, in the big cities now and even outside them, you know, with the Pizza Hut and the McDonald's and the Burger King on every corner."[57]

But for the people in less developed areas, whether in the developing nations today or most of America until recently, the coming of chains has increased rather than decreased both the variety and quality of restaurant food. "When I was growing up" in 1950s Little Rock, recalls the economist Michael Cox, "whenever we went out to eat, we'd eat at a place called Franke's Cafeteria. You'd get your tray, go down the line, and get your food. It wasn't much different from the food at home, and there was certainly no atmosphere. But Mom didn't have to cook." A progression of burger joints, then steakhouses, then fried chicken and pizza, then Chinese food gradually increased the choices. "If you look in the [Dallas] phone book," marvels Cox, "in 1970 there wasn't even any pizza delivery."[58] It is this sense of history—of what actually existed before the "homogeneous" chains arrived—that is missing from the snide stasist dismissal of what the political scientist Benjamin Barber calls "McWorld."[59]

The antichain critique also assumes that history stops with Burger King and Kentucky Fried Chicken, locking restaurant patrons into greasy homogeneity forever. In fact, consumers' tastes become increasingly sophisticated over time, making life tougher for chains catering to the lowest common denominator and opening opportunities for niche marketers with higher-quality offerings. When chain operators get together for conventions, they hear warnings that baby boomers "were weaned on fast food but became expert in a lot of things. They won't settle for some fast-food compromises."[60]

Though it remains a popular, and potent, platitude, the stasist notion that homogeneous mass culture was a permanent phenomenon has been falsified by experience. As the anthropologist Grant McCracken notes, "Where once the most important product was the guarantee of sameness and uniformity, what 'sells' increasingly is variation (at least in design). All of the 'waterfront' and 'downtown' renovations of the last 10 years have made this plain. The rise of the local (micro) brewery makes this plain. . . . Everywhere we look we see the great institutions and inclinations of uniformity giving way to the play of variation and heterogeneity."[61]

The same innovation and response that produced the chains in the first place—the same pattern of discontentment and solution—has pushed forward, creating diverse alternatives. When it identifies widely shared dissatisfactions, stasist social criticism itself becomes a form of dynamic feedback. Criticism, whether of scientific ideas, commercial institutions, or social structures, is essential to innovation and, in the best cases, progress. Having inherited the inventions of the past, we become dissatisfied and look for improvements. From that continuous search comes the open-ended future—the infinite series.

CHAPTER THREE

THE INFINITE SERIES

Early one morning in June 1993, David Gelernter, a Yale computer science professor, went to his office and opened his mail. A package exploded. The resulting injuries cost him most of his right hand, some muscles in his right arm, and much of the sight in his right eye. He considered himself lucky to survive. Three other targets of the same bomber were not so fortunate.

Almost two years later, Gelernter got a letter from his attacker. "If you'd had any brains," it said,

> you would have realized that there are a lot of people out there who resent bitterly the way techno-nerds like you are changing the world and you wouldn't have been dumb enough to open an unexpected package from an unnamed source. . . . If the developments you describe [in the book *Mirror Worlds*] are inevitable, they are not inevitable in the way that old age and bad weather are inevitable. They are inevitable only because techno-nerds like you make them inevitable. If there were no computer scientists there would be no progress in computer science.[1]

The letter was the first proof that the Unabomber's attacks had political content, that Gelernter and others had been singled out because their work advanced technology and learning.

Gelernter was a strange target because he was not then, and is not now, a computer enthusiast. A painter, poet, art critic, and biblical commentator as well as a scientist, he opposes the rapid introduction of computers into schools, fearing that multimedia entertainment will displace critical thinking and traditional literacy.[2] He has dissented from mainstream cyberculture by supporting laws to require new communications and encryption technologies to allow government wiretapping.[3] He describes himself as "one of the very few persons in the field who doesn't *like* computers."[4]

But Gelernter does believe in progress. Indeed, he is arguably one of the last old-fashioned progressive technocrats, a technophile who wants a better future but sees it as a product defined by authority and achieved according to plan. His touchstone technology is not the personal computer but the public work—the highway, dam, or bridge—and his great hero is Robert Moses, the "nearly unstoppable parks commissioner" who shaped New York City.[5] In the late 1930s, Gelernter writes wistfully, "people had the remarkable idea that they could build the future: ponder it, design it, construct it. We feel differently today. We have little sense of control over the future."[6] Gelernter longs to master the future, to hold it still. He shares that longing, though little else, with his attacker, and with the bomber's intellectual sympathizers.

The series of bombs represented one reactionary's attempt to bring the future under control—to wipe out individuals whose pursuits, uncoordinated and independent of one another, might create new patterns, new orders of human life. "We do not believe that progress and growth are inevitable," he wrote Gelernter. The attacks sought to destroy the open-ended future at its source, to impose stasis by eliminating the enterprise that generates change. The bomber's leading rationalizer, Kirkpatrick Sale, likened the bombings to political violence in the Middle East and elsewhere: "If you live in a complex, ever-changing world where you are denied control over your life, as you see it, by a massive forceful regime that uses subtle and artful means of manipulation as well as outright power and regimentation, you might well hate it so deeply that the only sensible way you could see of hurting it, of trying to end it, would be violence, even murder. . . . It would behoove us, I think, to pay less attention to the means by which that reasoning is expressed and more to the conditions that give rise to it."[7]

With its cavalier attitude toward murder, Sale's statement is morally repulsive. It is also analytically wrong. The conspiracist suggestion that the open-ended future is created by a forceful "regime," analogous to a political dictatorship or an occupying army, represents a deep misunderstanding of the dynamic processes Sale and the bomber so detest. In reality, the "complex, ever-changing world" is the product not of a powerful central mind but of millions of different trials and errors, experiments and results—done in parallel and without coordination.

There is no dictator, no "forceful regime." No one is in charge. Specific undertakings, such as a scientist's research program or a business's marketing campaign, may proceed according to plan. But they in turn contribute to a much larger, evolving system that "lives" with no more overall direction than an ecosystem or cell. It is that living, natural system that reactionaries seek to blow apart and technocrats want to freeze.

The dynamist concept of trial-and-error evolution is very different from the concept of progress popular earlier in this century—the goal-directed, progressive ideal for which Gelernter is nostalgic. We make progress not toward a particular, certain, and uniform destination but toward many different, personally determined, and incremental goals. In a global sense, "progress" is the product of those parallel individual searches: the extension of knowledge and the gradual improvement of people's lives—an increase in comfort, in life options, in the opportunity for "diversified, worthwhile experience."[8] Progress is neither random Darwinian evolution nor teleological inevitability.

This diverse, decentralized process makes technocrats uncomfortable—no one is in charge, and the results are unpredictable—but it strikes reactionaries as downright evil. They find its ambition unseemly, its results disruptive, its values perverse. Open-ended trial and error represents a willful rebellion against fate, a refusal, in their minds, to honor what is and what has gone before. It views civilization as an ongoing process rather than an eternal state. It overvalues the future and encourages discontent. Writes the British philosopher John Gray, in an essay calling for greens and conservatives to make common cause against dynamism:

> The idea of progress is detrimental to the life of the spirit, because it encourages us to view our lives, not under the aspect of eternity, but as moments in a universal process of betterment. We do not, therefore, accept our lives for what they are, but instead consider them always for what they might someday become. In this way the idea of progress reinforces the restless discontent that is one of the diseases of modernity, a disease symptomatically expressed in Hayek's nihilistic and characteristically candid statement that 'Progress is movement for movement's sake.' No view of human life could be further from either Green thought or genuine conservative philosophy.[9]

The allegedly "nihilistic" statement, which Gray breaks off in midsentence, concludes, "for it is in the process of learning, and in the effects of having learned something new, that man enjoys the gift of his intelligence." Hayek's claim is that striving for knowledge and improvement is, in and of itself, a worthwhile exercise of the highest human qualities, even if it does not produce an unquestionably better world.

Hayek is making the weakest possible claim for progress, which he defines as "the cumulative growth of knowledge and power over nature."[10] That claim does not depend on any demonstrable increase in prosperity, comfort, or happiness. It simply allows the human spirit to flourish. Most dynamists—most especially the mundane problem solvers and experimenters who drive "progress" without ever thinking in such grandiose terms—look for, and often find, less abstract benefits.[11] Progress does not mean that everyone will be better off in every respect. But under ordinary circumstances, for the random individual, life in a dynamist society tomorrow will be better, on the whole, than life today. It will offer more variety, more opportunity, more options, more knowledge, more control over time and place, more life. It will address more sources of dissatisfaction (though it may also call attention to new ones) and create more sources of delight. And while it will not perfect moral character or avert foolish ideas, its continuous processes of criticism and correction will, over time, curb excesses and limit damage.

Contrary to the critics who sling the epithet *utopian* at anyone who suggests that life might get better over time, dynamists do not envision utopia, for utopia is by definition static, an unchanging state of perfection. To dynamists, progress is a process, not a product. Christopher Lasch, although himself an emphatic reactionary, understood that much. In *The True and Only Heaven: Progress and Its Critics,* he accurately captured (and rejected) the dynamist concept of the open-ended future. What was original about that idea, he wrote, was

> not the promise of a secular utopia that would bring history to a happy ending but *the promise of steady improvement with no foreseeable ending at all.*
> . . . The idea of progress never rested mainly on the promise of an ideal society—not at least in its Anglo-American version. Historians have exaggerated the utopian component in progressive ideology. The modern conception of history is utopian only in its assumption that modern

history has no foreseeable conclusion. We take our cue from science, at once the source of our material achievements and the model of cumulative, self-perpetuating inquiry, which guarantees its continuation precisely by its willingness to submit every advance to the risk of supersession. (Emphasis added.)[12]

That process is driven not just by "techno-nerds" but by everyone who solves problems, adopts new products or new ideas, or combines familiar things in unfamiliar ways. Not every experiment or idea is a good one, but only by trying new ideas do we discover genuine improvements. And there is always more to be done. Every improvement can be improved still further; every new idea makes still more new combinations possible. In this context, the future is indeed an "infinite series," just as the Agrarians charged: an open-ended progression of invention, learning, adaptation, and change.

How we view that search for improvement—whether we celebrate it or denounce it, surf it or try to tame it—is the question that most obviously defines the dynamism–stasis split. Its answers and their implications are found not just in theory but in the textures of everyday life. Understanding progress, then, is critical to understanding both the dynamic vision and its opponents. To choose between the future and its enemies, we must first understand why that future is created and how—the demand for progress and the supply.

Just about every morning, sometime between 6:00 and 6:30, I wake up and glance at the clock perched four feet from my head. Its glowing red digits tell me that it is not yet time to get up, and I happily roll over to sleep for another hour or so. Every time this happens, I am amazed. And every couple of weeks, I get a sharp reminder of why that amazement is justified. On those mornings, the clock is nothing but a dark blur, its digits smeared into a bright discoloration with no hint of meaning. That is the way the world—all the world more than a foot or so away—looks to my naked eyes. No one who sees the world this way can simply scoff at the notion of progress.

Eyeglasses to correct nearsightedness were invented around the year 1500, two centuries after reading glasses.[13] For me in the late 1960s, they were miracle enough. The trees once again had leaves, the chalkboards words. Contact lenses came a decade later. More miracles:

peripheral vision, much sharper and more consistent focus, no annoying smudges, no slipping down my nose. And I did look better.

Another decade passed. My hard lenses had been replaced by supposedly better gas-permeable ones, safer because they let in more oxygen but never as satisfactory as the old contacts I could wear eighteen hours at a stretch. The dry air of Los Angeles made a difficult situation worse. The lenses would often start to hurt within a few hours, driving me back to glasses and all the shortcomings I thought I'd escaped. Finally, a new optometrist hit on a solution: disposables, which had been on the market only a couple of years. They were superwet and got thrown away before they could get grungy. Unlike rigid lenses, they came in off-the-shelf sizes—they were easier to fit than shoes—and could be quickly and cheaply replaced if lost. As an added bonus, I could keep them in for two weeks at a time. So now I wake up amazed.

My demand for progressively better lenses recapitulates much of a century-long search. The history of contact lenses stretches back to an obsessed late-nineteenth-century Swiss physician named A. Eugen Fick, who had glass lenses ground to his specifications, conducted extensive experiments on rabbits, and himself wore the first human contact lenses—for two whole hours. Fick envisioned all sorts of uses for the lenses, both therapeutic and cosmetic. He recorded most of the major problems contacts posed and explored some possible causes.[14] Over the next century, eye specialists, later joined by polymer chemists, experimented with lens materials and sizes, with various ways of making impressions of the eyeball, and with numerous wetting solutions—all in pursuit of a lens that would match the shape of the patient's eye, would provide the right vision correction, and could be worn for long stretches of time without harm or irritation.[15]

Contact lenses provide a microcosm of the demand side of progress: the trial-and-error process by which dissatisfaction breeds innovation and improvement. The inventors are still at work, and the perfect contact lens remains always out of reach. If people can wear lenses all day, they want to wear them all night, too, and that raises new safety hurdles. Soft lenses are easier to fit and wear, but they also require more care, leading doctors to worry about maintaining sterile conditions. Disposable lenses, which come packaged in sterile solutions, attempt to deal with that problem. But if lenses can be cheap enough to dispose of every week or two, why not unwrap a new sterile pair every day and avoid the risks of overnight wear? The challenge then becomes to push costs down far enough to make such lenses affordable.

Each problem solved leads to new demands and, sometimes, to new problems. It is an open-ended series: lenses that change eye color, lenses that protect against ultraviolet radiation, lenses that correct astigmatism, lenses that require less care, lenses that tear less easily, lenses that can be more safely slept in, and on and on. Someday we may expect our contact lenses to function as computer screens and navigation guides, to see infrared or enhance night vision. Or we may displace them altogether with laser surgery or other procedures, as yet undiscovered.

None of this process is unique to contact lenses. Similar problem-solving drives all innovation, technical or otherwise. Authors revise their books, cooks fiddle with their recipes, teachers try new techniques, and parents even hope to do better with later-born children. Rarely, however, do we discover perfection; one advance merely creates opportunities for more. The imperfections of the world (and our tendencies to notice them) generate the demand for progress.

Far from a utopian concept, this sense of progress acknowledges that life is not perfect, that any improvement requires ingenuity and work, and that different people have different notions of what constitutes a "better" idea. "Form follows failure," is how civil engineering professor Henry Petroski, whose popular books explore the histories of such mundane objects as zippers and forks, sums it up:

> The form of made things is always subject to change in response to their real or perceived shortcomings, their failures to function properly. This principle governs all invention, innovation, and ingenuity; it is what drives all inventors, innovators, and engineers. And there follows a corollary: Since nothing is perfect, and, indeed, since even our ideas of perfection are not static, everything is subject to change over time. There can be no such thing as a "perfected" artifact; the future perfect can only be a tense, not a thing.[16]

Contrary to the traditional technocratic vision, here the very nature of progress dictates an inherently open, and imperfect, future.

Fix one problem and others arise. Or having solved the more serious problems, we turn to others we never worried about before. Carmakers refine the placement of cup holders; dishwasher manufacturers cut noise and design fold-down racks; Procter & Gamble produces Tide Free for the allergy prone. An opportunity is a problem no one has solved, or addressed, or even considered. Post-it notes sprang from one man's discontent with the bookmarks that kept falling out of his choir hymnal. "Though no prior need for the little sticky notes had been articulated," writes Petroski, "once they were in the hands of office workers all sorts of uses were found, and suddenly people couldn't do without the things."[17]

The procession of imperfections, and the opportunities they present, never ends. Even so ancient and accepted an artifact as a dinner table is anything but perfect. Ideally it "ought to be variable in size and height, removable altogether, impervious to scratches, self-cleaning, and having no legs," notes a design scholar quoted by Petroski.[18] New furniture designs are in fact introduced every year—some offering functional improvements, others aesthetic innovations. This process is not a matter of "built-in obsolescence," the critic's dismissive term for every new consumer good; people keep their furniture for generations. Rather, new designs represent continuous attempts at improvement, or adaptations to environmental changes, such as shrinking families who require smaller tables or computers that demand reconfigured desks.

In some cases, the imperfections and improvements are in how we make things rather than in the things themselves. Throwing pots on a wheel replaces piling up coils of clay and smoothing them together. Power looms supplant hand looms. Desktop publishing displaces traditional paste-up with T-squares, wax, and X-Acto knives. Sometimes the new process is designed to save time, sometimes to improve quality, sometimes to conserve resources (and, by doing so, to reduce costs). My colleague Lynn Scarlett, an expert on recycling and solid waste issues, is fond of tearing soda cans in half to demonstrate how little metal they contain compared to the days when ripping one apart was a sign of virility and major muscles. From 1961 to 1996, the weight of a twelve-ounce soda can dropped by almost 80 percent, as manufacturers—under competitive pressure to find any incremental advantage—figured out ways to shave the thickness of cans and use new materials.[19]

Contrary to the scare stories of reactionary greens, many innovations substitute ingenuity for physical resources, reducing environmental impacts. That is particularly the case as technologies are refined and enter the phase of incremental improvement: The more farmers and manufacturers learn about chemical fertilizers or pesticides—how they work, how to deliver them, how to combine them with other farming techniques—the smaller the quantity necessary to produce the same results. From 1982 to 1992, the amount of corn U.S. farmers produced for every pound of pesticide used jumped 18 percent, the amount of soybeans 117 percent, wheat 6 percent, and cotton 16 percent.[20]

Petroski's thesis suggests another important insight into the nature of progress. Although science is the customary model for philosophers interested in evolutionary epistemology, it is not, in fact, the best analogy to capture the infinite series. True, science provides interesting instances of thesis, empirical test, analytical feedback, and response—of argument in action and the benefits of criticism. It does, as Lasch suggests, "submit every advance to the risk of supersession." It is indeed a dynamic process.

But science studies the natural world, which is finite. And the reductionist project of modern science sets further limits. It looks for fundamental principles, for scientific laws. Scientists could, in theory at least, discover all those laws. They could find what *Scientific American* writer John Horgan calls "*The Answer.*" We could arrive at the end of science—and Horgan suggests we are approaching it—with nothing left to do but catalog beetles or engage in unfalsifiable speculations about the beginning or end of time.[21] Whether Horgan is right, and I suspect he is not, the end of science in this sense is at least theoretically possible.

Technology is different. So is art. So is general human culture, that elaborate extended order of institutions and practices with which we are constantly experimenting (often without realizing any broader implications of our actions). Technology, art, and culture are based not on uncovering a few fixed facts but on coming up with new combinations of ideas, testing them, finding their faults, trying possibly better combinations, and so on. Petroski's endless imperfections are part of this story—the demand side. But there is a supply side, too, a reason the infinite series is not only desired but possible. That reason lies in combinations.

Economist Paul Romer explains the general point this way: There have been 10^{18} seconds since the Big Bang, and there are 10^{88} particles in the known universe. Those are very large numbers—the smaller is a million million million—but they are dwarfed by the number of ways things (or ideas) can be combined. Even something as simple as a deck of cards can be rearranged in unimaginably numerous ways. There are 10^{68} possible card decks, which means that any order you happen to shuffle has probably never appeared before. And card decks offer a relatively modest number of combinations: Recombining the 1s and 0s on an ordinary 1.4 megabyte floppy disk could generate $10^{3,500,000}$ different bit strings. A cow is one example of the possible combination of certain atoms—an amazing "machine" for turning grass into protein. Who knows what others might be possible?

"The naive intuition that people have about limits to growth is profoundly wrong," says Romer. "There is a scarcity of physical objects, but that's not the constraint on what we can do."[22] The real constraint is not the number of objects but the ways of combining objects or ideas—a number of possibilities that makes the number of atoms in the universe look close to zero by comparison. We are limited, in a very real sense, only by our imagination and the time in which we have to exercise it. That time includes not simply our own life spans but the creative legacies of past generations: the experiments, inventions, and knowledge on which we can build.

The power of combinatorics appears throughout the theory of technological creativity. But it is not the limited province of "technonerds." Technology, art, and culture all interact; they are not distinct realms but manifestations of the same experimental, creative impulse. And they can reinforce each other. Robert Wise, who edited *Citizen Kane*, recalls how cinematographer Gregg Toland's technical experiments gave the director more options:

> By having the deep focus he was able to give Orson [Welles] a lot more leeway in how he moved his actors and staged the scenes, and freed him up. . . . We'd always had this problem of cinematography not being able to carry somebody in the foreground as sharply in focus as somebody 20 feet back. Gregg had for a number of years been working on new lenses—faster lenses—that would allow him to pour more light in, to stop down and get a greater depth in these scenes, and that's one of the things I think that gave *Citizen Kane* the kind of dynamics that it has, extraordinary dynamics compared to other films of the time.[23]

As the child Charles Foster Kane plays in the snow outside a window, the adults inside are in equally sharp focus, discussing his fate. In this case, art interacts with technology, giving a visionary director new and better ways to tell the story—increasing the number of available combinations of actors and light.

As film progresses, technically and artistically, it also develops a visual vocabulary, conventions that audiences learn to interpret: point-of-view shots, dissolves to mark the passing of time, cuts between actions happening simultaneously but in different places. The history of film, like the history of literature, offers not only techniques but also a store of allusions on which new works can draw, for serious (*Pulp Fiction*) or comic (*Wayne's World*) effect. New art does not replace old art. We do not lose *King Lear* to get *Ran* or Laurence Olivier's *Henry V* to get Kenneth Branagh's. But each new creation can make still more new art possible. Without "Marlowe's mighty line," the refinement of blank verse, we would not have *Hamlet* or *Paradise Lost,* each of which in turn has begotten countless descendants.[24] The more things that have been created already, the more that can be created in the future.

Herbert Simon, the Nobel laureate whose students were puzzled by the spontaneous ordering of cities, explains this process in evolutionary terms. It is, he suggests, analogous to the creation of niches in the biological world:

> The larger and richer the collection of building blocks that is available for construction, the more elaborate are the structures that can be generated.
>
> If there is such a trend toward variety, then evolution is not to be understood as a series of tournaments for the occupation of a fixed set of environmental niches, each tournament won by the organism that is fittest for that niche. Instead evolution brings about a proliferation of niches. The environments to which most biological organisms adapt are formed mainly of other organisms, and the environments to which human beings adapt, mainly of other human beings. Each new bird or mammal provides a niche for one or more new kind of flea.
>
> Vannevar Bush wrote of science as an "endless frontier." It can be endless, as can be the process of design and the evolution of human society, because there is no limit on diversity in the world. By combinatorics on a few primitive elements, unbounded variety can be created.[25]

In human society, a similar combinatorial process creates what the anthropologist Grant McCracken calls "plenitude": the "sheer number and variety of social species," and of their technological, artistic, cultural, institutional, and intellectual equivalents. Teenagers mix cultural characteristics—hairstyles, fashion, musical tastes, hobbies, attitudes, slang—to produce new and distinctive categories: "rockers" and "b-girls," "hippies" and "punks," "skaters" and "goths." Popular musicians combine elements of old genres to produce new ones, fusing punk and heavy metal to create grunge or creating such unlikely combinations as bagpipe funk and swing punk; classical cellist Yo-Yo Ma incorporates Cajun music and Texas fiddle into his repertoire. Parents grow discontented with the public schools, and a "breathtaking speciation of educational philosophy" emerges from private alternatives.[26] New niches are being created all the time, and every possible niche seems to fill up immediately, generating still more new niches.

Plenitude can make progress harder to notice, and seemingly less impressive. When progress is just a matter of getting more stuff, it's relatively easy to recognize and to measure. Refrigerators, elevators, and smooth, modern highways were exciting in the late 1930s, writes Gelernter: "Technology was a less capable yet far more wonderful thing in 1939 than it is today."[27] We tend to recognize dramatic changes, not subtle improvements. It's harder to appreciate the dispersed advantages of customization and choice, because, by their nature, they serve the needs of the few rather than the many. Yet it is just such improvements that constitute much of the material progress we experience today.

In this regard, we can think of technological progress as a series of stages. First, a truly new technology is invented and spreads far enough for everyone to discover that a large demand for it exists. It then enters what we may call the "extensive" stage, where the major challenge for producers is to distribute the same basic technology to as many people as possible. This extensive stage is analogous to producing more crops by simply bringing more land under cultivation—the original use of the term *extensive* in economics. During this period of increasing quantities, improvements are made mostly in mass production or distribution, rather than customization or subtle aspects of product quality. And having the technology at all is a source of wonder.

Eventually the maturing technology reaches the "intensive" stage, where incremental improvements and niche products—increases in quality—become important. This intensive phase is analogous to farming the same amount of land more efficiently and, like such farming, it raises the specter of diminishing returns to innovative effort.

For developing countries, extensive progress—the spread of such well-established goods as adequate and varied meals, basic housing, electricity, automobiles, televisions, and refrigerators—is the major issue. Producers know what consumers want; the question is how to deliver it profitably. Meat packers must develop the refrigerator car and feed lot, automakers the assembly line. The expansion of Wal-Mart throughout rural America, bringing nationally branded products, represents a relatively recent example of extensive progress, one widely denounced by reactionaries. Once people have the basic extensive goods, however, customization and quality improvements become important, and where opportunities lie is less obvious. Major new inventions that might permit a new stage of extensive development are the great mystery, the challenge to would-be innovators.

Comparing the 1990s to the 1930s, Gelernter attributes the loss of wonder to the removal of contemporary technology from everyday concerns: "Technology then dealt in the tangible and the everyday, not in strange stuff like software and silicon."[28] But the glamour fields of computers and biotechnology are exactly the ones that stir today's public imagination (including the imagination of malicious reactionary bombers). They are the technologies undergoing rapid, extensive development; hence, they attract a disproportionate amount of attention.

Immersed professionally in the esoteric world of basic research, Gelernter writes critically that "relatively few technologists are intrigued by the question of how Mrs. Schwartz can shave half an hour off her weekly trip to the shopping mall. We have more significant things to worry about. We have goals that are more important than merely making people's lives easier in modest ways."[29] That is not, however, what is actually going on. Intellectual authorities may not glorify, or even notice, modest, intensive improvements in everyday life, but technologists are busy making them. To disprove Gelernter's gloomy assertion, we need only join the hypothetical Mrs. Schwartz on a trip to the supermarket to visit the shampoo, or detergent, or feminine hygiene–product aisle.

There we will find an enormous array of choices, many of them recent inventions. Far from mindlessly identical items, differing only by packaging or brand name, these products embody sophisticated applications of chemistry, materials science, and extremely high-tech manufacturing. The plenitude can be overwhelming—evoking the scene in *Moscow on the Hudson* where the Soviet immigrant played by Robin Williams faints at the sight of an American coffee aisle—but the influence of Mrs. Schwartz's demands for ever-improving, ever-more-customized products is undeniable.

At a West Los Angeles supermarket, for instance, I catalogued fifteen varieties of Procter & Gamble's Always sanitary napkins, examples of ever-intensifying progress. Disposable sanitary napkins date only to 1920. The self-sticking technology that liberated women from uncomfortable and barely functional belts (and that helped create all those niches) was developed only in the early 1970s.[30] Those intensive improvements, and rarely acknowledged products, make a tremendous difference in women's lives. Stifling mundane, intensive progress can even have political consequences. Interviewed shortly before the 1996 Russian presidential elections, Muscovite Olga Vladimirov explained her intended vote to the *Los Angeles Times:* "How could any woman who remembers the indignity of scrounging around the city and standing in endless lines for cotton wool even think about going back to life under the Communists? I didn't even know what a tampon was before the democrats came to power."[31]

In fact, Soviet planners emphasized extensive progress—heavy industry and the military—and deprived consumers of the subtle advantages of tampons, McDonald's, and shoes that fit. American observers, counting up the tons of steel (often inaccurately) but disregarding their quality, overestimated the strength of the Soviet economy. By the *glasnost* era in 1990, Soviet economist Victor Belkin was telling Americans that the Soviet gross national product was at best 28 percent of U.S. GNP, about half the Central Intelligence Agency's estimate. Once you factored in waste and extremely low-quality goods, he said, the Soviet standard of living was about that of China, much lower than U.S. analysts had believed.[32]

In the United States, by contrast, intensive progress has been rapid—leading to the opposite error: a tendency to understate economic progress by ignoring improvements in quality and choice. The consumer price index (CPI) may include shampoo, but not the added safety of replacing a glass bottle with an unbreakable plastic one; a pair of slacks, but not the improvement of wrinkle-free fabric; housing, but not the now-standard central air-conditioning or the stain-resistant carpet; an automobile, but not its increased working life. The CPI does not pick up the convenience of 24-hour toll-free numbers or super-markets and pharmacies open around the clock. These improvements are real, but they are much harder to count. So when they show up in higher prices, it's easy to attribute the increase to inflation. The result of ignoring incremental, intensive progress is a systematic underesti-mate of the standard of living.

Recognizing these problems, among others, the so-called Boskin Commission recommended in late 1996 that the CPI be adjusted downward.[33] The commission's report was roundly denounced by critics with a stake in a gloomy vision of the future. "If the Boskin Commission is right," scoffed economist Dean Baker of the left-lean-ing Economic Policy Institute, "our children and grandchildren can look forward to an incredibly prosperous future."[34] That prospect, he seemed to think, was too absurd to be believed.

For all his misplaced gloom, it turns out that Gelernter is on to something. Technologists are no longer *celebrated* for making improve-ments in everyday life. Our collective attitudes toward progress—the attitudes suggested in the popular press, in movies and books, by politicians, scholars, and acceptably "serious" pundits—reflect stasist values. Technocrats like Baker (and Gelernter himself) assume that progress requires firm central direction and that dynamism itself destroys the possibility of progress.

Meanwhile, reactionaries denounce Mrs. Schwartz's desire for new-and-improved products as petty, wasteful, and dangerous—at best the product of corporate manipulation, at worst the reflection of selfishness and greed. Environmentalist Stephanie Mills writes con-temptuously of the "debased human protoplasm" served by a local hypermart that "sells clothes, food, sporting goods, electronics, build-ing supplies, pets, baked goods, deli food, toys, tools, hardware, gee-gaws, jim-jams, and knick-knacks."[35] The Calcutta-based Consumer Unity and Trust Society denounces the spread of consumerism, with its toothbrushes, ceiling fans, and refrigerators, to India's poor.[36] John Gray declares open-ended economic growth "the most vulgar ideal ever put before suffering mankind."[37]

And in his influential 1976 book *The Cultural Contradictions of Capi-talism,* the sociologist Daniel Bell all but blames the fall of bourgeois civilization on the desire for improved products. Drawing on such examples as plate glass windows, washing machines, refrigerators, and automobiles, he concludes:

> The cultural transformation of modern society is due, singularly, to the rise of mass consumption, or the diffusion of what were once considered luxuries to the middle and lower classes of society. In this process, past luxuries are constantly redefined as necessities, so that it eventually seems incredible that an ordinary object could ever have been considered out of the reach of an ordinary man. . . . Taken all together, mass consumption meant the acceptance, in the crucial area of life-style, of the idea of social change and personal transformation, and it gave legitimacy to those who would innovate and lead the way, in culture as well as in production.

The result of this infinite series, Bell argues, is a culture of hedonism, "a world of make-believe in which one lives for expectations, for what will come rather than what is."[38] Bell the socialist thus anticipates Gray the Tory, who worries about "the restless discontent" fostered by the idea of progress. Innovation, novelty, and an eye toward the future, Bell suggests, undermine the Puritan virtues and will therefore destroy capitalism. (The entrepreneurial or inventive impulse figures nowhere in his vision of how capitalism works.) It is not just materialism that concerns him but the very impulse toward improvement. The endless pursuit of knowledge—or of improved paper clips, new musical forms, or better management practices—that delights dynamists appalls the stasis-craving social critics who have shaped the Western *Zeitgeist* for decades.

Technology, the cliché goes, gives us nuclear bombs and pollution. Rare is the new idea that does not go bad. "Every mature technology brings a minimal immediate gain, followed by enormous long-term liabilities," declares the social critic Theodore Roszak. "The computer is the latest entry in history, still bright with promise to its enthusiasts, but surely destined to join the lengthening file of modern technological treachery that Aldous Huxley began compiling in his *Brave New World*."[39] It is not enough, such critics argue, for new ideas to improve *some* things; they must bring unalloyed benefits or face denunciation for "treachery." No trade-offs are allowed, even for inventions that do more or less what they promise.

Learning through trial and error necessarily means experimenting with things that won't work at all. Since many attempts to correct the world's faults fail, critics pronounce stasis the best policy. Declares Gray, "A sound conservative maxim in all areas of policy . . . is that we should be very cautious of innovations, technological or otherwise, that have serious downside risks—*even if the evidence suggestive of these risks is inconclusive, if the risks are small, or if their magnitudes cannot be known*" (emphasis added).[40] We would do better, this view holds, to shun new ideas and the risks they entail, to prefer the devil we know to the devil we don't, to halt the infinite series.

Dynamism generates progress through trial and error, experiment and feedback. Both components of the process are crucial. As the economic historian Joel Mokyr notes, "If every harebrained technological idea were tried and implemented, the costs would have been tremendous. Like [biological] mutations, most technological innovations are duds and deserve to be eliminated. Yet overcoming the built-in resistance is the key to technological progress: if no harebrained idea was ever tried, we would still be living in the Stone Age."[41] This principle is not limited to technological ideas; it applies to all innovations. But in many areas of life, both trial and error—the freedom to experiment and the ability to fail—have been undermined by stasists uncomfortable with the inevitable risks such an evolutionary system entails. Disapproval of risk taking permeates our culture and shapes our law. Sometimes we forbid taking risks. Sometimes we spread the consequences from the risk taker to others. Either way, we squelch the learning that is essential to progress.

Consider the advice dispensed by *Vogue* medical columnist Isadore Rosenfeld, M.D., on disposable, extended-wear contact lenses. Three of the four experts he surveyed, Rosenfeld writes, say sleeping in the lenses "is not safe," an absolute statement:

> My own position is that removing the lenses at night takes no more than a minute or two, and, after all, you don't need them while you're sleeping (unless you're having nearsighted dreams). Even if you've been keeping your lenses in at night and haven't had trouble thus far, you still face an additional risk of infection. . . . There is good news on the horizon: I'm told there are lenses in development that will permit adequate passage of oxygen to the eye and will likely be safer for overnight wear.[42]

As consumer information on the inherent hazards of sticking pieces of plastic in your eyes and then going to sleep, Rosenfeld's column is perfectly reasonable. He questions cornea authorities and presents up-to-date research. And I can testify from excruciatingly painful personal experience that extended-wear contact lenses do entail the risk of corneal ulcers. But would we have contact lenses at all, much less those safer "lenses in development," if everyone shared Rosenfeld's attitude toward risk taking? We can only imagine what he—or any other sensible person—would have advised the obsessed Dr. Fick when he was placing ground-glass lenses over his eyeballs and observing the results.

Confined to the pages of a fashion magazine, Rosenfeld's preference for progress without risk is a benign fantasy, no more dangerous than the lingerie ad it follows. But it is, in fact, a fantasy. Risk and courage are essential to innovation. Among technologists, the importance of "early adopters" is widely acknowledged. Without people willing to pay the high prices that let innovators develop markets, improve processes, and drive down production costs, we would not have computers, stereo equipment, or contact lenses. But money isn't the only currency that finances new ideas. Other early adopters pay by willingly taking risks on unproven innovations, whose benefits likely come with flaws or side effects. These risk takers provide critical feedback both to innovators and to potential later adopters. The information they supply helps determine whether a new idea will flop altogether or get a chance to prove itself to a wider public.

Just about every new idea goes through a debugging process. When bank credit cards spread in the 1960s, the losses bordered on catastrophe. Issuing banks lost millions of dollars in theft, fraud, and bad debts. Consumers screamed about receiving unordered cards in the mail—a technique banks used to quickly establish a large enough network of cardholders to interest retailers. Pundits denounced the cards and warned of a nation of "credit drunks." Representative Wright Patman, the powerful chairman of the House Banking and Currency Committee, crusaded against bankcards and threatened to regulate them out of business. A foe of chain stores in the 1930s, Patman remained a steadfast opponent of shopping innovation throughout his career. He was a classic reactionary using technocratic means to block new ideas.

Testifying before Patman's committee in 1968, Federal Reserve Board governor Andrew Brimmer patiently defended the messy process of experimentation. The knee-jerk reaction against credit cards, he warned, threatened all innovation in financial services. Imagination, he implied, should be encouraged, not outlawed:

> We need to be careful not to discourage banks from experimenting in developing improved ways to serve the public, including consumers. Certainly banks have been criticized in the past, often with justification, for their failure to recognize developing needs for credit and for lack of imagination in devising ways to meet these needs. In determining whether statutory restrictions upon bank credit cards are needed, care should be taken not to deny the public the advantages of continued innovation in the provision of banking services.[43]

Mass card mailings managed to dodge regulation until late 1970, long enough for banks to blanket most metropolitan areas with credit cards, and for the cards to become an established part of American retailing.[44]

As for the risks (and losses) the banks themselves took, they were as necessary as they were painful. Figuring out how to make the system work required trials, errors, and more trials. Joseph Nocera puts it this way in his history of the "money revolution" that made bankcards and mutual funds the credit and investment tools of the middle class:

> Most credit card veterans now view the late 1960s as a time of madness, culminating in staggering losses to the banks, public embarrassment, and federal legislation. But they also now believe that the madness was necessary. From that chaos emerged the electronic credit card system that now exists. Without it, bank credit cards might never have become what they are today: the plastic symbol of the money revolution.[45]

No one had ever created a multibank credit card network before, so no one knew in advance how to do it. The pioneers could not possibly anticipate and correct ahead of time everything that might go wrong. They had to rely instead on their ability to adapt and learn.

The political scientist Aaron Wildavsky described two basic strategies for dealing with risk: anticipation, the static planning that aspires to perfect foresight; and resilience, the dynamic response that relies on having many margins of adjustment:

> Anticipation is a mode of control by a central mind; efforts are made to predict and prevent potential dangers before damage is done. Forbid-

ding the sale of certain medical drugs is an anticipatory measure. Resilience is the capacity to cope with unanticipated dangers after they have become manifest, learning to bounce back. An innovative biomedical industry that creates new drugs for new diseases is a resilient device. . . . Anticipation seeks to preserve stability: the less fluctuation, the better. Resilience accommodates variability; one may not do so well in good times but learn to persist in the bad.[46]

Many circumstances demand a mixture of both strategies. But in a rapidly changing environment—whether the changes spring from human action or natural phenomena—resilience is essential. Silicon Valley is built on resilience. Companies seek to establish partnerships with other vendors rather than try to do everything themselves. Employees job-hop from place to place, confident that if one employer closes shop they can find work elsewhere. Technologists work to get products out as quickly, rather than as perfectly, as possible. People do the best they can at the moment, deal with problems as they arise, and develop networks to help them out. Unexpected shocks are inevitable; the goal, then, is to foster adaptability.[47]

Resilience is enhanced by the dynamic processes and combinatoric options of the infinite series. Silicon Valley's many companies make it more resilient against economic shocks than a region that depends on a few vertically integrated firms. Similarly, richer, more technically advanced places bounce back more quickly from natural disasters than do poorer places with less cushion and fewer methods of response. Contrary to reactionary dreams of self-sufficient static utopias, places that routinely trade with the outside world are also more resilient. In an emergency, they can call on material resources and moral support from outside their stricken region. The people who piled their cars with provisions and drove to aid the victims of Hurricane Andrew represented a resilient response to disaster, a response dependent on flexible tools and decentralized reactions.

When the Kobe earthquake struck in 1994, the region's wealth and large stock of construction equipment sped cleanup, even though Japan's anticipation strategy, which had promised quake-resistant roads, railroads, and buildings, had failed. Indeed, the official bias toward anticipation made things worse. With regular telephone service down, officials refused to let Nippon Motorola give out free cellular phones because the authorities didn't want to issue the phones identification numbers. The Kobe city government turned away volunteers because, says an official, "we couldn't verify the trustworthiness of the people who volunteered, so we could not take responsibility for them."[48]

Kobe was hurt by another form of technocratic stasis as well: sheltering established ideas and enterprises from competition. Laws to protect small shops limited supermarkets that wanted to reopen. Other restrictions blocked home-building companies from bringing in American carpenters able to handle prefabricated or 2-by-4–based construction.[49] A more flexible system, one without legal bias toward small stores or particular construction methods, would have been much more resilient.

Such protectionist policies enforce stability at the cost of stifling both resilience and progress. They eliminate the checking process essential to trial-and-error learning, the way by which we identify the "failures" that new forms might correct. By protecting small stores, Japan blocks competition that would encourage shopkeepers to improve customer service, lower prices, or carry more varied product lines—and that might quickly spread successful new techniques. Until relatively recently, much of New York City effectively did the same. But in the mid-1990s, large-scale retailing hit the city. *The New York Times* took note of the effects in a front-page article, leading with the tale of stationery store owner Michael Jacobs, who had "re-created his business in the megastores' image":

> He bought uniforms and name tags for his employees, and walkie-talkies so they would not have to shout to one another over customers' heads. He began accepting returns. He extended his hours, opened on Sunday for the first time, and last Christmas hired his 14-year-old son, Andrew, as doorman. Every new touch, Mr. Jacobs admits, was borrowed from the bigger players across the avenue.
>
> "I made it into the 20th century by following these other stores," Mr. Jacobs said. "It's like going to college for getting the customer in your store—you have to pick up and steal these little ideas."[50]

Competition provides not only useful criticism but a continuous source of experiments. It gives people like Jacobs the ideas with which to create still more progress and encourages them, too, to come up with incremental improvements. By picking winners, stasist protectionism eliminates this learning process, which includes learning what does *not* work.

"Premature choice," warns the physicist Freeman Dyson, "means betting all your money on one horse before you have found out whether she is lame."[51] Protecting established interests from new challengers is one form of premature choice. But technocratic planners also sometimes kill existing alternatives to force their new ideas to "succeed." To protect the space shuttle, NASA not only blocked competition from private space launch companies, it also eliminated its own expendable launchers.[52] Such preemptive verdicts often mark public works projects. Planners pick an all-purpose winner, squeeze out alternatives, and eliminate any real chance of experiment and learning.

Consider the infamous Denver International Airport (DIA). Aviation officials touted the $4.9 billion project as essential to keep up with the region's growth. They promised it would be a vast improvement over the old Stapleton Airport, which was often socked in by bad weather. But its sponsors foisted DIA on unwilling customers. The airport is twenty-five miles outside Denver, pretty much in the middle of nowhere, while Stapleton was just fifteen minutes from downtown. To make matters worse, there are no hotels near DIA. And the new airport's cost per passenger is somewhere between $11.75 and $18.14, depending on how you count—substantially more than either the $4.59 at Stapleton or the $9.91 promised by former Mayor Federico Peña.[53] Frequent travelers resent the inconvenience and the generally higher ticket prices. "I liked Stapleton better," one told *The Denver Post.* "You could literally leave about 45 minutes before your plane departed. With DIA, you have to leave an hour and a half before." A flight attendant expressed a common sentiment: "It's a beautiful airport. But we hate it."[54]

On the airport's first anniversary, journalists had trouble reaching a simple verdict on DIA. There were complaints all right—lots of them. But some passengers liked the spiffy new airport, with its marble floors and inviting shops. And flight delays had in fact dropped dramatically. The first-anniversary stories were confused, lacking a central theme.

The reporters had missed the main problem: The city had eliminated the most obvious source of feedback—competition from the old airport. It had made DIA a protected monopoly rather than an experiment subject to competitive trial. By shutting down Stapleton, DIA's political sponsors had made it impossible to rule the new airport a definite error. No matter how many complaints passengers lodge, officials can always point to other advantages. At the same time, however, DIA's monopoly keeps it from becoming an accepted success. Without a genuine trial, we simply have no way to tell whether travelers (or airlines) would rather trade a convenient location for fewer weather-related delays. One airport must fit all. Love it or hate it, if you're flying from Denver you don't have a choice.

Another common way to protect experiments from feedback is to pass the costs of errors onto someone else. The conservative writer David Frum argues that such false signals undermine bourgeois virtues to a far greater extent than Bell's "cultural contradictions" would do alone. Frum seeks public policies that would restore the connection between personal actions and outcomes:

> Twenty years ago, an economist named Sam Peltzman noticed that drivers who wore seatbelts, while suffering far fewer accidents than drivers who did not, inflicted far more. The safer the driver personally felt, the more carelessly he drove. The welfare state functions as a political safety belt, reducing the riskiness of all of our lives; and just as with real safety belts, there are what Peltzman called "feedback effects" from our newfound sense of personal security. . . .
>
> Why be thrifty any longer when your old age and health care are provided for, no matter how profligately you act in your youth? Why be prudent when the state insures your bank deposits, replaces your flooded-out house, buys all the wheat you can grow, and rescues you when you stray into a foreign battle zone? . . .
>
> We cannot rescind the emancipation of appetite; but we can make its indulgence riskier by canceling the welfare state's seductive invitation to misconduct.[55]

As with the Denver airport, we can never say for sure which protected decisions—which "emancipations of appetite"—would have survived a true test.

Insulating mistakes from early feedback can make their cost astronomical. Instead of adjusting when corrections are relatively inexpensive, such "experiments" allow negative results to compound until they can no longer be ignored—and often cannot be corrected. The savings and loan debacle was such a disaster. It was the product, from start to finish, of technocratic planning and static assumptions. First, federal regulations fixed the thrifts' institutional forms and business practices, forcing them to lend specifically for home purchases and to pay interest at rates limited by law. Locked into undiversified portfolios of long-term loans, the S&Ls were designed as static institutions in a static environment. They developed a complacent corporate culture, secure in the knowledge that they had a ready market for loans and that federal law gave them a quarter-point interest edge over banks in attracting deposits. The government also promised that in the unlikely event an S&L went belly up, depositors would get their money back. Nothing was supposed to change: not the demand for houses, not the price of money.

Suddenly, in the 1970s, interest rates began to rise rapidly. Nobody had expected the increase, least of all the S&Ls. And they were not resilient. To keep up with inflation, depositors began pulling their money out of thrifts and putting it into high-interest money market funds. Prohibited by law from adjusting their strategy, the S&Ls faced ruin. So beginning in 1980, Congress partially deregulated the industry, allowing thrifts to raise interest rates paid on deposits and to jump into riskier businesses. Lawmakers did not, however, eliminate the seat belt of deposit insurance. To the contrary, they made the insurance even more generous, raising the ceiling from $40,000 to $100,000 per account.

Under the circumstances, the result was quite predictable: major risk taking by the S&Ls. The thrifts were still stuck with long-term, low-interest mortgage loans that didn't bring in enough income to pay off depositors. They needed to find big returns to make up the difference. Thanks to deposit insurance, they faced few consequences if their new investments went bad. So insolvent thrifts, often called "zombies," began to take greater and greater risks in an attempt to earn enough to cover their debts (which, for a bank or S&L, means making good on deposits). Some of their speculative real estate deals and "junk bond" investments look irresponsible, even crazy, in retrospect. But they made perfect business sense. If the deals worked out, the thrifts kept the profits. If those investments went bad, the federal government would cover the losses.[56] Most of the zombies' high rolling did not pay off. These S&Ls became more and more insolvent, deeper and deeper in debt. The errors could not continue forever. In the end, cleaning up the S&L mess cost $481 billion, about $417 billion of it from the taxpayers.[57]

*   *   *

Pursued long enough, insulated action will produce a public backlash against "progress" and a legally enforced bias against enterprise and experimentation. The S&L bailout quickly turned into a rhetorical club for business bashers, not a symbol of social insurance. It made people suspicious of risk-taking financial institutions in general. The technocracy of forced change often begets the technocracy of complete resistance.

Consider the development and redevelopment of cities, a process shaped as much by political planning as by real estate supply and demand. In Gelernter's golden age, Robert Moses willfully remade New York City. "He gouged great gashes across it, gashes that once had contained houses by the hundreds and apartment buildings by the score," writes the biographer Robert Caro. Moses was the quintessential technocrat, determined to shape the future to his sense of order and destiny. Squelching all opposition, he razed neighborhoods and spent tax money with abandon and without accountability. His West Side Improvement project cost at least $180 million in Depression-era dollars.[58] Unhindered by the constraints of competition or limited budgets—or the need to buy land from consenting sellers—Moses practiced "progress" without limit or feedback. He was a man of action who neither submitted his experiments to trial nor acknowledged the potential for error.

Moses believed, he wrote, in "the courageous, clean-cut, surgical removal of all of our old slums. . . . I am against phony compromises, however labeled, which look to patching up a few buildings here and there. . . . There can be no real neighborhood reconstruction, no superblocks, no reduction of ground coverage, no widening of boundary streets, no playgrounds, no new schools, without the unflinching surgery which cuts out the whole cancer and leaves no part of it to grow again, and spread and perpetuate old miseries."[59] And so, in the 1950s, Moses directed slum clearance programs that drove thousands of residents from poor but functional neighborhoods into dangerous areas and even more horrifyingly decrepit housing—or into once-middle-class brownstones that were subdivided into increasingly crowded new slums. Gripped by a static vision in which people could be surgically removed without consequence or spillover, Moses eradicated entire niches in the ecology of city housing and covered up the results.[60]

Nor was he alone in such efforts. The same attitudes, methods, and surgical metaphors permeated the planning profession. Over the fifteen years beginning in 1949, about a million Americans were evicted from their homes to make way for federally financed urban renewal projects. Justified in the name of improving cities, these sweeping efforts were protected from competitive feedback that might indicate what city residents actually wanted. The whole point of such activities, in fact, was to upset the housing patterns and businesses that had evolved through the normal dynamic processes of city life.

"The consequences of a typical federal urban renewal project are often harsh," wrote the economist Martin Anderson in his 1964 book, *The Federal Bulldozer.* "People are forcibly evicted from their homes, businessmen are forced to close their doors, buildings, good and bad, are destroyed—all in the name of an appeal to some higher 'good,' the public interest."[61] In the late 1950s, the West End of Boston, among the most famous urban renewal projects, went from a vital, if poor, multi-ethnic neighborhood to a concrete maze of overpasses and a few high-rise apartment buildings. In the process, some twelve thousand people were run out of their homes, almost always into more expensive but not necessarily better apartments.[62] Living within walking distance in the early 1980s, I found the former West End nearly impenetrable and utterly repellent, a dead zone. At the time, having no idea of its history, I wondered how such a wasteland could have grown up in the midst of an otherwise vibrant area.

The reason was simple: Developers in urban renewal areas didn't have to find buyers willing to pay more than the old neighborhood had been worth to its previous owners. Like Soviet farmers feeding livestock with subsidized bread, these developers were encouraged to destroy value rather than create it. They could buy land at about 30 percent of what cities paid to acquire it—and that acquisition itself, through eminent domain, had already eliminated the ability of private owners to refuse to sell for a "reasonable" sum.[63] Avoiding competition and thwarting resistance to planners' statist schemes was, argues Anderson, what the program was all about:

Again and again—from bankers, politicians, newspaper editors, businessmen, and even religious leaders—I heard statements like these: "Well, I've tried to buy property in that area of town, but the owner won't sell at a reasonable price. Somebody has to *make* him sell at a 'fair' price. Who does he think he is, standing in the way of the whole city?" Or, "We need at least a whole block to do anything worthwhile; we can't fool around trying to buy a lot here and a lot there. Besides some old man may feel attached to property that's been in his family for years. We can't wait for him to die. *We need the tool of eminent domain.*"[64]

Eminent domain effectively shut down the economic feedback that would have told city planners and developers that people just didn't want to live the way technocrats envisioned, that the planners' versions of "progress" did not, in fact, make life better.

Eventually, of course, such high-handed attitudes—and the devastating consequences the federal bulldozer had for city life—created a backlash. Neighborhood resistance began to block even voluntary development. New bureaucratic barriers were erected: environmental impact reviews, landmarking regulations, architecture reviews, hearing after hearing. "Rights of resistance and control have been carved into law," writes the urban planning scholar Sidney Plotkin. "Friction has been built into the system. . . . More and more, owners and citizens act on the belief that change must be conditioned on the consent of the governed, especially when the consequences of innovation threaten to hit dangerously close to home."[65] Cities have replaced one form of technocratic stasis with another. Innovation has become the enemy, "not in my backyard" the rallying cry. Consistent only in their dedication to central control, technocratic authorities still vest themselves with the power to decide which experiments can proceed and which trials will be cut off, which futures are possible and which can never be.

Compared to the alternatives, dynamist trial and error is a very humble process. It invests no one with decisive power, assumes no one is omniscient or even particularly wise. It cherishes the unheralded inventor willing to test a new idea. It acknowledges human differences and permits diverse approaches. It recognizes that most ideas will fail—and turns that weakness into a powerful lever for progress. "There is no way to find the best design except to try out as many designs as possible and discard the failures," writes Freeman Dyson.[66] Trial and error understands that life is unpredictable.

Dynamists may dream great dreams but they make modest claims. The infinite series promises not perfection but learning, not godlike oversight but diffused expertise. It makes progress mostly in baby steps. We are, it admits, fallible and largely ignorant. We have not discovered the one best way to live, nor are we likely to. But we can, and have, improved our lot, building on the discoveries, insights, and experiments of the past.

At the very center of the dynamic vision, then, is a recognition of the human condition—of the limits of our minds but also of their potential. How to think about knowledge is for dynamists not an esoteric challenge for philosophers but a central, organizing question.

CHAPTER FOUR

THE TREE
OF KNOWLEDGE

He was twenty-four years old, and people were expecting him to do the impossible.

Steve Gibson laughs when he remembers. After Princeton, he'd gone to work on Wall Street, first for Alan Greenspan's economic forecasting firm, then for Bear Stearns. Very quickly, he'd learned that forecasting is an inexact science, that even 1,100-variable Fortran models running on room-sized computers are subject to fudge factors. If the computers' forecasts conflicted with senior economists' intuitions, the staff fiddled with the models until the "right" answer popped out.

Gibson also learned that a lot of people would rather have utterly meaningless predictions than no predictions at all. "They'd call and say, 'What's your forecast for'—fill in the blank. 'What do you think inflation's going to be in the year 2000?'—these five- to ten-year forecasts," he recalls. "And I would *literally* say to them, 'We don't have a forecast out that far. If you would like, though, I will make one up for you *right now*.' And nine times out of ten they'd say, 'Oh could you? That'd be great.' " It didn't matter that Gibson was just a kid, the most junior of junior analysts, or that the prediction was a complete and admitted fabrication. All that mattered was that the callers could go back to their bosses and say, "Well the people at Bear Stearns say . . ."[1]

We hate not knowing the future. Soothsayers are as old as history. But the kind of soothsaying that runs on giant computers, that fills the pages of business publications and informs the decisions of legislators and regulators, is different from old-time magic. Rather than tap omniscient forces operating outside time, it claims scientific knowledge of the present, or at least of everything important about the present. Drawing on that information, it then predicts what people will do and how their actions will shape the world. Or it tells them how they must act and assumes it can foresee the results.

Sometimes this soothsaying is limited and relatively harmless, just one more factor in the trials and errors that compete to shape a more pleasing future. In the late 1980s and early 1990s, for instance, many retailers turned to consultants to predict which women's fashions to stock. Using impeccable demographic data, the consultants homed in on a central fact: Consumers were getting older and fatter. But the inferences they drew—forget youth, novelty, or sex appeal, and go for the basics—could not have been more wrong. What actually sold were slinky slip dresses and curvy, miniskirted business suits. Retailers who followed the reductionist consultants' advice got stuck with unwanted inventory, and the entire industry slumped.

"Never have so many people been employed in analyzing fashion, and never has fashion business been so dismal," commented *New York Times* fashion critic Amy M. Spindler. "As in any design field, fashion sells when something innovative is presented, something no consumer could have anticipated. . . . But most consultants, even if they are sharply tuned to changes in the demographics of the world, know little about fashion's X-factor, the unknown quantity that makes an item seem hot to a consumer."[2]

The world is full of X-factors, the unarticulated and unrealized knowledge that can be elicited only by experience and experiment. Informed by younger friends that the latest Washington hot spots were cigar-and-martini bars, an out-of-town visitor figured the young folks must be slumming in fusty old K Street steakhouses. "I was as usual totally wrong. As [a hypothetical 1978] planner would have been totally wrong," he later told a conference on industrial policy. "Because this was not a steakhouse that had somehow acquired a second clientele. This was built from the ground up for 22 year olds with so much facial jewelry that they would set off airport metal detectors." Moral of the story: "It's extraordinarily difficult to tell which products will be the successful ones."[3]

It is possible to discern patterns and to test that analysis against others'. But the competition—the test—is crucial. Most predictions are wrong, and the more specific the claim, the more likely the error.

When in 1983 *Forbes* confidently ran a list of "names you are not likely ever to see in The Forbes Four Hundred," the story had a perfectly good theory: that inventors rarely get rich off their creations. But the author got too specific. Third on the list of people unlikely ever "to transcend the $125 million mark in net worth" was none other than Bill Gates, who went on to become the richest man in the world.[4]

In his bet with Paul Ehrlich, by contrast, Julian Simon was able to predict confidently that the prices of five metals would decline from 1980 to 1990. His prediction was based on a dynamic understanding of resource use; his mental model assumed increasing knowledge about alternative sources and applications, feedback from prices, and competitive pressures to do more with less. Simon bet only on the general trend, however, not on specifics. He did not try to say in advance which innovations would lead to the price declines, nor did he project the exact magnitude of the drops. Of those things, he admitted ignorance.

Like the *Forbes* list, politically imposed stasist plans often get very specific. They admit no X-factors and no learning. They *know* that high-definition television will take off (and will do so in the form pioneered by the oh-so-scary Japanese) and that cigar-and-martini bars will not. Stasist plans do not consider how people might adjust to new circumstances, and they don't factor in new inventions.

"Most experts believe that without deep changes in both industry behavior and government policy, U.S. microelectronics will be reduced to permanent, decisive inferiority within ten years," wrote MIT's Charles Ferguson in a famous 1988 *Harvard Business Review* article. He called for a government-directed policy to help U.S. chip companies threatened by foreign competition and denounced the "fragmented, 'chronically entrepreneurial' industry" of Silicon Valley. As authorities to back up his prescriptions, he cited

> a wide number of university researchers and senior personnel of my acquaintance in the U.S. Defense Department, the CIA, the National Security Agency, the National Science Foundation, and most major U.S. semiconductor, computer, and electronic capital equipment producers. My conclusion, after meetings with groups in the U.S. Defense Science Board, the White House Science Council, and others, is that only economists moved by the invisible hand have failed to apprehend the problem.[5]

Ferguson and his mandarin contacts just couldn't envision an industry driven by microprocessors, software, and networks rather than memory-chip manufacturing. Instead, they assumed an essentially static world, anticipated disaster, and demanded industrial policy.

Ferguson's ideas were not adopted by either businesses or government. Yet ten years after he predicted an industry "reduced to permanent, decisive inferiority," American information technology companies lead the world. Had chip makers followed his advice, clinging to commodity technologies and stifling entrepreneurship in an effort to build larger firms, the industry would have indeed gone down the drain. "Economists moved by the invisible hand," who understood the dynamic patterns of the industry but did not try to predict its exact evolution, knew more than Ferguson's "experts"—for the very reason that they recognized the limits of their knowledge.

Technocratic plans assume the very things they try to enforce: that the world is simple and easily controlled, that it changes only in predictable ways, that it can be mastered. They suppose that the planners have all the relevant information and know exactly how the world works. The urban renewal programs of the 1950s and 1960s were neat, logical expressions of a certain understanding of city life, as neat and logical as the fashion consultants' projections. But the planners recognized neither the bustling vitality that appeals to city dwellers nor the personal space that draws people to the suburbs. They thought that plazas surrounding high-rise apartment buildings—which looked great in architectural drawings—would somehow duplicate the open space of suburban lawns; instead, such projects lacked both the urban convenience of nearby places to mingle and shop and the suburban attractions of privacy and green space. These technocrats scorned the critical information embedded in the lives of both city dwellers and suburbanites: the "tacit knowledge" expressed in relationships and habits and conveyed through webs of economic and social connections.[6]

More recently, the Environmental Protection Agency has evaluated California's smog-reduction regulations not by measuring actual pollution levels but by cranking computer models. The models neither permit radically new ideas for cutting pollution nor incorporate unexpected changes in the human environment. They cram any new technology or information into the same old framework. By 1996, when California developed a plan to comply with the 1990 Clean Air Act amendments, the state had ample data indicating that a small percentage of "gross polluters" contribute the majority of vehicle pollution—and that the most effective way to spot such cars is through roadside "remote sensing," analogous to radar guns for catching speeders. Under EPA rules, however, officials could not fully adapt their smog-reduction program to this new information and technology. Instead, they had to create an awkward hybrid that sticks remote sensing onto established programs of periodic smog checks and trip reductions. "The public cares about results—cleaner air," says Lynn Scarlett, who chaired the California Inspection and Maintenance Review Committee, which was responsible for developing a plan to meet EPA requirements. "EPA cares more about whether folks are complying with permit procedures and technology mandates."

EPA predictions also take a simplistic view of human behavior. The agency's rigid models make room for scheduled inspections, but not random smog checks or their deterrent effects. And the models assume that population will grow, never that it will shrink or change in composition. Projections made in the late 1980s thus missed southern California's post–Cold War economic downturn, which reduced growth rates and traffic; yet those projections remain, feeding regulations. The agency's predictions presume that both behavior and knowledge are essentially fixed. And they force 17 million motorists to live accordingly.[7]

Predictions go wrong because there are many possible sources of error: environmental shocks, bad or incomplete models, bad or incomplete data, sensitivity to initial conditions, the ever-branching results of action and reaction. Writing of technology, the physicist Freeman Dyson notes that its inherent unpredictability makes centralized decision making hazardous:

> Whenever things seem to be moving smoothly along a predictable path, some unexpected twist changes the rules of the game and makes the old predictions irrelevant. . . . A nineteenth-century development program aimed at the mechanical reproduction of music might have produced a superbly engineered music box or Pianola, but it would never have imagined a transistor radio or subsidized the work of Maxwell on the physics of the electromagnetic field which made the transistor radio possible. . . . Yet human legislators act as if the future were predictable. They legislate solutions to technological problems, and they make

choices between technological alternatives before the evidence upon which a rational choice might be based is available.[8]

Many important developments take place out of view of the pundits. What business analyst in the 1970s would have looked to rural Arkansas to find the future of retailing? Yet that's where Wal-Mart emerged. It took Jimmy Carter, a born-again Southern Baptist immersed in Bible Belt culture, to recognize the political potential of evangelical voters—who were there all along. In retrospect, fashion consultants could trace those miniskirted business suits to the characters of *Melrose Place*. Not so surprising after all. The critical "local knowledge" is out there, but it's hard to collect.

Unexpected events or patterns often make perfect sense in hindsight. But the very difficulty of predicting the future points up how little we know—or can know—about the present. The present is, after all, the basis of all prediction. Management guru Peter Drucker, among the most perceptive of trend spotters, declares emphatically that "I don't speculate about the future. It's not given to mortals to see the future. All one can do is analyze the present, especially those parts that do not fit what everybody knows and takes for granted. Then one can apply to this analysis the lessons of history and come out with a few possible scenarios. . . . Even then there are always surprises."[9]

Knowledge is at the heart of a dynamic civilization—but so is surprise. A dynamic civilization maximizes the production and use of knowledge by accepting widespread ignorance. At the simplest level, only people who know they do not know everything will be curious enough to find things out. To celebrate the pursuit of knowledge, we must confess our ignorance; both that celebration and that confession are central to dynamic culture. Dynamism gives individuals both the freedom to learn and the incentives to share what they discover. It not only permits but encourages decentralized experiments and competitive trial and error—the infinite series by which new knowledge is created. And, just as important, a dynamic civilization allows its members to gain from the things they themselves do not know but other people do. Its systems and institutions evolve to let people develop, extend, and act on their particular knowledge without asking permission of a higher, but less informed, authority. A dynamic civilization appreciates, protects, and nurtures specialized, dispersed, and often unarticulated knowledge.

Not surprisingly, how we think about knowledge—like how we think about progress—is one of the questions over which dynamists and stasists clash. These competing visions simply do not imagine knowledge in the same way. To dynamists, knowledge is like an ancient, spreading elm tree in full leaf: a broad trunk of shared experience and general facts, splitting into finer and finer limbs, branches, twigs, and leaves. The surface area is enormous, the twigs and leaves often distant from each other. Knowledge is dispersed, shared through a complex system of connections. We benefit from much that we do not ourselves know; the tree of knowledge is too vast. For stasists, by contrast, the tree is a royal palm: one long, spindly trunk topped with a few fronds—a simple, limited structure.

We all know many things we can't explain. Some are basic and widely held: how to breathe, sleep, and walk; the meanings of words and tones of voice; the structures of sentences. Breaking down such routine human activities into their component parts, understanding how they work, and uncovering the knowledge hidden in ordinary life is the stuff of specialized sciences unfamiliar to most people. For the rest of us, the knowledge we share remains unarticulated.

So, too, does much of the knowledge we do not share. A swimmer cannot say how he stays afloat, nor an editor truly account for what makes an interesting, appropriate article. Artists know their art in ways they could never define. Laughter is universally human, but what we find amusing varies widely by time and place, culture and generation, personality and circumstance. Explaining a joke is the fastest way to kill it.

The personal ads all sound alike not because tastes are homogeneous but because the important differences are so hard to express. My idea of a tall, handsome, funny, kind, intellectual man may have very little in common with yours; depending on our own heights, we might even argue over the definition of "tall." But even if we agree that a particular man has all these qualities, the list is not complete. No litany of attributes can capture the nuances that inspire love. We simply know it when we see it. Such "tacit knowledge" is why arranged marriages work better when marriage is seen as a business transaction or the advantageous melding of families rather than as a communion of emotionally close individuals.

Books on writing or videos on golf, however instructive, never capture the essence of the activity at its best. Nor can the tips they offer be comprehended in any meaningful way by people who neither write nor play golf. Absorbing such advice requires an insider's understanding. Observed the chemist and philosopher Michael Polanyi, whose 1958 book, *Personal Knowledge,* is among the most influential explorations of tacit knowledge:

> Maxims are rules, the correct application of which is part of the art which they govern. The true maxims of golfing or of poetry increase our insight into golfing or poetry and may even give valuable guidance to golfers and poets; but these maxims would instantly condemn themselves to absurdity if they tried to replace the golfer's skill or the poet's art. Maxims cannot be understood, still less applied by anyone not already possessing a good practical knowledge of the art. They derive their interest from our appreciation of the art and cannot themselves either replace or establish that appreciation.[10]

We must know the art in question before we can understand—much less give—advice about it.

In everyday life, we take our intimate knowledge for granted. We just assume that there are naturally things we know deeply that other people don't, things that are hard to explain. We shape our lives and circumstances by acting on that knowledge. But we are rarely conscious of doing so. And the more tacit the knowledge, the less we think about it. We also rarely realize how much knowledge we have access to, how much is embedded in the things and customs, services and routines we encounter every day.

It is thus easy to fall prey to stasist rhetoric that promises to dumb down the world, especially since stasists almost never put it that bluntly. They don't even talk much about knowledge. They don't say they want to forbid us to act on tacit knowledge unless we first give them a "good reason." They don't admit they want to deprive us of the creativity and knowledge of others. Instead, reactionaries offer paeans to "self-sufficiency" and "independence," extolling the authenticity, humanity, and stability of living without trade or specialization. Technocrats meanwhile pledge "efficiency," "standards," "fairness," or, the catchall, "problem solving." Like Charles Ferguson or Ross Perot, they promise to find experts to gather and apply all important knowledge.

Reactionaries idealize a world in which everyone knows pretty much everything, in which we fully understand every artifact we use and know every person with whom we interact. Their vision appears to celebrate competence and personal knowledge, but in fact it exalts ignorance. It sucks most of the knowledge out of life. Reactionaries despise the specialization of "scientific management," which breaks manufacturing tasks down into highly regimented component activities. But they also reject less rigid divisions of labor: the specialization that allows for professional writers, lab technicians, mechanics, hairdressers, or farmers—in short, the nonsubsistence economy in which people do the things they're good at and develop deep, often tacit, knowledge of something in particular.

"The specialist system fails from a personal point of view because a person who can do only one thing can do virtually nothing for himself," writes the farmer-essayist Wendell Berry, whose agrarian ideas are popular among both greens and traditionalists. No one, of course, truly "can do only one thing," but Berry explains by example: "In living in the world by his own will and skill, the stupidest peasant or tribesman is more competent than the most intelligent worker or technician or intellectual in a society of specialists."[11] The alternative to specialization is the great reactionary dream: a return to peasant life.

In their quest for efficiency and expertise, technocrats too assume a sort of omnicompetence. Although they may draw on "the best experts," they presume that someone in charge can assimilate all relevant information. They issue prescriptions that depend on their own imagined "topsight" (the term is David Gelernter's)—the notion that everything important can be seen from above.[12] So, for instance, Charles Ferguson and his high-level contacts assumed they could engineer the microelectronics industry to function more efficiently. Addressing the Reform party's 1996 convention, Ross Perot envisioned "a [Perot] White House, a House, and a Senate carefully, thoughtfully, and rationally working to solve our country's problems. . . . I've spent the last 40 years designing, engineering, testing, and implementing complex systems and making them work successfully in a cost-effective manner. So without realizing it, I have been training for this job" of president.[13] Nor, for all his egomania, is Perot the only politician who trusts his own universal expertise. In our technocratic system, that assumption is ubiquitous.

Few lawmakers, however, can possibly know the relevant details of the problems they set out to solve. In part, this is because they have other expertise. The members of Congress widely admired in Washington circles usually have deep local knowledge of what it takes to get bills passed. They know House and Senate rules, can intuit when to push for a compromise and when to hold out, and understand the personalities and interests of their colleagues. But people like Robert Byrd, John Dingell, Ted Stevens, Bud Shuster, and Edward Markey are not exactly inspirational figures in the rest of the country, nor have Bob Dole and Ted Kennedy been able to translate their particular expertise into national success. Their Washington reputations stem from their intimate knowledge of legislative processes, knowledge that is as little appreciated outside the Beltway as other local knowledge is appreciated within it.

For problems outside their legislative turf, members of Congress make do with a very broad overview. Remarks Representative Rick White (R-Wash.), a critic of congressional attempts to regulate cyberspace: "When Congress focuses on an issue, Congress sees the big, big, big, big, big, big, big, big picture. They're the ultimate big picture people. And they really don't understand the details."[14] Working without details, let alone intimate knowledge, they pass laws that force us to explain the unexplainable, to give "good reasons" for choices we can barely articulate to ourselves.

Often the reactionary and technocratic perspectives overlap. We then see prescriptions designed to reproduce a static past, but without any detailed sense of how we got to the present. Pat Buchanan may not share his reactionary allies' zeal for self-sufficient peasant villages, but he joins them in opposing international trade. "Where did the steel come from that turned the Mon Valley of Western Pennsylvania into an industrial graveyard, if not from Marshall Plan–rebuilt Europe and Japan?" he writes, repeating similar lines in political stump speeches.[15]

To restore 1950s-style industries and the lifestyles that surrounded them, Buchanan proposes high tariffs. But slumping demand for steel can be traced to new, lighter auto designs as well as to foreign competition,[16] and homegrown minimills have been as fiercely competitive with big steel as the Japanese or Koreans.[17] To say that the minimill workers of Darlington, South Carolina, or Crawfordsville, Indiana, should suffer to save the old-time mills of Pennsylvania—or to denounce the industrial creativity that led to minimills and lighter cars—would be much less popular than bashing foreign trade. But it would provide a fuller, more honest account. For every economic or social transformation, there is a complicated story, loaded with nuance and detail, that is hard to understand from afar. Both reactionary and technocratic appeals omit those nuances and details. They strip the tree of knowledge down to its trunk, lopping off "extraneous" branches, culling "superfluous" twigs, and creating a barren structure that can be captured in a glance.

Unsophisticated dynamists, however, can be their own worst enemies. Too many Internet advocates, for instance, imagine that theirs is the first endeavor ever to be attacked and dictated to by the ignorant. "We have government by the clueless, over a place they've never been, using means they don't possess," says Electronic Frontier Foundation cofounder John Perry Barlow.[18] Barlow's criticisms are echoed by many less famous Netizens. These declarations suggest that legislators know nothing about cyberspace because it is high tech and special, more important than the grubby industries of the past. In such complaints, Netizens imply that vital knowledge is the possession of a cutting-edge elite rather than something we all have, each according to our particular surroundings and circumstances. They turn what could be a powerful understanding of the world into mere special interest pleading, often with a grandiose tone.

In "A Declaration of the Independence of Cyberspace" Barlow declares to would-be regulators: "You do not know us, nor do you know our world. . . . You have not engaged in our great and gathering conversation, nor did you create the wealth of our marketplaces. You do not know our culture, our ethics, or the unwritten codes that already provide our society more order than could be obtained by any of your impositions."[19] All true, but hardly unique to the regulation of cyberspace. The creators of Post-it notes and plastics, TV shows and trucks, anyone who has ever hired an employee, built a building, or educated a child—all understand firsthand what it means to be governed by the clueless. Cyberspace is not the first dynamic culture that technocrats have tried to thrust into a stasis field; it is only the most recent.

Many dynamists, particularly of a high-tech inclination, also get mixed up about the knowledge economy. "Information wants to be free" is a popular slogan, and Barlow himself proclaims that in cyberspace, "whatever the human mind may create can be reproduced and distributed infinitely at no cost."[20] The instant duplication of digital data or documents is a genuinely significant phenomenon. But it does not make transferring *knowledge* free—or even cheap. Knowledge is not, in fact, easily ordered, moved, or collected.

This is an important point, because it crystallizes the choices stasists want us to make, choices they often obscure. Kirkpatrick Sale, for instance, argues that we can and should have towns that are self-sufficient in everything but knowledge:

> Self-sufficiency, I must add, before I am badly misunderstood, is not the same thing as isolation, nor does it preclude all kinds of trade at all times. It does not require connections with the outside, but within strict limits—the connections must be nondependent, nonmonetary, and noninjurious—it allows them. And in one area, it encourages them.
>
> There are no barriers to knowledge, and it would be foolish to imagine constructing them. Indeed, it may be the self-sufficient society that most needs information from without—about new techniques and inventions, new materials and designs, and innovations scientific, cultural, technical, political, and otherwise.[21]

Sale simultaneously imagines a world of ever-increasing, freely flowing knowledge and autarky, equilibrium, and stasis. He assumes that knowledge is easily created and transferred—and that it can flourish outside the turbulent civilization he despises. Nothing could be further from the truth.

As Polanyi suggested, much of our most important knowledge is tacit—difficult to articulate, even to ourselves. Contrary to Sale's imaginings, such knowledge is expensive to share, assuming it can be transferred at all. It is "sticky," in management scholar Eric von Hippel's term: "costly to acquire, transfer, and use in a new locus."[22] Von Hippel notes, for instance, the difficulty of duplicating a scientific apparatus. Subtle information about the lab environment, or procedures that people at the original site take for granted, can make the difference between success and failure. "It's very difficult to make a carbon copy," says a researcher quoted by von Hippel. "You can make a near one, but if it turns out that what's critical is the way he glued his transducers, and he forgets to tell you that the technician always puts a copy of *Physical Review* on top of them for weight, well, it could make all the difference."[23]

As a result of this stickiness, tacit knowledge often travels only through apprenticeship, the trial-and-error process of learning from a master. (A form of "apprenticeship" is essentially how as children we learn such complex basic skills as speech.) Writing in the 1950s, Polanyi argued that the art of scientific research, as opposed to the scientific information that can be taught in a classroom, had still not passed much beyond the European centers where it had originated centuries earlier: "Without the opportunity offered to young scientists to serve an apprenticeship in Europe, and without the migration of European scientists to the new countries, research centres overseas could hardly ever have made much headway."[24] The Nazi-induced exile of European scientists to America, followed by decades of American prosperity and loose immigration restrictions on scientists, effectively moved much of this tacit knowledge to the United States. Today American science plays for Asian-born researchers the role Europe once played for Americans.

Reconstructing sticky knowledge without the guidance of a master is difficult in part because critical information may be hidden even from expert eyes. When Steinway & Sons resumed making a discontinued upright piano in the early 1980s, it had no diagrams or specifications to work from. (Over the past several decades, the company has begun to create such records from existing pianos.) Instead, company "guru" John Bogyos first took apart an old piano he had at home and made drawings from it. Then, knowing from his half-century of experience that some of the specifications still didn't look right, he tracked down an old foreman, who filled in the gaps. Bogyos explained to *Atlantic Monthly* writer Michael Lenehan:

> The specifics of it was, the soundboard, which is a very important segment for tone in the piano, was an even thickness throughout, and I know that this is not so. From all history, as far back as you can go, they wouldn't ever make the soundboard one thickness throughout. They'd make it that way, but then they'd take away from certain areas to make it more flexible. But I could not find this on my piano. And when I got the foreman's pictures, showing me where, I found it on my piano too. I really looked. I drilled holes in the damn thing. But you see, just by looking, I couldn't see it. Everything is so hidden.[25]

Translating the sticky knowledge about how to build the upright into a written form that could be used by future craftsmen required not only dissecting an existing piano but tapping both the intuition in Bogyos's head and the unsystematic notes and photos that the retired foreman had kept. It was a hard, complicated process. Contrary to Sale, there are indeed "barriers to knowledge." Like the piano soundboard's secrets, much important knowledge is "so hidden."

In fact, articulation is so difficult that it is relatively rare, compared to the scope of what we know. Michael Kass, a computer graphics designer doing cutting-edge work on digital animation for Pixar Animation Studios, talks about the excruciatingly difficult process of mathematically modeling the way fabric moves, as, say, the wrinkles propagate across a shirt when you move your arm. After Kass and his colleagues had made progress on their fabric models, they discovered the hard way that they knew very little about how clothes are made. They built an animated jacket as a simple T, with the arms coming straight out of the armholes at right angles. But in real jackets, that sort of construction produces strange bunching around the ..rmpits, which is exactly what it did on the screen when they simulated the underlying physics. Real sleeves slant downward to avoid that problem—a bit of rarely articulated knowledge hidden in every jacket.[26]

The scarcity of articulated knowledge increases the rewards for turning tacit knowledge into easily shared information or products, from jackets to animation software. The difference between a top-flight writer and a mediocre one is often the ability to produce Alexander Pope's ideal of "what oft was thought but ne'er so well expressed," whether in a clear instruction manual, a moving tribute, or a powerful political speech. Former presidential speechwriter Peggy Noonan is famous not merely because she has a marvelous way with words but because she can capture the personality and cadences of the particular speaker, a task requiring her to elicit or intuit much tacit knowledge. Rather than making them sound like Peggy Noonan, she gave Ronald Reagan and George Bush better language with which to express *themselves*.

Moving sticky knowledge from one location to another generally takes a large investment up front and many iterations, the trial-and-error equivalent of an apprenticeship. Hired to create cakes for a British retailer, a Danish bakery made five generations of samples, each slightly more to the retailer's tastes (and, presumably, to its customers'). The bakery knew cake ingredients and baking techniques; the food retailer knew British preferences and dessert customs; to create a successful product required merging both sets of sticky knowledge.[27]

In some cases, a literal apprenticeship may be needed. The management scholar Ikujiro Nonaka tells the story of Matsushita Electric's efforts to develop a home bread-making machine in the mid-1980s:

> They were having trouble getting the machine to knead dough correctly. Despite their efforts, the crust of the bread was overcooked while the inside was hardly done at all. Employees exhaustively analyzed the problem. They even compared X rays of dough kneaded by the machine and dough kneaded by professional bakers. But they were unable to obtain any meaningful data.
>
> Finally, software developer Ikuko Tanaka proposed a creative solution. The Osaka International Hotel had a reputation for making the best bread in Osaka. Why not use it as a model? Tanaka trained with the hotel's head baker to study his kneading technique. She observed that the baker had a distinctive way of stretching the dough. After a year of trial and error, working closely with the project's engineers, Tanaka came up with product specifications—including the addition of special ribs inside the machine—that successfully reproduced the baker's stretching technique and the quality of the bread she had learned to make at the hotel. The result: Matsushita's unique "twist dough" method and a product that in its first year set a record for sales of a new kitchen appliance.[28]

Once embodied in a cake or a bread machine, the baker's knowledge can be widely distributed, enjoyed by people who could not duplicate his mastery with their own hands. The same is true of Bogyos's piano diagrams (or the piano itself), Pixar's digitally animated movies, and Noonan's speeches. Articulation is hard, scarce, and well rewarded. But once the knowledge has a home—tangible or intangible—that can be duplicated, then it can spread easily.

"The hallmark of modern consciousness is that it recognizes no element of mind in the so-called inert objects that surround us," writes Morris Berman in *The Reenchantment of the World*.[29] In the sense that he means it, Berman is quite correct; modernity is antianimistic. But we do in fact live in an enchanted world, surrounded by objects brimming with intelligence—the objects of our own making, objects whose "element of mind" is so great no single person can possess it all. The wonder of the bread machine and the piano is that they contain so much knowledge, available even to the ignorant. They are the exotic fruits of our vast tree.

And they frighten reactionaries. The specialization such inventions require, they counsel, makes us vulnerable and weak, too dependent on other people and too removed from our animal nature. A specialist, says Berry, "has not the power to provide himself with anything but money. . . . From morning to night he does not touch anything that he has produced himself, in which he can take pride."[30] (Tell that to the highly specialized piano maker or, for that matter, to the software programmer, musician, or ace real estate agent whose work product cannot be touched and yet is a source of pride.) "A self-sufficient bioregion," promises Sale, "would be more economically stable, more in control of investment, production, and sales, and hence more insulated from the boom-and-bust cycles engendered by distant market forces or remote political crises."[31] This is not in fact true, as "self-reliant" and starving North Korea attests. Trade creates resilience, while economic busts and political crises function at home as well as abroad. "Self-sufficiency" merely adds to those shocks the ancient fears of famine, disease, earthquake, fire, and flood—and a cushion limited to whatever happens to be in the bioregion. In investment terms, this supposedly safe strategy amounts to an undiversified portfolio.

But, say reactionaries, the richness created by specialists is self-indulgent. Our transportation and economic networks give us things we have no business wanting. "The frivolity of strawberries in January, asparagus in December, and wheat or soybean products that taste like chicken is simply never acknowledged," writes Berry, critiquing an article on the "agricultural revolution."[32] This abundance leads, in Christopher Lasch's words, to "desiccation," particularly for people who work with their brains:

> Air-conditioning and central heating protected them from the elements but cut them off from the vivid knowledge of nature that comes only to those who expose themselves to her harsher moods. Exemption from manual labor deprived them of any appreciation of the practical skills it requires or the kind of knowledge that grows directly out of firsthand experience. Just as their acquaintance with nature was limited to a vacation in some national park, so their awareness of the sensual, physical side of life was largely recreational, restricted to activities designed to keep the body "machine" in working order.[33]

Our true nature, these writers imply, lies not just in physical exertion but in forced mediocrity and limited ambition—in providing ourselves with food, shelter, and clothing but little else, and doing so as poorly as our individual talents might allow.

This vision permits few additions to the store of human knowledge and few benefits from the brilliance of others. At its extreme, it is an airbrushed fantasy, far more frivolous than strawberries in January. Even Sale's self-sufficient bioregions somehow manage to support universities, hospitals, and symphony orchestras—presumably complete with lab equipment, exquisitely crafted instruments, and highly trained specialists.[34]

This frivolous vision has real-world consequences. Couched in the protectionist rhetoric of "national sovereignty" and "self-sufficiency," the illusion of abundance without specialization helps cement stasist alliances of Buchananite nationalists and "steady-state" environmentalists to oppose international trade. That is its political manifestation. Culturally, and more significantly, it devalues our accomplishments; it tells us that we know nothing if we do not know everything, that we can take no pride in doing a few things well. It erodes our appreciation for what a dynamic civilization can achieve: its ability to "know" more than anyone can express.

Tacit knowledge is a special case of a more general phenomenon: local knowledge, the things people "on the spot" know that are specific to time, place, and circumstance and aren't seen at a distance. It is this information, vast and particular, that forms the branches and twigs of the complex tree of human knowledge. Local knowledge both drives and responds to the dynamic processes that reactionaries seek to abolish and technocrats long to replace.

Although local knowledge may be articulated, and thus available to those who ask, it is not widely shared. Interpreting its significance may require still more pieces of obscure, dispersed information. Reporting on Steinway, Lenehan discovered that the skin of a certain small Brazilian deer is critical to covering a particular part of the piano's hammer shank—not a trade secret, but not exactly common knowledge or even information most people would understand.[35] More famously, the expensive consultants IBM hired in the late 1950s to gauge the potential market for the Haloid Company's new xerographic photocopier pegged it at five thousand machines, tops, leading IBM to decline a joint venture. Haloid's salesmen, meanwhile, were out asking customers how much special paper they bought for the existing nonxerographic copiers. Journalist David Owen recounts:

> In Philadelphia one day, one of the salesmen stopped by the local Social Security office, which used one of the coated-paper machines.
> "How much of that paper do you use?" he asked.
> "What do you mean—how many carloads, or what?"
> The Haloid man's eyes lit up. "*Carloads*"?[36]

The information was out there, dispersed among potential customers, but it wasn't easy to gather unless you happened to ask the right people the right questions. And to appreciate its significance beyond the budgets and supplies of a particular Social Security office, you also had to know about Haloid's new technology—itself at that time an example of local knowledge. Haloid later changed its name to Xerox, after its extraordinarily successful and no longer obscure machine.

Local knowledge is dynamic, constantly adjusting to new ideas, information, and events. It is, in part, the outcome of decentralized trial and error, of the infinite series of innovation and progress. But it also responds to every possible sort of environmental change: weather and tastes, personal moods and political revolutions, shortages and gluts. It is often transitory and elusive. The person on the spot knows which vegetables look particularly promising at that day's market; how to shape a job to play to a specific employee's current strengths and help correct her weaknesses; how the football schedule affects the demand for hotel rooms; what the look on a student's face suggests about how well he understands the material; how a regular customer likes his hair cut, his eggs cooked, or his hedge trimmed; the particular and fluctuating value of location, location, location.

By its very quantity and nature, local knowledge cannot all be collected in a central place. It encompasses too much detail, requires too much understanding of context and circumstance, and changes too frequently. It is thus the source of much of the unpredictability and many of the X-factors that confound would-be soothsayers. When David Gelernter says it's "crazy for each senator and congressman not to have a software model of the country on his desk," he believes he is quarreling with a hardware-driven industry that stubbornly refuses to think carefully about the real potential of computers.[37] But he's really beating hi~ head against fundamental limits—the bounds of our ability to gather even numerical data, much less to collect, codify, and constantly update often-tacit local knowledge. Legislators do not lack for models, which agencies, think tanks, and lobbyists' consultants regularly crank out. What they don't have, and cannot have, is certainty or significant detail. Nor can they know all the ripple effects their actions will set off. At best, they can understand the potential of Freeman Dyson's imagined Pianola; the best software in the world won't inform them of future Maxwells.

In his seminal 1945 article, "The Use of Knowledge in Society," Friedrich Hayek put the problem of local knowledge at the center of economic thought:

> The peculiar character of the problem of a rational economic order is determined precisely by the fact that the knowledge of the circumstances of which we must make use never exists in concentrated or integrated form but solely as the dispersed bits of incomplete and frequently contradictory knowledge which all the separate individuals possess . . . There is beyond question a body of very important but unorganized knowledge which cannot possibly be called scientific in the sense of knowledge of general rules: the knowledge of the particular circumstances of time and place . . . To know of and put to use a machine not fully employed, or somebody's skill which could be better utilized, or to be aware of a surplus stock which can be drawn upon during an interruption of supplies, is socially quite as useful as the knowledge of better alternative techniques.

Markets, Hayek observed, operate as a "system of telecommunications," collecting scattered information and relaying it through price signals to interested parties. The signals adjust rapidly when circumstances change: "The marvel is that in a case like that of a scarcity of one raw material, without an order being issued, without more than perhaps a handful of people knowing the cause, tens of thousands of people whose identity could not be ascertained by months of investigation, are made to use the material or its products more sparingly; that is, they move in the right direction."[38]

Prices are, indeed, powerful, immediate signals of changes in local conditions: A cotton crop fails in China, and the resulting shortfall is reflected in more expensive cotton. Garment makers substitute synthetics, including polyester. The increase in demand drives up the price of polyester resin, spurring resin makers, whose stocks feed not only fiber but also film plants, to invest in new capacity.[39] The resin makers need know nothing about the cotton crop or why it failed; they simply respond to the demand for their own product.

But prices are not the only way markets express and elicit local knowledge, because there is more to local knowledge than supply and demand. We not only adjust to changes, we create them. The progress that comes from improving the things we know well—which Henry Petroski encapsulates in the phrase "form follows failure"—depends on local knowledge. Art Fry knew he didn't like bookmarks falling out of his hymnal, and he also knew that 3M had created an "unglue" that was looking for an application. Combining this knowledge led to Post-it notes.[40] Sam Walton created Wal-Mart out of his deep understanding of both rural markets and efficient distribution systems. While other discounters concentrated on cities, he built stores in small towns, clustering them around central warehouses.[41] Betty Friedan tapped her own experiences and feelings, as well as information gathered as a journalist, to write *The Feminine Mystique*. It became a best-seller with lasting cultural impact because, by articulating her own tacit knowledge, Friedan gave voice to the inchoate discontent of a generation of educated, talented women who couldn't figure out why housework wasn't enough to satisfy their ambitions.[42]

Fashion has no monopoly on X-factors. All sorts of customers, for ideas as well as products, know more than they can articulate. So do third-party innovators, who often find unexpected ways to get the most out of new inventions. 3M developed cellophane tape originally so a bakery could seal moisture-proof packages. But no sooner was the tape on the market than customers started finding new uses for it: wrapping packages, repairing ripped curtains, making labels, even lining the ribs of dirigibles.[43] Peter Drucker, who tells many such stories, recounts how an Indian engineering firm marketed a bicycle with a small engine. The bike didn't sell well, but in one region customers kept ordering just the engine. The company investigated and discovered that farmers were using the machines to run small irrigation pumps. It switched businesses and became the world's leading maker of such pumps.[44] Seemingly chaotic innovation, bubbling up from a multitude of individual plans, allows us to benefit from the knowledge and creativity dispersed beyond the obvious centers of invention.

Such messy processes frustrate technocrats, who deem them wasteful. Gelernter criticizes the hardware innovation and software improvisation that drive the personal computer industry. "A killer app is a piece of software that shows up—everybody buys the Apple II to get VisiCalc and everybody buys the Mac because of PageMaker. The whole idea of the killer app is if I'm a hardware company I can build a computer with no plans for it whatsoever—put it out there with absolutely no intention of anything in particular for it to do—and I assume that that killer app will materialize from the atmosphere," he says contemptuously. "And so far it always has." Improvising has "worked so beautifully" that software development is "completely chaotic," lacking an overall intellectual structure.[45]

As a software scholar, Gelernter is entitled to his frustration. Yet the advances produced by improvisation, adaptation, and the race to improve hardware are hard to imagine coming from machines developed as integrated products. Dedicated word processors were thriving, after all, until they were displaced by multiuse PCs. The "killer app" approach allowed manufacturers to tap complementary skills they themselves did not possess. Inventing the Macintosh, developing PageMaker, and redesigning publishing procedures and magazine layouts to take advantage of desktop production all require different knowledge bases. To centralize knowledge for the sake of planning and "efficiency"—the technocratic dream—we have to throw away vast amounts of local knowledge.

Depending on topsight can easily lull us into imagining that we see not only the "big, big, big, big, big, big, big, big picture" but the whole, including the critical details. At a distance, it is easy to think that other people just don't know what they're doing—especially when you can override their decisions by decree rather than through persuasion or competition. In a famous 1910 case, Louis Brandeis convinced the Interstate Commerce Commission to deny the railroads any increase in freight rates. The railroads pointed to rising wage costs, general inflation, and a need to upgrade their roadbeds—arguments that might very well have prevailed. But Brandeis declared that while it was true that costs were rising, the railroads could economize: "Scientific management," the efficiency techniques pioneered in manufacturing by

Frederick W. Taylor and others, would make up the difference. An expert witness testified that scientific management could save the railroads $1 million a day, a figure that became a popular slogan and won Brandeis the case. But, recounts Thomas McCraw in his Pulitzer Prize–winning history, *Prophets of Regulation,*

> Subsequent events in the railroad industry all but proved that scientific management had much less relevance for transportation and other service industries than it did for manufacturing. . . . And by the time of the war emergency of 1917–18, the railroads had fallen into such desperate financial straits that the federal government temporarily took over the entire industry. After a brief study, the government instituted by fiat very large across-the-board rate hikes about the size of the combined increases the railroads themselves had requested in the years between 1910 and 1918. It would have been hard to devise a clearer demonstration of the insubstantiality of Brandeis' argument of 1910.[46]

Against Brandeis's topsighted expert, the railroads' managers were insufficiently articulate. They knew his arguments were wrong, but, especially as unsympathetic witnesses, they couldn't convince the commission, or the public, that they knew their business. They could not persuasively convey their local knowledge of railroad operations.

In a contemporary culture far less enamored of engineering and efficiency than Brandeis's, it's easy to criticize turn-of-the-century technocrats for hubristically overriding local knowledge. But the same impulse exists today. *New York Times Magazine* writer John Tierney once devoted a column to a satirical meditation on New York City's "public servants turned management consultants," who demand laws regulating such business details as the security around automatic teller machines and the pricing of salad bars and dry cleaning. Imagine, he suggested, what such great entrepreneurial minds could do if they just had the chance to go into business for themselves: "Applying their talents privately could absolutely *invigorate* the economy." For example,

> Overhauling the [dry cleaning] industry will require someone with more initiative than the ordinary immigrant—someone like Councilwoman Kathryn Freed. At the hearing, when the dry cleaner mentioned the problem with the automatic press, Freed suggested, "Your automatic machine should be a little more adjustable." Eureka! A technolog-

ical breakthrough that had eluded the industry's best minds! A few more innovations like that and our economy could be booming again.[47]

Many debates over risks, including those surrounding FDA approval of new drugs, are about whether a central agency should determine the "one best way" for everyone. The tax code is loaded with credits and deductions designed to skew spending and investment away from the trade-offs suggested by local conditions (including individual tastes and values) and toward those favored by Congress. In the name of consumer protection, the Agriculture Department even dictates the proper way to make pizza. All frozen pizzas must, by law, contain tomato sauce, regardless of what, in context, consumers expect. To market a sausage and herb pizza with pesto sauce, world-renowned chef Wolfgang Puck had to throw tomato into the sauce—hardly the common meaning of "pesto."[48]

One-size-fits-all requirements frequently get absurd when stuck into an unexpected local context. A contract incorporating four levels of affirmative action—corporate, city, state, and federal—tells a sign construction company to "assign two or more women to each Phase of the construction project." But, notes company president Tama Starr, "One of the phases is structural installation, which entails landing big steel and welding it while perched on a scaffold 100 feet or more above the ground, sometimes in zero-degree weather. For some reason, I don't get a lot of female applicants for this position."[4]

The early Clinton administration was notable for its technocratic bias against local knowledge, most famously in its complicated health care scheme but also in lesser-known proposals. As a candidate in 1992, Bill Clinton pledged to require all employers to spend at least 1.5 percent of payroll on formal worker training or to pay the equivalent into a government training fund. The idea came from the Commission on the Skills of the American Workforce, headed by Ira Magaziner. The commission's 1990 report swept aside any objections or variations based on local knowledge. Qualifying expenses would include "only accredited courses that form part of a formal certification program or a college degree program," not on-the-job training. "This proposal may appear burdensome to small companies that do not compete internationally or perceive no need for training," it said. "But the most equitable initiative is one that treats all companies and institutions uniformly."[50] (The administration's proposal quietly died.)

Even in his 1996 incarnation, "triangulating" toward the political center, Clinton busily pushed ideas designed to steamroller all sorts of local knowledge: If curfews or school uniforms are good for some children, they must be good in general. If some women need to stay in the hospital for forty-eight hours after childbirth, all women must. If some companies can give workers time off for PTA meetings, all should be required to. The administration never gave up the concept behind the training tax or, for that matter, behind Brandeis's invocation of scientific management—that any idea that works in one situation should be forced on everyone. That different standards might be appropriate for different people in different circumstances remained as foreign to the new Clinton as to the old.

Such blindness is not unique to the Clinton administration, which is simply following old technocratic patterns. Bureaucratic rule making, whether public or private, favors uniform treatment even when that means disregarding local knowledge. At their best, bureaucratic rules gain predictability at the cost of nuance: When you go to McDonald's, you know the menu will be the same, whether you're in Dallas or Duluth. You know you'll be able to buy a Big Mac and can count on a minimum level of quality. But keeping things standardized means limiting the available options and the ability to adapt. Fine restaurants are notoriously difficult to duplicate, because their quality depends on the staff's particular skills, local knowledge, and continuous improvement of the menu and atmosphere. The same is true of social service organizations that respond to the personal needs of their clients.

Since government rule making seeks to treat all citizens the same, to ensure equity, it has a particular tendency to disregard local knowledge. The Occupational Safety and Health Administration fined Judy's Bakery, a small shop in Evanston, Illinois, $2,500 for not having a written Material Safety Data Sheet for "hazardous" chemicals and $500 for not having an accident log on the wall. Yet the store's only chemicals are ordinary household bleach and pink liquid dishwashing detergent, and it had no accidents to record.[51] A Berkeley company had to give up plans to offer on-site day care for employees' children when it discovered an irresolvable conflict between its building permit, which limited the number of walls it could have, and state day care regulations, which required a separate entrance, separate bathrooms, and a separate kitchen for the facility. The day care code also demanded far more outside play area than an urban site could offer; using city parks, which the company had planned to do, was not a legal option. City regulators, the personnel manager complained to me, "claim to be liberals, but most of them are only liberals if it's what they want."[52]

Even at its most flexible, technocracy demands that people give a "good reason" for actions that depend on hard-to-articulate knowledge. That may sound reasonable and uncontroversial. But articulation is, as we've seen, difficult and costly. And reasonableness is in the eye of the beholder. Consider the vague rhetoric propounded in congressional hearings on TV violence. Lawmakers demanded that writers and producers articulate and justify their creative choices. Creators and network executives hemmed and hawed and talked about Shakespeare. Seemingly absurd hypotheticals, such as banning *Schindler's List* from broadcast TV, were bandied about. And, having declined to articulate what they *don't* like, members of Congress passed a law requiring V-chips to screen out violence (and other undesirable material) according to a single, still-to-be-determined standard that is somebody else's problem.

Local, often tacit, knowledge is at the heart of the issue. In statement after statement, all concerned were quick to say that, as one researcher put it, "We should be distinguishing between *Schindler's List* and *Terminator 2*."[53] The notion of banning a serious movie about the Holocaust because it contains violence and nudity was, everyone seemed to think, utterly absurd. No restrictions should cancel out the local knowledge that says that, whatever its violent or sexual content, *Schindler's List* is a good, important movie, worthy of being on TV. Yet the very first show to be broadcast with a TV-M rating—the rating that, once V-chips are installed, would block it—was none other than *Schindler's List*. And the next day Representative Tom Coburn (R-Okla.) blasted NBC for the movie's "violence . . . vile language, full frontal nudity and irresponsible sexual activity. It simply should never have been allowed on public television."[54]

The clash between Coburn's assessment and the broad public sentiment that broadcasting *Schindler's List* was not just tolerable but morally good illustrates the significance of local knowledge to this issue. Tastes and values differ, often profoundly. Even if everyone did agree that the V-chip should not keep viewers away from *Schindler's List,* what about *Star Trek: Deep Space Nine* (sometimes among the week's most violent broadcast shows)? *America's Funniest Home Videos? E.R.? The X-Files? The X-Men?*

Parents have diverse opinions about what constitutes appropriate material for their children to watch. Some worry about sexual innuendo, some about violence, some about political or religious content, some about general mindlessness. The problem isn't merely with ratings that aggregate detail into age groups, a complaint some V-chip supporters had about the networks' original approach. It's that the level of detail can never be enough. What's unacceptable sexual innuendo to one parent is a mild joke to another. Nor can ratings of any sort evaluate how to trade off "redeeming social value," or just plain good art, against otherwise problematic levels of sex or violence. The *Schindler's List* problem is inescapable.

For their part, writers and producers "hide behind the First Amendment" because it protects people from having to give a "good reason" for their creative choices. They want the discretion to create what they consider good (and commercially successful) art, freedom that requires that they exercise judgment based on their difficult-to-articulate understanding of audience and storytelling. Writers' workshops, after all, pay well for such insights—and even then the lessons are often superficially expressed; they convey maxims that would require an apprenticeship to fully understand.

Legal procedures necessarily suck the knowledge out of particular situations, limiting us to whatever can be easily and convincingly articulated. Physical evidence works relatively well in the courtroom; complex personal assessments don't. Consider employer-employee relations, the regulated arena most like personal matchmaking and therefore most affected by tacit knowledge and judgment calls. Employment law second-guesses those relationships, substituting the knowledge of distant jurors and regulators for that of the people on the spot.

It can even second-guess artistic judgment. In 1997, actress Hunter Tylo successfully sued the producers of *Melrose Place* for firing her when, shortly after she was cast as a seductive, adulterous vixen, she revealed she was pregnant. During her pregnancy, she gained forty-seven pounds, but the jury "felt she could still play a vixen," the foreman said after a $5 million ruling in Tylo's favor. The soap opera's creative team had not convincingly articulated their reasons for not wanting to use a pregnant woman to play the siren's role. "Even if she gained 47 pounds or whatever, she's still a beautiful person," said a juror, adding that he personally found pregnant women "a lot prettier."[55]

If fully enforced, current employment law would all but eliminate management discretion, forcing employers to reduce complex individuals to a few easily documented traits and to govern them according to written, inflexible rules. In challenges to employee evaluations, for instance, courts have ruled too subjective such characteristics as "temperament, habits, demeanor, bearing, manner, maturity, drive, leadership ability, personal appearance, stability, cooperativeness, dependability, adaptability, industry, work habits, attitude toward detail, and interest in the job." Comments legal writer Walter Olson, "One wonders what is left."[56] Whatever it is, it's got to be easy to explain—which means it will be awfully formulaic and impersonal.

Employment law also drains local knowledge out of company policies, forcing managers to ignore what they know about individuals' circumstances. Olson notes that "over a wide range of situations, provable inconsistency is more legally dangerous to an employer than foolish consistency." As a result, job credentials, leave policies, and rule enforcement become absolutely rigid: "Fear of the leniency-for-one, leniency-for-all rule leads some companies to discipline or even fire workers they'd rather have retained. Compassionate leave is doled out with an eyedropper on advice of counsel. At the extreme, the totally rule-bound company begins timing people's bathroom breaks."[57]

Rather than allow learning and evolution, rigid, technocratic standards freeze the status quo, preventing experiments that might produce new and improved ways to organize work. They drive workplaces toward a static state that neither admits ignorance nor values knowledge, and that can be quite inhumane. A dynamic system, whether a single organization or an entire civilization, requires rules. But those rules must be compatible with knowledge, with learning, and with surprise. They must allow the tree to grow, not chop it into timbers. Finding those rules is the greatest challenge a dynamic civilization confronts.

CHAPTER FIVE

THE BONDS OF LIFE

Overhearing that I was working on a chapter about rules, my seven-year-old niece, Rachel, ran into the room. "I know some rules," she said, rattling them off rapidly. Her list is:

1. Look both ways before you cross the street.
2. Check to see how deep the water is before you dive.
3. Don't take others' medicine.
4. Never eat old mayonnaise, or mayonnaise that has been left out of the refrigerator too long.
5. Never bother a big dog when it is eating, or any kind of dog.
6. Never leave a thumbtack where someone will sit on it.
7. Never take a ride with a stranger.
8. Always check over your work.
9. Always tell the truth, or you might get into more trouble.
10. Never look straight at the sun.
11. Check the lights before you put them on the Christmas tree.
12. Always stick with your buddy.[1]

Like *The Rules,* the book for husband hunters that enjoyed a boomlet in 1996, Rachel's list is not binding on anyone. It is just the distilled and simplified wisdom of experience. Such rules of thumb help us navigate the world, so much so that we rarely think about them, except when reminded by children. Rachel's rules are themselves the products of the infinite series of trial-and-error learning. Most have exceptions, from accepting a friend's aspirin to politely pretending to like a hideous wedding present, and we expect to apply them selectively. Rachel's rules assume, rather than override, our tacit knowledge. We may choose to violate them with or without a good reason, and to bear the consequences that naturally follow. (Maybe we're just curious about what happens if you eat old mayonnaise.)

Most of our public debate over rules, however, is about making detailed rules such as Rachel's into mandatory, no-exception laws: Always keep new mothers in the hospital at least forty-eight hours. Never build a day care center without a big yard. Always put tomato on pizza. These rules are rigid and drained of local knowledge. The consequences of breaking them flow not from the actions themselves—whose results may be neutral or even positive—but from external law enforcement. The rules establish narrowly defined categories for all times and circumstances, hindering progress based on new combinations. That is the technocratic way (sometimes to reactionary ends), and it does not permit much evolution.

By dispersing knowledge and control, a dynamic society takes advantage of the human quest to create and discover. Dynamism allows the world to be enriched through the decentralized, trial-and-error experiments in which we all engage when left free to do so. While reactionaries seek rules that would ban change and technocrats want rules that will control outcomes, dynamists look for rules that let people forge new bonds, invent new institutions, and find better ways of doing things. Like the laws of physics and chemistry, which permit the simplest of particles to form complex combinations, dynamist rules allow us to create the bonds of life—to turn the atoms of our individual selves, our ideas, and the stuff of our material world into the complex social, intellectual, and technological molecules that make up our civilization. Such rules enable competitive processes and effective feedback; they do not dictate results. They change slowly, and their workings are predictable. They respect the limits of knowledge. They are, in the legal scholar Richard Epstein's phrase, "simple rules for a complex world."

Stasists, by contrast, have little tolerance for the world's complexity. They want to simplify life, to hold it still. Reactionaries would prefer flat prohibitions: No new stores. No new technologies. No new social arrangements. No trade. No migration. Such simple rules would forbid, rather than permit, complexity and infinite combinations.

But it's hard to impose such blanket prohibitions. Their overt intolerance scares the general public, and interest group lobbying can generally manage to carve out exceptions. Technocrats, who seek control rather than stability, have a politically viable alternative: complex regulations to make the world simple. Through a million tiny, specific rules, decreed and adjusted to cover each new situation as it arises, they promise to mold the future to the one best way.

This thicket of technocratic regulations stifles diversity and innovation. It also creates an alienated, confused, and sometimes terrified citizenry. Although they promise security, ever more complicated rules actually make the world uncertain. They deprive people of the benefit of their own local knowledge, of the reliable and familiar facts of how their immediate world works, while simultaneously creating new sources of instability: new rules to master, or to guess at, before acting. As plumbing contractor Lindsey Peet describes the Americans with Disabilities Act's detailed instructions for building bathrooms: "It's just one more set of forms to fill out, one more thing to worry about, one more way you have to watch yourself."[2]

Environmental regulations, often established under the simplest of slogans, are notoriously difficult to obey. In a 1993 survey of corporate general counsels, *National Law Journal* found that "only 30 percent of the attorneys believed that full compliance with the matrix of U.S. and state environmental laws was possible." One respondent summed up the situation: "Too many regulations. Some are in conflict. Some are unclear."[3]

Along similar lines, many of the frustrations Daniel Pink identifies among "free agents" spring from the manipulative complexity of the income tax code. As aggravating as it may be for salaried employees, the tax code is far more frustrating for the self-employed, who find themselves spending precious time and money on compliance and accountants.

"Hyperlexis," as the legal scholar Peter Schuck has dubbed the extension of technocracy to every aspect of life, makes all sorts of endeavors unintelligible without expert help. It thus gives those specialists a stake in increasing the law's complexity, making them technocrats out of self-interest if not conviction. And it frightens everyone else. As Schuck observes:

> As the body of rules grows more dense, the legal landscape becomes more thickly populated and harder to traverse. Concealed declivities, sudden detours, arterial congestion, unexpected cul-de-sacs, puzzling signs, and jarring encounters abound. . . . Experienced guides equipped

with maps and special know-how are essential, for only the initiated can lead a newcomer through the honeycomb of enclaves, each with its local patois, exotic cuisine, peculiar customs, and belligerent pride. . . . If the complex legal landscape contains many pitfalls for the governors, it is *terra incognita* for the governed. . . . Intelligible only to experts, the law is likely to mystify and alienate lay citizens whose intelligence it often seems designed to mock.[4]

By turning everyday life into terra incognita, complex rules make not just the future but the present an unknown country.

Even when technocratic rules aren't intentionally designed to require a static future, they often assume one. In doing so, they stifle experimentation and stamp out plenitude. Consider the thirty-year struggle against hidebound cosmetology regulations. Back in 1966, the heretic was Vidal Sassoon, the renowned British hairdresser whose precision cuts freed straight-haired women from the confines of permanents, teasing, and gobs of hairspray. New York's state cosmetology regulations allowed no such innovations. To practice his trade there, Sassoon was supposed to take a test based on the sort of hairdressing he hated. After two of his best stylists failed the exam, he refused to take it, although he had long ago learned the old-fashioned skills needed to pass. "The test requires that I do finger waving, reverse pin-curling, and a haircut in which you thin as you cut—things that haven't been used since Gloria Swanson was in silent movies," he said. "I simply cannot take it on the grounds that it violates everything I've worked for for 21 years."[5]

With high-profile stunts like giving actress Mia Farrow a $5,000 haircut on a Hollywood sound stage, Sassoon made the state regulators look ridiculous for questioning his authority over his own work. Only after the state cosmetology board said it would update the exam did he finally take the test, still in its old form. The real test of Sassoon's new ideas was in competition for respect and customers—and there he won a decisive victory. "Some 30 years after his tangle with that angry little bureaucrat swathed in wash and wear, Sassoon's empire continues to grow," writes Grant McCracken, the anthropologist who also discusses plenitude. "It includes 22 salons with some half a million clients. His four academies train over 15,000 students a year. None of these students is instructed in finger waving or the reverse pin curl."[6]

Rigid cosmetology regulations still obstruct evolving styles, however. Today's upstart hairdressers labor in deliberate obscurity, often working illegally. Like Sassoon, many are immigrants, not from the fashionable streets of London but from West Africa. They do intricate braiding, locking, and weaving on black women's hair. By freeing their clients from straighteners and hot combs, the styles the braiders create have liberating effects similar to Sassoon's blunt cuts—and are equally unwelcomed by licensing rules that never imagined such techniques. In 1996, California state regulators fined the Braiderie, a specialized salon in San Diego, for "aiding and abetting" unlicensed hairstyling by African immigrants.

Braiders use no chemicals and often learn their craft from relatives or friends. Most do not even offer haircuts, so their work is completely reversible. To ply their trade legally, however, they need a license, which requires as many as sixteen hundred hours of formal training, can cost as much as $7,000, and must include courses on chemical treatment.[7] The training itself is shaped by the law's rigid categories, curtailing the imagination of students and teachers.

"I have been around to cosmetology schools and beauty colleges to try to promote the idea of a natural haircare system, and what I find is that they teach based on what the law requires them to learn," says JoAnne Cornwell, chair of the Africana Department at San Diego State University and, in her nonacademic life, a third-generation hairstylist who has developed a trademarked technique for creating very fine locks. "So you can go into an environment like that and do a free demonstration until you're blue in the face, and they think it's cute and ethnic, but they have no motivation whatsoever to include it in the curriculum, because they'll never be tested on it."[8]

Writing about Sassoon's battles, McCracken notes that "there is something intrinsically odd (even unsettling) about using a bureaucrat to govern the world of style. In the last few years, we have learned to rethink government, to get it out of the places it shouldn't be (especially the bedroom and the marketplace). The idea that it ever presumed to control the world of style is too strange to bear contemplating."[9] In the world of style, X-factors and rapid change are so obvious that stasist regulation seems silly, which is why both Sassoon in the 1960s and African-style hair braiders in the 1990s have attracted good press and public sympathy. As McCracken's mention of "the bedroom and the marketplace" suggests, however, fashion is not the only area of life affected by unarticulated knowledge, diverse per-. sonal preferences, and constant experimentation and feedback. Technocratic rules disregard those factors in all sorts of endeavors. And, as with the world of style, the technocrats rarely retreat when challenged.

In fact, they often go on the offensive, contending that their critics want a chaotic society with no rules at all. It's an effective argument. If it is "odd" and "unsettling" to stifle dynamic processes with stasist rules, it is equally unsettling to imagine a civilization with no rules. Just as biological life would be impossible if chemical processes were arbitrary, so social life would disintegrate if its rules fluctuated unpredictably. The real question is not whether "rules" in general are good or bad. It is what sort of rules are necessary and appropriate to support dynamic systems.

It's a difficult question, best tackled not through deductive reasoning but through empirical observation. There are many dynamic systems in the world, many areas of life that evolve and improve through trial-and-error learning: from Jim Dowe's digital organisms to global financial markets, from adaptable architecture to international science. Looking across these various processes, it is possible to find patterns in the rules that make them possible—though, like Polanyi's maxims for playing better golf, we can fully apply the rules to a specific case only when we understand that particular system. This chapter, then, can only begin the exploration of dynamist rules by laying out some general principles. As an overview, dynamist rules:

1. Allow individuals (including groups of individuals) to act on their own knowledge.
2. Apply to simple, generic units and allow them to combine in many different ways.
3. Permit credible, understandable, enduring, and enforceable commitments.
4. Protect criticism, competition, and feedback.
5. Establish a framework within which people can create nested, competing frameworks of more specific rules.

These principles are very different from the Rachel-style rules that our technocrat-dominated political discussions have led us to equate with "governance." And, as we shall see, dynamist rules apply to a broad array of circumstances. They are not limited to politically enforced laws.

Any dynamic learning system must follow those principles. But the system itself need not be a global one. It may be nested inside a larger dynamic order: a flexible business, of the sort encouraged by Arian Ward or Tom Peters, inside the larger economy, for instance, or even a department within a larger, evolving company. And, as the fifth rule suggests, within broader dynamic systems, there is also room for more-rigid rules, serving other purposes. If McDonald's wants to make its menus the same everywhere or a basketball coach wants to require his team to stick to one set of plays—in each case, valuing consistency above innovation—dynamic rule making permits that trade-off too, as long as there is competition.

Once upon a time, the prospect of a "new world" in the Americas inspired political philosophers to think about the state of nature and how civilization evolves out of it. From that philosophy, and inherited legal traditions, came new constitutional regimes and experiments in self-government. Settling new territory requires serious thought about fundamental rules, thought that not only shapes the new world but can reshape the old. This is a matter not simply of philosophy but of practice, since pioneers must evolve new rules to govern the new landscape.

That is why cyberspace is more than a technological fad, why its governance has become a contentious legal issue, and why it attracts enormous amounts of both dynamist and stasist comment. The "settlement" of this virtual world has forced its pioneers to consider how and when rules work. Through trial and error, experimentation and competition, they have evolved technical standards, etiquette, and boundaries of various sorts. That computer programs are themselves strings of rules, which in turn depend on more-fundamental rules embedded in hardware or lower-level software languages, means that even a nonphilosophical programmer has a practical knowledge of rule structures. And for the more ambitious, developing the virtual frontier offers a chance to explore and create rules that enable other people to generate rich, dynamic systems of their own.

Back in 1985, when personal computers were strange and wondrous inventions just filtering into American homes, Chip Morningstar and his colleagues created an online world in which Commodore 64 owners could meet, play, and communicate with each other. The computers were simple, the modems slow, but the world—

called Habitat—quickly became complex.[10] Habitat provided its users with an animated landscape, props, activities, and cartoon personas called avatars. Users could send each other e-mail or converse through text in word balloons. Working from this underlying structure, Habitat's virtual citizens developed a wide variety of social activities and institutions. They invented games and dance routines, went on treasure hunts and quests, published a newspaper, threw parties, got married and divorced, founded religions and businesses, wrote and sold poems and stories, and debated weighty issues.

Developing Habitat, and watching it develop on its own, made Morningstar think seriously about how rules shape societies and what the limits of rule making are. "It was a small but more or less complete world, with hundreds and later thousands of inhabitants," he recalls. "And I, along with my coworkers, was God." In theory, the programmers made the rules, knew them thoroughly, and could change them at a stroke. But their godlike powers weren't as limitless as they seemed. Says Morningstar:

> Again and again we found that activities that we had planned based on often unconscious assumptions about user behavior had completely unexpected outcomes (when they were not simply outright failures). The more people we involved in something, the less in control we were. We could influence things, we could set up interesting situations, we could provide opportunities for things to happen, but we could not predict nor dictate the outcome.[11]

If there were chinks in the rules, the players found them. A few enterprising souls spent hours shuffling between a "Vendroid" machine selling dolls for 75 tokens and a pawn machine in another region buying them for 100 tokens. When the arbitrageurs had enough profit to buy crystal balls for 18,000 tokens, they repeated the same procedure with a pawn machine paying 30,000 tokens, until the Habitat money supply had quintupled overnight. When questioned about the source of their new-found wealth, they replied, "We got it fair and square!"

"Unintended consequences really have to do with naive people believing that there are no holes [in the rules]. It's very easy to seduce yourself into thinking that you've got everything under control," says Morningstar. "And the reality is, it's almost never true."[12] Clever people will always come up with ideas no central rule maker has conceived. A dynamic world's rules must allow for adaptation, change, and recombinations. The invention of "marriage," for instance, revealed the limits of Habitat's very narrow concept of property. No avatar could enter another avatar's turf unless the owner was present. When avatars got married, the system operators joined their territories so they could pop from one to the other instantaneously. But the two turfs did not become one, so a husband avatar couldn't enter his wife's side of the house unless she was there.

Over and over again, Habitat's designers ran into the limits of their own knowledge. Creating a rich online world with many interacting users was very different from designing a game to be used by one or two people at a time. The range of tastes and knowledge all those people brought to Habitat quickly overwhelmed the ability of designers to foresee how users would react. A treasure hunt that took weeks to build lasted less than a day, after a single Habitat resident quickly discovered a critical clue; the winner had a great time, but most of the other players barely got started. The system's operators soon realized the value of letting users create their own games. "It's not that they could necessarily do things that were as good as some of the things that we had the facilities to do," says Morningstar. "But the things which they did were much more directly in tune with what people immediately wanted—because they were much more directly in contact with themselves."[13]

This, then, is the first characteristic of dynamist rules: *They allow individuals (including groups of individuals) to act on their own knowledge.* They recognize that people are "more directly in contact with themselves" than any rule maker can be. This principle arises naturally from the dynamist understanding of knowledge as dispersed—a spreading elm rather than a vertical palm—and runs directly counter to the stasist notion that someone in charge knows best. Rules, then, must be simple and general, a foundation on which people can build, not a detailed blueprint for exactly what they must construct. The rules must respect the "knowledge problem," the limits of what any authority can know.

The knowledge problem helps explain why lawyer Philip Howard's prescription in his book, *The Death of Common Sense*—giving bureaucrats discretion to use "common sense" in applying technocratic regulations, rather than hamstringing them with rigid legalisms—may curb some excesses but will eventually break down.[14] To understand the nuances of a situation, to see it from the inside, a regulator would need the very sort of local knowledge that is time-consuming to acquire and difficult to articulate. Even when outside officials sincerely try to balance costs and benefits, they lack the information necessary to make that calculation. It is hidden in the hearts and minds of diverse people with diverse tastes, with many different assessments of costs and benefits.

Many people, including New York state regulators, believed that Sassoon's hairstyles defied common sense. "We're not going to be told what to do by these damn foreigners, especially those Limeys. Over there, you can't tell the difference between the boys and the girls!" declared the head of the state's cosmetology department.[15] Even friendlier officials thought the regulations perfectly sensible. But hairdressers and their customers will always know much more than outside regulators about their own circumstances and preferences. The alternative to honoring that knowledge is imposing a false uniformity, a single, rigid model of how the world must be.

Using "common sense," technocrats still pick winners and, therefore, also losers. The "knowledge" at stake is not only information but values, tastes, and individual expression. Cosmetology regulations, complains JoAnne Cornwell, "help perpetuate a negative self-perception on the part of women with naturally textured hair: Our hair is wrong. Our hair is bad."[16] Giving regulators broad discretion means empowering majorities—or their bureaucratic representatives—to impose their "common sense" on minorities. To people for whom hairdressing obviously includes chemical treatments, Cornwell's views defy common sense. Howard's prescription does not resolve that dispute.

Once in place, regulatory discretion can become a powerful force for reactionary stasis, as has happened in the French cities controlled by Jean-Marie Le Pen's neofascist Front Nationale. Exercising the broad discretion that French technocracy gives whomever happens to run the government, Front representatives have banned nonpork alternatives from public school cafeterias, forcing Jewish and Muslim children to conform or go hungry; closed market booths selling African and West Indian foods "on the grounds that only locally grown produce can be sold"; and overridden the decision of local booksellers to give a book fair award to author Marek Halter, declaring that he is an unfit honoree because "he comes from Poland, is a naturalized French citizen, is in favor of immigration and of imposing a cosmopolitan culture on France." Avignon-based writer David Zane Mairowitz reports in *Harper's:*

> In Orange, Mayor Jacques Bompard decided that the public library would henceforth be directly answerable to the *mairie* (or town hall). Suddenly books that did not reflect Front ideology began disappearing from the shelves—including works on the French Revolution (the sentiment *"Liberté, Égalité, Fraternité"* is anathema to the Front), collections of stories from North Africa, and any book with illustrations showing the races mixing. Also included, of course, were any works hostile to the party.[17]

Case-by-case common sense can curb excesses when there is widespread agreement, but it does nothing to permit plenitude. It still substitutes the regulator's local knowledge (and prejudices) for the values and the far more specific, often tacit, knowledge of the parties involved.

We have in fact invested juries with exactly the kind of discretion Howard urges for regulators. We ask jurors to rule on all sorts of things about which they know very little, including complex trade-offs. Their decisions, as a result, are often more random than rational. The difficulty isn't that jurors are lay citizens rather than experts. It's that they are asked to second-guess decisions without the requisite local knowledge, knowledge even an expert—and such trials usually present plenty of expert witnesses—wouldn't have. Looking at a single case, they are expected to substitute hindsight and hypotheticals for the dispersed knowledge conveyed through market processes and the tacit knowledge acquired through experience and embedded in habits and routines.

The consequences have not been pretty, as Walter Olson notes in *The Litigation Explosion:*

> Someone hurt himself using a caustic drain cleaner, or playing with fireworks, or trying to pull a carving knife out of its original holder. Should the product maker have to pay? The most widely used set of modern guidelines invites the jury to consult at least a dozen factors in answering this question. They include the likelihood that users will hurt themselves with the product; the probable seriousness of those injuries; the danger signals, if any, communicated by the "obvious condition of the product"; the ability of users to avoid danger by being careful; the user's likely awareness of the dangers and how avoidable they are; and the general public's knowledge of the same thing.

Got that figured out? There's much more. The bewildered jury must then consider the product's usefulness; whether it could have been made safer without making it less useful or "too expensive to maintain its utility"; whether other products on the market might serve the same need and not be as unsafe; and on and on. This meandering list of things to keep in mind might be useful as an agenda for a talk-show discussion of product safety. What it is not is law. Not surprisingly, many companies have decided to flee the uncertainty by declining to market useful products frequently found on the scene in injuries, from football helmets to life-saving drugs. Businesses will forgo quite a bit of short-term profit rather than roll the dice on a standard that they can never know for sure whether they are complying with.[18]

The problem is not that businesses sometimes lose lawsuits. It is that the rules are unpredictable. Rather than very specific rules enforced with broad discretion (and hence uncertainty), a dynamic vision calls for general rules on which actors can depend—a reliable foundation on which to build complex, ever-adapting structures that incorporate local knowledge.

Some of those structures may themselves be elaborate new schemes of rules. But such rules will be voluntarily subscribed to, allowed to evolve, and able to incorporate detailed knowledge of particulars. They will operate as separate, nested systems within the general rules. And they should not be confused with the fundamental rules that, in fact, allow such specific-purpose rules to develop.

Nested rules that evolve to thoroughly incorporate local knowledge can sometimes solve very tricky governance problems. The political scientist Elinor Ostrom studies how communities develop effective ways to share "commons" used by many people and owned by no single entity. Grazing land and fishing sites are classic examples of commons. Economic theory predicts that such common property will be overused, since everyone has an incentive to draw as much as possible from it rather than to conserve. But Ostrom finds many examples of cooperative institutions evolving to regulate commons use effectively, to everyone's benefit. Many such institutions have lasted for hundreds of years. They have developed through trial-and-error learning, with the rules made by the same people who must abide by them.

In the 1970s, for instance, the fishers of Alanya, Turkey, faced a crisis. Overfishing threatened to deplete stocks and was leading to sometimes violent conflict. Production costs were rising. So, recounts Ostrom, members of the local fishing cooperative began more than a decade of experiments to find a way to assign fishing spots. Eventually they arrived at a stable solution that preserved both the peace and the fish stocks. It gives each fishing boat two turns at each fishing location over the course of the year and spaces out the sites so nobody blocks neighboring nets. The assignments are essentially self-enforcing, since anyone who tries to steal a good spot out of turn will be caught by its rightful claimant.

This privately administered system evolved within the broader law. National legislation permits local cooperatives to make such arrangements, and local authorities officially accept the list of site assignments each year. Instead of trying to impose a particular result, the law protected the process by which new local rules could develop peacefully. That law allowed, indeed fostered, new bonds.

Local knowledge was absolutely critical to developing the Alanya system, which required a great deal of fine-tuning and information about specific sites. "Central-government officials could not have crafted such a set of rules without assigning a full-time staff to work (actually fish) in the area for an extended period," notes Ostrom. "Fishing sites of varying economic value are commonly associated with inshore fisheries, but they are almost impossible to map without extensive on-site experience."[19] The Alanya rules got better over time, as the fishers refined them through trial and error. Designed to solve particular problems by the people affected, this new layer of rules—really a new social institution—does not need to be simple or general. It has specific goals and is subject to competition, from both Alanya fishers with alternative proposals and other fisheries with different arrangements. Like a new technology, business, scientific theory, social arrangement, or work of art, it is the *product* of dynamic processes.

The shipping container is a marvelous invention. It revolutionized and expanded international trade by allowing goods to move from trains to trucks to ships without ever being unpacked. Containers look alike, regardless of their contents, and they can contain just about anything from chainsaws to Barbie dolls. They are completely generic.

In their chronicle of how the Internet was built, *Where Wizards Stay*

Up Late, Katie Hafner and Matthew Lyon use containers as a metaphor to describe how the Internet's underlying data-transfer rules (called transmission control protocol, or TCP) work. Just as shipping containers can carry anything across varied transportation modes without disruption, so TCP allows "packets" of data to move from network to incompatible network, letting computers of all different sorts communicate with each other.[20] What's inside the "container," or packet, is irrelevant. By providing a way to bond wildly different computer networks, this basic protocol made the Internet possible. And because they were built to be extremely general, TCP and its companion, Internet Protocol (IP), allowed the Net later to encompass technologies and uses its designers never imagined. Rather than prescribe a particular purpose for the network, TCP/IP established rules that allowed for surprises.[21]

Again, the settlement of the electronic frontier—or, in this case, its creation—suggests something about the rules that foster dynamic systems. Write Hafner and Lyon:

> Whatever structure [the Network Working Group members] chose, they knew they wanted it to be as open, adaptable, and accessible to inventiveness as possible. *The general view was that any protocol was a potential building block, and so the best approach was to define simple protocols, each limited in scope, with the expectation that any of them might someday be joined or modified in various unanticipated ways.* The protocol design philosophy adopted by the NWG broke ground for what came to be widely accepted as the "layered" approach to protocols.
>
> One of the most important goals of building the lower-layer protocol between hosts was to be able to move a stream of packets from one computer to another without having to worry about what was inside the packets. The job of the lower layer was simply to move generic unidentified bits, regardless of what the bits might define: a file, an interactive session between people at two terminals, a graphical image, or any other conceivable form of digital data. Analogously, some water out of the tap is used for making coffee, some for washing dishes, and some for bathing, but the pipe and faucet don't care; they convey the water regardless. The host-to-host protocol was to perform essentially the same function in the infrastructure of the network. (Emphasis added).[22]

Bits, water, shipping containers—these are all generic. Similarly, the nineteenth-century midwestern grain trade took off once the Chicago

Board of Trade figured out how to turn individual sacks of grain into a generic commodity that could be stored and traded interchangeably, based on very broad grades.[23] On a like note, the author Stewart Brand praises the adaptability of generic old factories, "the plainest of buildings," which can be turned into apartments, shopping centers, offices, restaurants, and countless other new configurations.[24]

These examples suggest the second characteristic of dynamist rules: *The underlying rules apply to simple, generic units and allow them to combine in many different ways.* In this sense, dynamist rules are, as communitarian stasists glibly charge, "atomistic." They do not specify which molecules must form, or which larger structures those molecules must, in turn, make up. But atoms rarely float free. And we have only to contemplate the variety of the world's DNA—human and otherwise—to glimpse the possibilities that arise when simple units combine in complex ways. Recall economist Paul Romer's vision of a cow as but one conceivable atomic combination for turning grass into protein.

From atoms to the alphabet, from music to math, the world's plenitude depends on very primitive units. Their meaning and purpose arise from the bonds they create: the way they fit together and the new building blocks these combinations then become. From this infinite series of bonds upon bonds, inspired by our imaginations and diverse tastes, we enrich the world.

Such bottom-up building is adaptable. While stasists create brittle systems by trying to specify every detail in advance, this second dynamist principle allows for flexibility. The many subunits permit many fine adjustments, encouraging gradual adaptation instead of radical, all-or-nothing change. They also accommodate varied needs and tastes. Urban scholar Anne Vernez Moudon notes how small, regular lots, competing construction styles, and strict but general legal rules led turn-of-the-century San Franciscans to build the diverse and adaptable Victorian houses that mark that city to this day. "Few cities, if any," she writes, "were built as rapidly with as varied a mix of house forms."[25]

Rather than try to design the city as a whole, San Francisco's rule makers created a generic block system. Within the blocks, individual home owners and builders had wide latitude to develop their own property to suit their needs and wants: They built detached, semi-detached, and row houses, even "detached row houses" with side yards but no side windows; they experimented with a variety of setbacks, bases, and facades; they included commercial buildings amid residences and stores on the first floor of homes. Patterns, such as putting commercial buildings on corners, emerged over time. As a whole, Moudon writes, "the architecture of the block was a potpourri of interpretations of loose rules of development, the result of uncoordinated decisions by pioneers."[26] Over the ensuing century, this potpourri proved remarkably resilient, able to adapt to changing demographics and lifestyles, new technologies (notably the automobile), and city growth.

Another way of expressing this second dynamist principle is the nineteenth-century legal historian Henry Sumner Maine's famous statement that "the movement of the progressive societies has hitherto been a movement *from Status to Contract.*"[27] A system of status determines connections and obligations by birth. Contract treats individuals as free and equal, creating their own bonds. Traditional contract law is as generic and flexible as Internet packet protocols. Writes Richard Epstein:

> The logic of mutual gain from voluntary exchange is perfectly general. . . . [It] is not role specific. It does not speak about one set of rules for employers and another for employees or one set for landlords and another for tenants. It does not create one set of rules for people who are rich and powerful and another set for those who are frail or meek. Instead, the law speaks about two hardy standbys in all contractual arrangements: A and B. These people are colorless, odorless, and timeless, of no known nationality, age, race, or sex. . . . The patterns of social life are determined not by some powerful central authority but by the repetitive and independent decisions of thousands of separate individuals pursuing their self-interest.[28]

Contract threatens those who aspire to "powerful central authority," whether over the homes and marriages of Habitat avatars, the shape of cities, or the hairstyles of African-American women. Through generic units, each treated equally, contract allows individuals to imagine—and create—arrangements beyond the plans of grand designers.

"Contract" does not inspire romance, however. Its very idealism makes it sound cold and calculating. We naturally do not see ourselves as generic, so talk of people as "colorless, odorless, and timeless" hardly appeals to our egos. Yet only by treating individuals as generic units can overarching rules allow us to take advantage of our own knowledge, to express our individuality and follow our own ideas; the alternative is to force everyone to conform to a few rigid, preestablished categories.

Not surprisingly, then, one of the most effective ways to attack dynamism is to suggest the superiority of status over contract. Reactionaries invoke the warm sentiment of fixed status roles that are, by definition, respecters of persons. Wrapped in enough evocative language, they can make the traditional constraints of class, race, sex, and geography—not to mention premodern medical care and backbreaking agricultural labor—sound positively humane. In a passage typical of this genre, the philosopher John Gray declares that humans' "deepest need is a home, a network of common practices and inherited traditions that confers on them *the blessing of a settled identity*. . . . Human beings are above all fragile creatures, for whom the meaning of life is a local matter that is easily dissipated: their freedom is worthwhile and meaningful to them only against a background of common cultural forms. Such forms cannot be created anew for each generation." (Emphasis added.)[29]

Through rhetorical sleight of hand, Gray conflates the desire for lasting commitments with an appeal for predetermined, inherited status roles. "Revealed preference," as the economists say, suggests that people do not crave "settled identity" but instead tend to seek novelty: We marry outside our ethnic groups; adopt foreign foods and fashions; invent new words, music, and visual art forms; develop new religious practices and beliefs. We leave our birthplaces to seek better lives elsewhere. We are forever fixing up our homes, changing our hairstyles, making up new stories.

Such innovations are rarely truly original, almost never "created anew for each generation." They are, rather, evolutionary variations on old themes. In our social and personal lives, as in the economic, scientific, and political realms, there is no scratch. We do not simply jettison the inherited or the familiar—but we do seek to improve on it. Honoring that pursuit, a dynamist world is, like the Internet, "open, adaptable, and accessible." By treating individuals as Epstein's "colorless, odorless, and timeless" A and B, dynamist rules allow us to forge new bonds—to join our ideas, our property, ourselves in "various unanticipated ways."

The alternative, much beloved of both technocrats and reactionaries, is to specify the exact shape of things, to reify detailed categories. The goal is to make a naturally fluid world static, to make labels permanent: Offices do not belong in homes. Private companies cannot carry regular first-class mail. A "doll" is subject to a 12 percent tariff; a "toy soldier" is not, making G.I. Joe a problematic case.[30] A full-time job takes five eight-hour days; four ten-hour days are not equivalent.[31] Zoned for industrial use, an otherwise adaptable factory building cannot be turned into retail space. Broadcast spectrum assigned to AM radio cannot be used for cellular phones. Whether such rules seem ideologically "conservative" or "progressive" depends on context, but they are consistently designed to impose stasis, to limit the bonds of the imagination. They assume categories cannot, will not, or should not change.

Nor are all static categories so technical, so seemingly dry and mercenary. In the late nineteenth century, railroads blasted through the granite of social status as surely as their builders dynamited mountains. On a train, paying passengers became contract's generic As and Bs—as odorless, timeless, and colorless as water in a pipe or bits on the Internet. All ticket holders were effectively the same, their contracts for carriage equally valid. So when black passengers bought tickets for unsegregated first-class cars, they expected their contracts to be honored, and they made them stick in court. But color was not an attribute dissolved without resistance.

The railroads, writes historian Edward Ayers, "neither wanted to police Southern race relations and then be sued for it nor to run extra cars. It was clear that white Southerners could not count on the railroads to take matters in hand" by blocking or expelling black passengers from their first-class cars. "Some whites came to blame the railroads for the problem," says Ayers, "for it seemed to them that the corporations as usual were putting profits ahead of the welfare of the region."[32] The critics were mostly right. The railroads were not civil rights pioneers but contract-bound, profit-seeking businesses for whom commerce was a "universal solvent." Outraged southern legislators, who already resented the railroads' economic power, passed laws requiring segregated accommodations. (It was one of these laws, passed by Louisiana in 1892, that the U.S. Supreme Court upheld in the famous "separate but equal" case, *Plessy v. Ferguson*.) Combining the technocratic lust to regulate business with the reactionary zeal to preserve social stability, Jim Crow laws imposed static definitions on a dynamic commercial culture inclined to treat customers as "colorless, odorless, and timeless."

Notions of the public welfare have changed, of course, but the idea that race is static has not. In a society dominated by contract, race remains among the most potent and problematic vestiges of status, officially honored in everything from electoral apportionment to the intimacies of family life. Under a federal directive, every American has been designated as either black, white, American Indian/Alaskan Native, or Asian/Pacific Islander, with further notation of "Hispanic origin" or "not of Hispanic origin." Individuals do not, however, cooperate with such prescriptions. Left to their own devices, enough people will create cross-racial families to make a mockery of static categories. A Georgia child with a black father and white mother is, his mother testified before a congressional committee, "white on the United States census, black at school, and multiracial at home—all at the same time."[33] (As a result of such objections the 2000 census will allow individuals to check as many racial categories as they choose.)

Such status-defying anomalies exist because, in one sense, John Gray is right. Home is indeed a deep human need. People seek bonds with those who complete their world, who allow them a place to fully realize themselves. Given the individuality of human beings, however, the homes we create quite often cross traditional status lines, linking us across imagined boundaries. Those new bonds disrupt the old categories, erase accepted labels. That disruption, and the resistance it encounters, has inspired art as well as law: "Deny thy father and refuse thy name, / Or, if thou wilt not, be but sworn my love / And I'll no longer be a Capulet," says Juliet.

Although miscegenation has traditionally been the great fear behind rigid racial boundaries, such status-defying bonds are not limited to romantic love. In recent years, transracial adoption has been more controversial than interracial marriage. In 1972, the National Association of Black Social Workers declared that "Black children belong, physically, psychologically, and culturally in Black families," and vowed to end the "genocide" perpetrated by transracial adoption.[34] Following their lead, state social service agencies have engaged in "race matching" of children with adoptive parents, refusing in many cases to place even biracial children with white parents.[35] The results have often been tragic. African-American children tend to stay in the twilight zone of foster care twice as long as their white counterparts. Some never find a permanent home. Nonblack foster parents often cannot adopt children they have raised as their own; indeed, asking to adopt can lead authorities to snatch the child from his home and place him elsewhere. [36]

Race matching, argues the legal scholar Randall Kennedy, hurts children in deep and abiding ways, condemning them "to the anxiety of having no family that is permanently and intimately one's own." In addition,

> It strengthens the baleful notion that race is destiny. It buttresses the notion that people of different racial backgrounds really are different in some moral, unbridgeable, permanent sense. It affirms the notion that race should be a cage to which people are assigned at birth and from which people should not be allowed to wander. [37]

This combination of insecurity and cages—and the resulting inability to shape one's own life by forming chosen bonds—is characteristic of the static world of status. The colorless, odorless, timeless A and B of contract, by contrast, permit an infinite series of combinations, encompassing the diversity of human beings and making a dynamic world resilient. Generic categories and general rules may sound cold, but they allow us to find our own sources of warmth.

Contract is not simply about categories. It is also about commitment. Contracts allow us to incur reciprocal responsibilities, to make promises others can rely on, and to establish reasonable expectations for future actions. Those obligations may be as limited as the agreement to deliver a particular good at a certain price or as open-ended as the devotion of parents to an adoptive child—but they are all binding. To speak in chemical terms, the bonds of life create compounds, not mixtures. Compounds can, of course, be broken up; they can be turned into new substances or returned to their original elements. Such transformation does not take place easily, however, and it exacts a cost.

A dynamic society, then, depends not only on preserving fluidity but on permitting permanence. To learn, we must experiment. But to experiment, we must commit ourselves. And we must find ways to cooperate with others, to extend trust. Here, then, is the third characteristic of dynamist rules, a complement to the second: *The rules permit credible, understandable, enduring, and enforceable commitments.* That means not only that the rules are clear and predictable, but that people can be held to their promises (or penalized for breaking them). This side of contract allows people to plan and to cooperate—to merge their talents, resources, knowledge, and ideas. It allows them to create zones of security, bonds they can count on. This security is essential not only to individual happiness but to growth, learning, and progress.

The great weakness of Habitat, says Chip Morningstar, was that its residents could not themselves create new places or objects within its virtual world. Nor could they build "their own little pockets of the universe," with their own rules. There could be no independently governed institutions. As a result, Habitat was a relatively limited world. And while its limits came in part from the primitive nature of the computers involved, that was not the biggest problem. The real issue was that allowing participants to add new objects or places meant letting them create software code that would then enter other participants' computers. That, says Morningstar, would require "inviting people inside trust boundaries that you just generally couldn't trust strangers in."[38]

Today, Morningstar and some of his former Habitat colleagues are involved with a new venture, called Electric Communities, that is designing widely applicable software to get around this problem. The goal is to allow "cooperation without vulnerability," to build both security and flexibility into software so that online worlds can evolve through the experiments and invention of their participants. The model is contract—a security system based on transferable "capabilities" rather than the static identity of passwords and "authorized user" lists.[39]

Virtual frontiers are not the only settlements that require rules allowing "cooperation without vulnerability." We can see similar patterns in the burgeoning cities of the Third World, where migrants from the countryside establish homes, businesses, marketplaces, and neighborhoods outside the law. In his influential 1989 book *The Other Path*, the economist Hernando de Soto and a team of researchers identified barriers to legal entrepreneurship or home ownership in Peru's cities: To comply with all the laws to start a small garment factory, they found, required 289 days, eleven different permits, and $1,231 ("thirty-two times the monthly minimum living wage"); acquiring state-owned wasteland on which to build modest homes, along with the necessary building permits, would take eighty-three months—just shy of seven years—and more than a half million dollars; opening a small store legally would consume 43 days and nearly $600. (None of these figures, which are strictly for legal compliance, includes such basic operating costs as sewing machines, building supplies, or store inventory.)

Concludes De Soto, "What we have here is bad law."[40] Peru's highly bureaucratic mercantilist regime represents a perfect melding of reactionary goals and technocratic means; it maintains a traditional social hierarchy through complex regulations administered by experts. The country's "bad law" cannot accommodate the creativity of Peru's ambitious former peasants, and so they defy it. In the face of the law's prohibitive costs in time and money, poor Peruvians have created an economy that operates illegally, yet provides services usually considered law abiding. This "informal sector" has developed almost half the housing in Lima, built or acquired street markets worth $41 million, provided almost all urban mass transport, and accounted for about half Peru's employment and nearly 40 percent of its gross domestic product.[41]

The law still matters, however, because bad law is only half the story. Informals also suffer, writes De Soto, "from the absence of a legal system that guarantees and promotes their economic efficiency—in other words, of good law." For that, Peruvian society pays a high price. Owners of land without a secure title cannot mortgage it to finance a business. They cannot confidently rent out all or part of a house, for fear that the tenant will claim to be the owner. They cannot be sure that any investment to improve their home will be theirs to keep or transfer. As a result, property without titles is more likely to remain in shantytown conditions than property with titles.[42]

Suppose, suggests De Soto, that he and a friend decide to start a button factory. He has a button-making machine and excellent skills; his friend has the necessary contacts to make the sales. They agree to split the proceeds sixty-forty, with De Soto, as owner of the machine, getting the larger share. But they have no way of enforcing the deal over the long term.

My friend goes very happily to his home and sees his wife. She says, "Now, wait a second. Think it over. This fellow, De Soto, you barely know him. This fellow, De Soto, after a year will know who your clients are, whom to sell to, when to sell, and how to sell to them. After a year, he won't need you. He will no longer keep on giving you 40 percent of the business." . . .

As a result, my friend will choose instead to associate with a relative—someone in his extended family. And that person won't produce buttons as good as mine. So they will have a little company that isn't going to be very prosperous. I'll have to do the same. I'll find someone to sell buttons who trusts me because he happens to be family of mine. But he just doesn't sell buttons the way my friend can sell buttons. And, therefore, the two talents that were required to make a successful industry in Lima will not be able to merge. Then some anthropologists from Cornell University will come to Peru and say, "Look at Peruvians. They like to work in small family units."[43]

Relying on family ties is only a compromise solution, providing trust but limiting possible alliances. When people cannot make binding, enforceable commitments, dynamic progress is severely hampered. While it's wrong to presume that people can't make their own arrangements, it's equally wrong to imagine that in all cases the deals will be self-enforcing.

Douglass North, an economic historian who won the Nobel Prize for his work on the relationship between institutions and economic growth, notes that "the inability of societies to develop effective, low-cost enforcement of contracts is the most important source of both historical stagnation and underdevelopment in the Third World."[44] The challenges of Third World and postcommunist development have demonstrated the power of North's once-controversial insight. Corruption and insecure contracts stifle economic development.

At best, entrepreneurial individuals find ways to shop for more reliable legal regimes. In the former Soviet Union, contracts are sometimes written to be paid not in currency but in natural gas, a generic product, for delivery in Germany and, hence, subject to the German rule of law. In other cases, contracts are backed with bank deposits in London or Bermuda and thus enforceable under British law.[45] But such international arrangements are hardly "low cost." Too often the only alternative is physical intimidation, either real, as with the Russian mafia, or implied. Esther Dyson tells of a Russian programmer friend who once sent over a couple of intimidating-looking, but actually quite peaceable, pals in hopes that his client would *think* they would use mafia-style violence and would complete some paperwork the local bureaucracy was demanding. (The ruse worked.)[46]

Well-functioning legal systems are particularly important when strangers interact—"This fellow, De Soto, you barely know him"—but even then they mainly exist never to be used. Rather, they establish "the shadow of the law" under which bargains can be made. The goal is not to inspire legal disputes but to settle or avoid them. The clearer the rules, the fewer the conflicts. Recognized procedures for registering property, for instance, may be all that is needed to make title transfers secure. Epstein notes the value of well-known rules, such as putting real estate sales in writing, in making bonds more certain:

> The writing is only a formality; the true heart is the substantive agreement between the parties over the terms of the contract of sale. . . . [But] an oral contract leaves open serious questions as to what was agreed over subsidiary terms (who keeps the fixtures? which side has to arrange the financing? when may the buyer move in?). The writing requirement, announced in advance and well known by all professionals who work in the business, thus *channels,* to use the standard phrase, complex negotiations into safe paths.[47]

Rules that eliminate ambiguity make it more likely that people will keep their promises, for the simple reason that they will understand what in fact they have promised. And they will know that those promises can be observed by third parties.

Rules that support commitments (and, if applicable, the courts to interpret and enforce them) sound unobjectionable. After all, reactionaries value stability and technocrats seek control, both of which commitments offer. But this side of contract, too, wrecks stasist schemes. "Cooperation without vulnerability" does not make society stable as a whole: It instead provides room for experimentation and new, unfamiliar bonds. It gives no one central control but, rather, permits many different arrangements, Morningstar's self-governing "little pockets of the universe."

Far from imposing stasis, contract fosters dynamic processes. It encourages specialization and allows an "extended order" to grow beyond the simple solidarity of intimates. Under such rules, De Soto's button company need not stay in the family, nor must it remain small. It can borrow money or extend credit, and possibly export. It can trust even faceless strangers. The security of cooperation without vulnerability permits the "footloose" society E. F. Schumacher attacked for disrupting peasant certainties.

Confronted with commitments that disrupt their visions, reactionaries and technocrats have several options. Most simply, they can refuse to recognize those agreements: remove children from their would-be parents; allow untitled property to be seized by nonowners; let railroads throw paying passengers off the train based on race. This is not simply a matter of court enforcement. For the bonds of contract to work, third parties must also honor them. If I sell you my house, the bank, the property tax collectors, and the neighbors all recognize the transfer. The hedge is now yours to trim, the plumbing yours to fix; if the gardeners or plumbers send me bills, I won't pay them. And if my friends or relatives enter your new home using keys they got from me, they and I are both in trouble—because everyone has agreed that the house is now yours. Our deal is enmeshed in other bonds.

But official recognition also matters. Family law, because it is still largely tied to status, is rife with examples of commitments unrecognized by the authorities. Legal disputes over surrogate motherhood hinge on whether courts will recognize the contracting couple's right to the child. Single-sex couples find their commitments to de facto spouses disregarded in matters ranging from hospital visitation to inheritance taxes. No-fault divorce laws nullify marriage contracts that require mutual consent for dissolution. Ignoring such commitments can, all by itself, erode them.

Alternatively, the bonds of contract can be actively broken and replaced by an order more to the liking of distant authorities. Sometimes this happens inadvertently, as when inflation erodes the value of a promised payment. More frequently, an existing commitment interferes with a technocratic vision of the proper shape of society. Universities, for example, give professors the security of tenure but have long included mandatory retirement, usually at age sixty-five or seventy, as part of the bargain. Now, however, they can no longer enforce the retirement contract. Federal law prohibits such "age discrimination," making tenured professors employees for life and forcing schools to offer expensive buyouts if they want to make room for younger faculty. The law has disrupted the progression from one generation of professors to the next and stuck universities with unproductive scholars who decline buyout offers. "The new law clogs the arteries," the retired historian Oscar Handlin, then seventy-eight, told *The New York Times*. "It won't allow young people to move in."[48]

Finally, bonds can be broken indirectly, by eroding the norms that enforce them. In many communities, geographic and otherwise, reputation is a far more reliable enforcement mechanism than the vagaries and expense of the courts. Protected in the United States by the First Amendment and in other free countries by traditions of open discourse, journalism and science operate almost entirely outside the courts. They are self-governing professions that trade in truth and rely heavily on trust. Journalists honor promises to sources, and scientists uphold standards of peer review, not, with rare exceptions, because they can be dragged into court but because their professional reputations are at stake.[49]

No one had to sue Janet Cooke—the *Washington Post* reporter who won a Pulitzer Prize, only to have her story (and much of her resumé) revealed as a complete fabrication—to punish her for breaching her commitments to her readers and *The Washington Post*. Mere public knowledge that she had falsified a story was enough to wreck her career. When she reemerged after fifteen years in obscurity, issued lame apologies, and said she'd like to return to journalism, Jim Amoss, editor of *The Times-Picayune* in New Orleans, expressed the nigh-universal industry reaction: A newspaper hiring Cooke, he said, "would be like a day-care center hiring a convicted child molester."[50]

For reputation to work, however, the rules must allow ostracism to take place. That means permitting criticism—and not only in extreme, well-publicized cases. Yet privacy advocates frequently attempt to limit the accurate information that credit bureaus and others can share about, for instance, whether tenants have paid their rent, wrecked their apartments, or caused problems for their neighbors.[51] And employment law has seriously eroded the ability of former bosses to give truthful references, especially about employees who have been fired. Saying anything bad can result in a defamation suit, while a positive reference can be grounds for a wrongful dismissal case.[52] There is something disconcerting about calling a newspaper editor for a job reference, only to be told that company policy prohibits any comment other than confirmation of employment.[53] Refusing to give references is increasingly common in all sorts of businesses, but it is especially troubling in a profession that depends on the free exchange of information and relies almost entirely on reputation to check bad actors.

*　　　*　　　*

Learning by trial and error means having the chance to try things. It also means finding out when they don't work, or when something else works better. That, in turn, implies that other people will get the chance to prove your ideas wrong, or inferior, or limited to a smaller audience than you imagined. Depending on whether you're trying a new physics theory, a supposedly improved laundry detergent, or a new style of music, "error" may be absolute or just relative to other people's alternatives and current tastes. Either way, progress through trial and error depends not only upon making trials but on recognizing errors. Criticism is at the very heart of the dynamic process of learning.

If, as Henry Petroski suggests, "form follows failure," then criticism, like invention, has a combinatoric quality. Petroski observes:

> The vast number of things that exist in the world today ensures that there will be ever more tomorrow, for virtually every existing thing is fair game to come under the scrutiny of someone restless and discontented who does not think "well enough" is sufficiently free of faults. The reactionary call to leave well enough alone is a futile one, for the advancement of civilization itself has been a history of the successive correction (and sometimes the overcorrection) of error and fault and failure.[54]

As Petroski hints, there is always pressure to block criticism: to shut off alternatives, shelter the familiar, stifle the imagination. Criticism is, after all, no fun for its targets. No one wants to be a failure, even a relative one. So reactionaries who fear disruption, technocrats who want to pick winners, and self-interested parties who want to shut out rivals can all be counted on to try to limit criticism and competition. The ability to resist this collusion against new ideas is perhaps the single most distinguishing feature of dynamic systems.

This, then, suggests the fourth characteristic of dynamist rules: *The rules protect criticism, competition, and feedback.* They allow the freedom to challenge established ideas and the freedom to offer alternatives—*criticism by expression* and *criticism by example.* And they make sure that no one has the privilege of conducting experiments insulated from the effects of failure. Dynamic, evolving systems have no guaranteed or permanent winners.

In many cases, allowing criticism is just that: a hands-off rule that keeps the powers that be from meddling. But protecting criticism also means policing attempts to silence critics by force. Left unchecked, terror can be an effective way of maintaining stasis. It worked well in the segregated South, where authorities did not control violent intimidation against blacks or whites who broke racial norms. By contrast, one reason the historical Luddites failed was that British authorities enforced the law against their violent acts. And the novelist Salman Rushdie remains alive and writing in part because the British government has protected him from religious vigilantes determined to kill him.

The greatest power to block criticism is, however, the legal force held by government. Unlike the Unabomber, legal authorities need not send bombs to random targets whose ideas they dislike; they can simply ban the expression of those ideas and enforce the ban with prison terms, a far more efficient approach. That is why government power is often the first tool stasists try to grab when they want to stop challengers—whether those challengers are disrupting traditional hairstyling, promoting dissident political views, or desegregating trains—and it is why dynamists are wary of laws that hinder competition.

Petroski envisions criticism by example, through the creation of new-and-improved artifacts. For such "criticisms" to work, their inventors must be able to enter the market, to compete with the ideas embodied in established products. That's why outsiders and upstarts love competition and hate barriers. Although their ideas may ultimately fail, they want the chance to succeed. To them, "competition" suggests not dog-eat-dog struggle but openness. It rewards quality instead of entrenching privilege. As Braiderie owner Ali Rasheed puts it: "We're looking for competition. . . . Competition is where it is, where the rubber meets the road. Let the market decide who should be working, who should be doing hair. A license doesn't make people come to you, and people don't stay away from you because you're not licensed. It's the quality of work you do."[55]

The economic historian Nathan Rosenberg imagines business start-ups and investment decisions as "economic experiments," explorations aimed at discovering better technologies and organizational forms. He emphasizes both "the freedom to conduct experiments" and the need to test them. And he stresses the danger of letting any single authority rig the outcomes:

> The need to expose investment decisions to the risk of being proven wrong implies the decentralization of decision-making authority, since

any central authority will have a strong motivation for withholding financial support from those who are bent on proving that the central authority made a mistake, or on imposing on the central authority the cost of scrapping splendid-looking facilities whose only fault is that some interloper has devised more productive facilities. . . .

Historically, one of the most distinctive features of capitalist economies has been the practice of decentralizing authority over investments to substantial numbers of individuals who stand to make large personal gains if their decisions are right, who stand to lose heavily if their decisions are wrong, and *who lack the economic or political power to prevent at least some others from proving them wrong.* Indeed, this particular cluster of features constitutes an excellent candidate for *the* definition of capitalism.[56]

If your goal is to impose a single, static vision, however, this "cluster of features" contains exactly the rules you must overturn. It permits turbulence and annoying questions. Stasis cannot survive a constant stream of alternatives, whether economic or intellectual. It can tolerate neither criticism nor uncertain outcomes.

That is why the need to limit competition is a constant theme among both reactionaries and technocrats. When Charlotte Allen tells fellow conservatives, "Don't let Wal Mart wreck *your* downtown," she is asking them to protect existing retailers from criticism—to outlaw the idea that stores can and should be different by making alternatives impossible to build. Supporters of centrally managed public schools similarly fear that competition from charter schools will prove disruptive and weaken technocrats' ability to control curriculum and values: "The disadvantaged population that charter schools are meant to help will find it hard to examine all the options, to elude the clever advertising, to shun fads," warns *Seattle Times* columnist David Brewster. "By putting the selection of schools firmly in parents' hands, you interfere with the way pluralistic public schools traditionally help children escape from a smothering family culture."[57]

The economic and intellectual spheres are not as easily separated as our political discussion often suggests. Rules that allow criticism by example often feed criticism by expression, and vice versa. In many cases, ideas embedded in products and processes are intimately connected with ideas expressed in words. Rasheed's braiding salons make not only a profit but an argument about African beauty. Rushdie's novels are not intangible abstractions but physical books, sold in public stores.

Even in the nitty-gritty of manufacturing, example and expression are bound together. When Toyota learned in 1970 that Volkswagen could change dies on a thousand-ton press in two hours, half the time it took the Japanese carmaker, the company set out to beat that competition. Achieving that goal after six months of hard work, Toyota pressed on, ultimately reaching a once-inconceivable three-minute changeover time.[58] This remarkable "Single Minute Exchange of Dies," or SMED, technique required both new thinking about how production is organized and enormous attention to detail. The rules of free trade, derided by reactionaries for their disruptive effects, spread these new ideas worldwide. Fierce competition from Toyota and other Japanese companies spurred U.S. automakers, which otherwise would have considered such fast changeovers impossible, to reinvent their own production. And along with that criticism by example came criticism by expression: books, articles, seminars, and consulting by the creators and students of SMED and other "lean manufacturing" techniques.

Similarly, the deregulation of satellites and cable television in the 1970s broke the broadcast networks' stranglehold on televised news. More-open rules made it possible for Ted Turner and Brian Lamb to launch new models of TV news—for-profit CNN's twenty-four-hour reporting and nonprofit C-SPAN's unmediated coverage. "This is the only place in the history of electronic communication where someone can approach a microphone with a speech, stand in front of the microphone, and complete their thoughts without any interference," boasts Lamb.[59] The postderegulation proliferation of news outlets, "criticism by example," has made media criticism, "criticism by expression," a booming business. There are both more models of "the way things ought to be" and more ways for people who take issue with the mainstream—or the upstarts—to voice their opinions.

As Petroski's nod toward "overcorrection" suggests, however, many "improvements" fail to excite anyone but their inventors. Robert McMath, director of the New Products Showcase and Learning Center, tracks not only successful new products but the far more common flops: ScotTowels Junior didn't fit on conventional paper-towel racks. Maxwell House ready-to-drink coffee couldn't be microwaved in its original container. Kleenex Avert Virucidal Tissues scared away customers with that deadly name.[60] What seemed like improvements couldn't survive the test of competition.

Dilbert cartoonist Scott Adams has made a fortune spoofing the stupid management fads that constantly sweep American business. His comic strip is a devastatingly effective form of criticism by expression, respected even by some of its targets. It is, says Tom Peters, "the classic backlash. We of *In Search of Excellence* were the backlash to the MBA dogma of the 1960s and '70s. *Dilbert* is the backlash to the management gurus of the last 15 years, starting with *In Search of Excellence*. That's life. It's called conjectures and refutations [the title of a book by the philosopher Karl Popper]. It's very Popperian."[61] Popper argued that we cannot prove our hypotheses, only submit them to tests that may refute them. The thesis of *Conjectures and Refutations* was, he wrote, "that *we can learn from our mistakes*" and that "*all* our knowledge grows *only* through the correcting of our mistakes . . . the method of trial and error."[62]

What's true for products and practices is true for ideas. Testing them is essential. As Jonathan Rauch notes, "We can all have three new ideas every day before breakfast; the trouble is, they will almost always be bad ideas. The hard part is figuring out who has a *good* idea."[63] Rauch's concern is protecting "liberal science," the process of continually checking intellectual hypotheses (not just natural science) through decentralized, rigorous, no-holds-barred discussion. He worries that rules against giving offense threaten that dynamic process. To work, Rauch argues, liberal science must allow criticism, without limiting who can participate or what they can say, and it must give no one the final authority:

> The notion that error is never a crime—may indeed be an inspiration—frees us to think imaginatively, even ridiculously. At the same time, the insistence that everybody be checked gives us some reassurance that the truly ridiculous will be weeded out. Herd-thinking and fad-following will always be part of human life, but over time liberal science does tend to correct itself. It shares with evolution, capitalism, and democracy this advantage of liberal systems: the capacity to be self-regulating, to be "led by an invisible hand" (order without authority). When opinion rushes to extremes, claims start being overblown, and then they become juicy targets for debunking. Pretty soon headlines appear along the lines of "Skeptics Are Challenging Dire 'Greenhouse' Views" and "Nuclear Winter Theorists Pull Back." . . . If you play the game well, you must be

imaginative in two ways at once: in dreaming up statements about the external world and in dreaming up ways to debunk them.[64]

Nor is scientific criticism limited to modifying "extremes." Completely different hypotheses compete, mustering data in their favor and attacking counterhypotheses: Geologists, chemists, astronomers, and paleontologists duke it out over whether the impact of an extraterrestrial body—a meteorite or asteroid—led to the extinction of the dinosaurs. Milton Friedman and Anna Schwartz write *The Monetary History of the United States* to show that "money matters," contrary to the received Keynesian wisdom. Within a decade, the theory of continental drift goes from geologic crankdom to how the world works.

Hypotheses that challenge established ideas may have a tough time—for good reason in most cases—but under dynamist rules they can't be squashed altogether, only marginalized. Anyone can start a journal; form a scholarly, political, or religious association; set up a Web page or discussion group. Anyone can try to persuade the world (or a significant portion of it) of their ideas. The freedom to persuade is central to a dynamic, learning system, whether the lessons are intellectual, cultural, religious, or economic. And that persuasion takes many forms, of both expression and example. Indeed, the two are not easily separated. "At the root of technological progress is a rhetorical environment that makes it possible for inventors to be heard. . . . Free speech leads to riches," writes the economic historian and rhetorician D. N. McCloskey.[65] Both showing and telling are important.

We swim in a sea of rules. Few are as fundamental as the four principles elaborated above. Rather, they are particular: company policies, traffic laws, religious strictures, etiquette conventions, professional ethics, grammar and syntax, game rules, software programs, university honor codes. Between the common law of contracts and "Never eat old mayonnaise" lie layer upon layer of increasingly specific rules.

The final characteristic of dynamist rules, then, is a rule about rule making: *Dynamist rules establish a framework within which people can create nested, competing frameworks of more-specific rules.* The overall framework allows Morningstar's "little pockets of the universe" to emerge, establishing their own rules. Competition—the option to leave one pocket of the universe for an alternative—permits such specific rule regimes to flourish without making the overall system rigid or inflexible. We can choose the bonds with which to shape, and reshape, our lives.

In *How Buildings Learn,* Stewart Brand examines how buildings are adapted to new uses over time—and what makes for resilient architecture that can "learn." His research provides a useful metaphor for dynamic systems in general. A building, he notes, contains six nested systems: site, structure (the foundation and load-bearing elements), skin (the exterior), services (wiring, plumbing, heating, etc.), space plan (the interior layout), and stuff. The farther out the system, the more permanent. Moving around furniture (stuff) is easy; altering a foundation (structure) extremely difficult. In a building, writes Brand,

> the lethargic slow parts are in charge, not the dazzling rapid ones. Site dominates Structure, which dominates the Skin, which dominates the Services, which dominate the Space plan, which dominates the Stuff. How a room is heated depends on how it relates to the heating and cooling Services, which depend on the energy efficiency of the Skin, which depends on the constraints of the Structure. . . . The quick processes provide originality and challenge, the slow provide continuity and constraint.[66]

A well-designed, adaptable building, he argues, respects the different speeds and different functions of these nested layers. It keeps them separate, allowing "slippage" so that the quick inner layers can change without disrupting the more permanent systems. (You don't have to tear up the foundation to fix the plumbing.)[67]

So it is with rules in a dynamic, learning system. The basic dynamist rules, like a building site or foundation, change slowly, if at all. That is why they must be extremely general. But on top of them, we build increasingly fluid, nested sets of more-specific rules. The rules of free inquiry, property, and contract that allow universities to form may not change much over time, for example. But the institution-specific codes governing curfews, library privileges, computer use, curriculum requirements, or admissions procedures can evolve rapidly, assuming that each institution is free to govern itself. (University rules lose much of their resilience when they're set by distant authorities, such as state boards of regents.) Between the general rules and the institution-specific codes lie other rules: the professional standards that govern scholars, the classification systems that catalog books, the Internet protocols that link computer systems. Nor must every school adopt the same, or even similar, rules. A system of free competition and criticism allows room for fundamentalist Bob Jones University and for free-wheeling Berkeley, for requiring senior theses at Princeton and co-op work internships at Northeastern. By choosing a university and leaving if they don't like it, students and faculty decide which rules they wish to be governed by. They don't have to agree on which rules are best for everyone. Nested rules accommodate diversity.

Like architects who imagine they can predict every future use of a building, however, stasist rule makers scorn nested rules. They believe that theirs is the one best way. They see single standards as efficient, even just. If they cannot imagine a pizza without tomato, they require that all pizza have it. If they want a big yard in their child's day care center, they demand big yards in all day care centers. From afar, they rewrite every personnel manual to forbid smoking and require carpools, to delete mandatory retirement and impose maternity leave. They are forever in search of the one best college curriculum (although, thankfully, rarely empowered to require it). In the name of consistency and "harmonization," they override competitive processes and local knowledge.

Nested rules, by contrast, recognize the diversity of human bonds. They protect plenitude—and voluntary community—by allowing individuals to choose the specific rules under which they prefer to be governed. They permit choice, competition, and learning, rather than imposing a single, static model.

The more that rules must compete for adherents, the more legitimacy they enjoy and the more local knowledge they can incorporate. "We reject kings, presidents, and voting. We believe in rough consensus and running code," declares the Internet Engineering Task Force Credo, and Internet rules have indeed evolved through trial-and-error competition. Net pioneers are intensely loyal to that process. Against demands for censorship and regulation, they reflexively propose flexible, nested alternatives: filtering software for many different tastes, voluntary Web site "trustmarks" indicating various audited privacy standards, access-provider terms of service enforced by banishing rule breakers. These ideas assume that diversity is valuable and that there is not, in fact, one best way. "The value of labels," writes Esther Dyson, "is that people can pick the rules that suit them, rather than be forced to operate in a one-size-fits-all environment where everyone has to follow the same rules. . . . The basic rule is that providers must disclose—label—themselves clearly and honestly. And they must do what they promise to do."[68] Contract, commitment, and competition permit diverse, voluntarily accepted nested rule sets.

Competitive systems can operate to check each other's excesses. Consider the codes governing the relations between U.S. corporations and their shareholders. The fifty states compete to offer standard corporation codes; companies can either use these default terms or tailor specific provisions in their corporate charters. (A company does not have to be physically headquartered in a state to claim it as the corporation's legal domicile.) Agreeable state rules, backed by well-established case law, can significantly cut the cost of doing business. The competition among states for incorporations and the taxes they bring makes legislatures responsive to new ideas and changing business conditions.

Equally important, company managers can't get away with adopting just any code that makes their lives easy. These rules govern a two-way agreement—between the business (essentially, its managers) and the shareholders. Opportunistic managers who try to use state laws to help themselves at the stockholders' expense are checked by another source of competition: the financial markets. So, for instance, when Pennsylvania passed a law designed to make hostile takeovers difficult, protecting managers but making stock less valuable, pressures from falling stock prices pushed most of the state's publicly traded companies to opt out of the law's provisions. Few other states adopted the same law, lest they lose incorporations.

The legal scholar Roberta Romano, who calls this federalist system of competing rules "the genius of American corporate law," writes: "As the Pennsylvania experience illustrates, the federal system provides a safety net against the consequences of harmful state laws. Some jurisdictions will have no or only mild takeover regulation, and this constrains how much other jurisdictions can act in this area and how much firms can take advantage of value-decreasing laws, especially when major commercial states such as Delaware and California have less onerous laws."[69] Having many sources of competing rules, rather than a single, national standard, makes finding good rules—and eliminating or limiting bad ones—more likely.

Easy international communication and shipping can turn technocratic standards originally designed to be one-size-fits-all laws into competing rules operating within a global system. This is famously true of the capital markets, which reward and punish local governance by moving money to more favorable regimes. But it also applies to other rules. Rather than submit to the Food and Drug Administration's extreme risk aversion, for instance, Americans can more and more easily use the Internet to buy medicines approved in other countries. Legal scholar Peter Huber writes of a friend who ordered an asthma drug from France: "He would not have bought a drug from China or Belize, but he was willing to trust France. The world's drug regulators, in short, compete for his custom."[70] Competition strengthens the legitimacy of the rules that survive.

And it makes the distinction between dynamist principles and technocratic rule making all the more clear. Dynamists seek not a world without rules, but a world in which rules govern the appropriate level of life. Rachel's rules exist in a dynamist world, infused with the knowledge accumulated through generations of trial-and-error learning. But such rules are the "stuff" of life, the particular maxims through which individuals govern themselves. They are not the "site" or the "structure" to which all of society must conform. Dynamist rules permit complexity and plenitude, even of rules themselves.

Competition among rules infuriates stasists. It thwarts their ambition to force everyone to conform to a single, static vision. It turns the grand designs they claim as "The Way" into just one more alternative, one more product in the marketplace of ideas. Global competition, which substitutes alternatives and exit for the one best way of political power, is a stasist bête noire. The green reactionary Jerry Mander frets that "democracy is already suffering its greatest setback, as a direct result of this de facto conspiracy" of technologies and markets.[71] "National governments have lost much of their power to direct their own economies," complains the historian Jeremy Brecher in The Nation. He warns of "cancerous, out-of-control globalization."[72]

As Brecher suggests, "cancer" is one of stasists' favorite metaphors to describe dynamic systems. It suggests that something is not right, that nature is out of whack, that things are running dangerously out of control. It turns life—the spontaneous evolution of human civilization—into something threatening and unnatural. And that is not surprising. Nature and artifice, wildness and control, spontaneity and planning take on very different meanings in dynamist and stasist thought.

CHAPTER SIX

CREATING NATURE

Eden is in Western myth the unchanging and pristine paradise, lost through overreaching and lamented ever since. In the biblical story, however, Eden is more complicated. It is a living, growing place whose life depends on water and human labor.[1] God plants the garden only after he has created man from the ground, and he charges Adam to work and keep the garden: to both improve and preserve it.[2] Humanity is to be the source of both change and stability. Adam is part of nature—his very name springs from the earth, *adamah*—yet he is also distinct from it.

Of course, no sooner has God created man, animals, and woman than the creator loses control of his creation. Genesis is the original Frankenstein myth. That man and nature could defy God has provoked theologians for centuries. We can leave the theological puzzles aside, however. Genesis suggests truths that do not depend on a particular religious tradition: Even in Eden, humanity occupies a garden, a place between static order and wild nature, a place we both work and keep. And no creation is completely under its creator's control. The world changes almost as soon as it is formed, and so does humanity. They change each other.

Yet the ideal of the untouched paradise, of orderly nature undisturbed by human action, still shimmers in many imaginations. Nature is a source of moral authority for some, of security for others. It offers standards and models. It is autonomous and eternal. "The chief lesson is that the world displays a lovely order, an order comforting in its intricacy," writes Bill McKibben in his best-selling book, *The End of Nature.* "And the most appealing part of this harmony, perhaps, is its permanence—the sense that we are part of something with roots stretching back nearly forever, and branches reaching forward just as far."[3] Throughout its long history, this image suggests, nature has not really changed. Its harmony and order are permanent, reminders of the beauty of stasis.

Changeless nature is not just a matter of utopian dreams. Those who seek stasis in the human world argue that they are following nature's way, that dynamism is not merely disruptive but unnatural. "The characteristic that best distinguishes flourishing ecosystems is never growth, but rather stability (a conservative virtue in its own right)," writes John Gray, the British philosopher, in his appeal for conservatives and greens to join forces. "This is a truth which is acknowledged in the discipline of ecology in all of its varieties. . . . Modernist political faiths which advocate the unlimited growth of population, production *and knowledge* . . . are effectively in rebellion against every truth we have established about order in the natural world" (emphasis added).[4] The open-ended future of discovery and learning is not merely disruptive but downright perverse. The infinite series, Gray maintains, defies the natural order of things.

Clearly, how we think about nature—and about artifice—informs how we think about the growth and evolution of human societies. If what is given by nature is good by definition, then to change it is evil. If nature supplies patterns, distinctions, boundaries, and essences for us to respect, then recombinations are immoral or dangerous. If stasis is the highest form of biological nature, then perhaps it is also the highest form of human society. If human beings and human work are fundamentally unnatural, set apart from the rest of the world, then we must choose either all-out war against nature or separation from it—destruction or quarantine.

If, however, nature is itself a dynamic process rather than a static end, then there is no single form of "the natural." An evolving, open-ended nature may impose practical constraints, but it cannot dictate eternal standards. It cannot determine what is good. If human beings, human work, human purposes, and human imagination are part of nature in some significant way, then neither destruction nor quarantine is an option. The distinction between the artificial and the natural must lie not in their source—human or not—but in their characteristics, in the way they relate to the world around them.

"Certain phenomena are 'artificial' in a very specific sense: they are as they are only because of a system's being molded, by goals or purposes, to the environment in which it lives," writes Herbert Simon in *The Sciences of the Artificial,* which seeks to give such fields as engineering, architecture, design, and administration the same sort of status and theoretical grounding that the natural sciences have. Artifice implies design, goals, external purposes. It requires control. Even the artifacts of nonhuman creatures, from wasp nests and beaver dams to the moistened sticks chimpanzees use to dig out termites, all extend their designers' control over the environment. Human artifacts, writes Simon, "are what they are in order to satisfy man's desires to fly or to eat well. As man's aims change, so too do his artifacts—and vice versa."

But artifice does not offer complete control. Simon notes that "those things we call artifacts are not apart from nature. They have no dispensation to ignore or violate natural law."[5] The artificial and the natural are bound together: The artificial serves its creators' purposes, subject to the limits of nature.

The natural, by contrast, does not require purposes. It simply is. Nature, lacking intent, is amoral. And natural systems are out of control.[6] Purposeless, undirected behavior is characteristic not only of ecosystems, weather patterns, or tectonic plates but of undesigned human systems, such as languages. English grammar is not more or less moral than Chinese; it simply is. And while linguists and copy editors may study or trim a language, as a gardener tends plants, no one can control the system as a whole. It is constantly evolving.

Natural systems often evolve from the purposeful activities of their members, however. Birds pick wild strawberries and excrete their seeds, making it more likely that the sweeter, redder berries that attract birds will reproduce. That natural selection has nothing to do with the birds' purposes and is not under their control. Squirrels bury acorns, encouraging the evolution of oak trees that produce nuts of a size and shape particularly appealing to squirrels. The animals' actions must fit within the broader biological system, but they also affect its future direction.[7]

This relation between decentralized actions and the natural systems that encompass them is even more apparent in the human world. When someone coins a word to capture a new attitude, invention, or idea, the new term must fit into the broader language, over which the word's creator has no control. And the new word affects the future evolution of the language. The same is true for an entrepreneur with a new product. He can directly control only his immediate economic environment (and even there his control is partial), not the economy as a vast, complex, natural system. But his success or failure will have ripple effects. Through such consequences, artifice is continually creating nature: generating new patterns and systems beyond anyone's control.

The tension between the natural and the artificial is a subject as old as philosophy or science, but the industrializing world of the late eighteenth and nineteenth centuries was famously obsessed with the question. We have inherited its romantic culture—a suspicion of nature tamed—as much as its technological arts and technocratic government. The romantics set emotion in opposition to reason, nature against artifice, humanity against technology. To preserve nature's purity, they recommended the quarantine of the human mind. That has never been a choice we could truly accept. It denies the fundamental links between body and mind, humanity and nature. In the name of authenticity, the romantic ideal counsels passivity and fatalism.

"As a 19th-century position, romanticism never broke with rationalism: rather, it was rationalism's mirror-image," writes the historian and philosopher of science Stephen Toulmin:

> Descartes exalted a capacity for formal rationality and logical calculation as the supremely "mental" thing in human nature, *at the expense of* emotional experience, which is a regrettable by-product of our bodily natures. From Wordsworth or Goethe on, romantic poets and novelists tilted the other way: human life that is ruled by calculative reason alone is scarcely worth living, and nobility attaches to a readiness to surrender to the experience of deep emotions. This is not a position that *transcends* 17th-century dualism: rather, it accepts dualism, but votes for the opposite side of every dichotomy.[8]

We have lived with this uneasy dichotomy for a century or more, alternately believing one side, then the other. It has never really suited us. It has never given us a satisfactory balance between body and mind, the natural and the artificial.

Understanding the relation between the natural and the artificial has recently assumed increasing urgency. Ours is, more and more, a biological era: an age defined by its insights into and power over the stuff of life itself. We are self-consciously, and quite literally, creating nature. How we understand what that creation means will determine much about our future. We must either choose between the rationalists and romantics—or their technocratic and reactionary derivatives—or we must find a different way.

So let us return to the garden. In *The End of Nature*, McKibben muses about the meaning of the greenhouse effect, which he argues has so transformed the atmosphere as to replace autonomous "nature" with a completely man-made world: "The greenhouse effect is a more apt name than those who coined it imagined. . . . We have built a greenhouse, a *human creation*, where once there bloomed a sweet and wild garden."[9] It is a striking line, adopted even by negative reviewers.[10] And it is quite peculiar. McKibben misses the obvious: Gardens themselves are human creations, which organize and rearrange nature. Natural processes continue in the garden—not everything is under the gardener's control—but those processes are channeled to human ends; in a garden, the natural is mixed with the artificial. Our very view of nature "sweet and wild" assumes human influence.

The artificiality of gardens was in fact the subject of much poetry in the English Renaissance, an age as concerned as our own with the relation between nature and artifice. In Andrew Marvell's "The Mower Against Gardens," for instance, the narrator is a veritable seventeenth-century Jeremy Rifkin, upset with the innovation that creates unnaturally colored flowers and trees without parents:

> *With strange perfumes he did the Roses taint,*
> *And Flow'rs themselves were taught to paint.*
> *The Tulip, white, did for complexion seek;*
> *And learn'd to interline its cheek: . . .*
> *No Plant now knew the Stock from which it came;*
> *He grafts upon the Wild the Tame; . . .*
> *And in the Cherry he does Nature vex,*
> *To procreate without a Sex.*[11]

Like the crossbreeding that produces tulips streaked with color, grafting is highly "unnatural," a high-tech process that was extremely difficult to discover and to master. We take grafting for granted only because we are used to it. Every vineyard is a colony of clones; every rose garden, cherry orchard, and bougainvillea-strewn trellis is artificial. In modern nurseries, plants regularly "procreate without a Sex."

We have long since stopped thinking about the artifice of tulips. Instead we imagine that real human influence on nature began a mere century ago, if not last month. In pursuit of a dynamic vision of nature and culture, however, the poet and critic Frederick Turner argues that we should rediscover Shakespeare's thoughts on the matter: that in sixteenth-century musings lie lost truths about the relation between the natural and the artificial and between the biological and economic worlds. "Shakespeare's core insight," Turner writes, "is that human-created value is not essentially different from natural value. The value that is added by manufacture, and the reflection of that value in profit, are but a continuation of nature's own process of growth and development."[12] On transforming nature, Turner quotes the disguised King Polixenes' response to the shepherdess Perdita in *The Winter's Tale*. Like Marvell's mower, Perdita eschews engineered flowers that add art to "great creating Nature." Polixenes argues:

> Yet Nature is made better by no mean
> But Nature makes that mean; so over that art
> Which you say adds to Nature, is an art
> That Nature makes. You see, sweet maid, we marry
> A gentler scion to the wildest stock,
> And make conceive a bark of baser kind
> By bud of nobler race. This is an art
> Which does mend Nature, change it rather; but
> The art itself is Nature.[13]

The quest for improvement, and for novelty, does not overturn nature. It recreates it. By understanding how biological processes work, we turn them to human ends. We do not overthrow nature, but cooperate with it, using nature's own art to create new natural forms. Our artifice alters the path of nature, but it does not end it, for nature has no stopping point, no final shape. It is a process, not an end.

On the oldest part of the newest land in the United States, the ever-expanding Big Island of Hawaii, is a place that looks like Eden: the Waipi'o Valley. It nestles, flat and green, between a slate-gray beach and verdant cliffs up to two thousand feet high. A stream winds through it, giving the valley its name, "curving water." The volcanic soil is rich, the rain ample, the temperature warm. For nine centuries, Waipi'o was Hawaii's breadbasket, its irrigated paddies supplying taro, whose starchy roots are mashed into *poi*. Fruit trees grow wild here—guava, mango, Java plum, banana—along with ginger, berries, medicinal plants, and edible ferns. The kukui, or candlenut tree, yields nuts that can be eaten or strung together and burned for hours of light. Wild horses and pigs roam the valley, and its water is full of prawn, fish, and escargot-like snails. Waterfalls dangle from the valley's back wall. Viewed from the plateau above, Waipi'o is a miniature world, small enough to cup in your hands. Except for the mosquitoes and a bit too much humidity, it does seem like paradise.

Yet there are few people here. And the stories Kelly Loo tells are full of hunger: How, as children in the valley, he and his friends used to swipe the food offerings their Chinese neighbors left for ancestral spirits. How he used to find eggs and hide them in the outhouse, hoarding them for himself. "What did I know?" he says. "I was a hungry kid."

Retired from a job with the water company, Loo now lives in a suburban-style home on the outlook above the valley, where amenities such as electricity and paved roads are available. He takes tourists down to the valley floor in his four-wheel-drive van, telling stories as he negotiates the forty-five–degree semipaved one-lane road. He also grows taro, and has the calloused hands and herbicide-loving attitudes of a farmer.

Loo is thoroughly at home among the valley's plants and animals, happy with a garden to work and keep, full of Hawaiian natural lore. But he does not wax romantic about how "stability" distinguishes "flourishing ecosystems." It is not human nature to prefer poverty and hunger to the comforts of cold beer and four-wheel drive.

Besides, Loo knows that nature is not stable.

On April 1, 1946, a fifty-foot-high wall of water slammed into this tranquil valley, flattening everything before it. The same *tsunami* killed ninety-six people in the city of Hilo, fifty miles to the south. The several hundred residents of Waipi'o escaped unharmed, but their homes and other buildings were destroyed. Today's valley has no sign of the houses, stores, or churches of Loo's boyhood. He points to a wild and vacant meadow where his home town once stood.

The Waipi'o Valley's current "natural" state is the result of that cataclysm—and, just as surely, of the pull of economic opportunity elsewhere. In the valley, and in the rest of the world, nature is more complicated than romantic visions of stability suggest. Waipi'o did not arise spontaneously, created by autonomous nature seeking its proper form. Many of its varied flora and fauna are imports, brought by the Polynesians who first settled the island and the Europeans who followed centuries later. Palm trees, taro, and bananas are not native to bare volcanic rock.[14]

Indeed, contrary to Gray's confident assertion about "the discipline of ecology in all of its varieties," ecologists no longer hold a static vision of nature. They no longer portray a balanced world that seeks equilibrium and is undisturbed in any major way by fire or flood, tidal waves or volcanos, drought or disease. The balance of nature "makes nice poetry, but it's not such great science," says the plant ecologist Steward T. A. Pickett.[15] Instead, current ecological science emphasizes turmoil and disruption: Constant changes create conditions in which different species thrive. Some of those changes have nothing to do with people, but others are driven by human artifice. Deliberately set, human-controlled fires appear to have shaped the African savannas and American prairies, while the rain forests of Latin America, like the islands of Hawaii, contain many plants imported by pre-European settlers.

"There is almost no circumstance one can find where something isn't changing the system," says the paleoecologist George L. Jacobson, Jr., who studies changes reflected in sediments and rocks. If nature does tend toward an equilibrium, he notes, "it's never allowed to get there, so we might as well not expect it to exist."[16] Nature has no end, no goal, no one best state. Daniel Botkin, one of the leading scholars of the "new ecology," writes that

> nature, never having been constant, does not provide a simple answer as to what is right, proper, and best for our environment. There is no simple condition that is best for all of life. Some creatures are adapted to disturbed environments, like the Kirtland's warbler, an endangered bird that nests only in forests that have recently burned. The warbler became endangered because of the Smokey the Bear policy of our century to suppress all fires as unnatural and undesirable. Other species, like sugar maple, are adapted to relatively undisturbed conditions. An environment that is "best" has many different conditions at different locations at the same time. The nature that is best is not a single, idyllic scene from a Hudson River School of painting, but a moving picture show,

mosaics on a video screen, many different conditions distributed in complex patterns across the landscape.[17]

From a scientific point of view, stasis is neither natural nor desirable. Interpreting the Endangered Species Act to enforce a hands-off policy has endangered numerous species, from butterflies and songbirds to grizzly bears, that depend on habitat not found in "climax" forests.[18] Different living things require different conditions; the diversity of life is encouraged by the dynamism of nature.

Assuming that nature will remain constant tends to backfire. Botkin began his career as the caretaker of New Jersey's Hutcheson Memorial Forest, an uncut stand of oak and hickory bought in the 1950s by Rutgers University. The forest's protectors assumed that leaving the woods alone was the best way to save it for posterity. The Hutcheson Forest was, said a 1954 article, "a cross-section of nature in equilibrium." Without human interference, the forest was expected to stay pretty much the same forever, each generation of trees providing for the next: "The present oaks and other hardwood trees have succeeded other types of trees that went before them. Now these trees, after reaching old age, die and return their substance to the soil and help their replacements to sturdy growth and ripe old age in turn."[19] In this patch of New Jersey, the experts believed, nature had found its balance.

But the oaks did not reproduce; maples began to take over. By examining fire scars in the stumps of dead trees, Rutgers researchers discovered the artifice behind their cherished nature. Before Europeans arrived in New Jersey, Indians had burned the underbrush every decade or so, presumably either to drive game or make travel easier. "These frequent fires cleared the understory, favored oaks over maples, and created the open forest of tall trees believed by naturalists in the early sixties to be original, constant, and unaffected by human influence," writes Botkin. The Indians weren't trying to produce a beautiful forest of hickory and oak; that particular mix of trees was a ripple effect, nature created as a consequence of art. Contrary to static assumptions about how ecologies work, Botkin warns, a place that is truly protected from human interference "may become a 'nature' nobody has ever seen before and perhaps nobody really wants."[20] By contrast, the "environment that we like, and that we think of as 'natural'" is often the creation of earlier human action.[21]

For ecologists like Botkin, a turbulent sense of nature in no way means that whatever humans do is good. It simply demands far more clarity about what human beings want from the environment and more research into how particular natural systems work. In some places, we may want to recreate the experience of nature as European explorers discovered it on the American continent three hundred years ago, a nature shaped by Indians' artifice. In others, we may want to preserve a particular species or maintain fishing grounds. Or we may have more global purposes, planting trees not for their own sakes but to soak up carbon dioxide, for instance. Achieving any of these goals—all of which are "artificial"—requires careful data collection, sophisticated and subtle models, and significant local knowledge. When Botkin's research team sought to understand the fluctuations in Washington State salmon populations, they got the most useful information not from the traditional theory of "maximum sustainable yield" but from an old-time fisherman, who knew that future supplies of salmon could be predicted by the water levels in the stream when they hatched.[22]

Far from trying to plough up biological systems, Botkin and his fellow ecologists are eager to preserve and extend them—to create the varieties of nature that environmentalists value. Botkin is suspicious of civil engineering to tame rivers and mourns the passing of the prairie; he thrills to the songs of sparrows and the howling of wolves, a symphony in the forest night. But he does not claim that "nature knows best." Rather, Botkin argues frankly for the *human* value of saving what he loves, for prairies as a connection to history and species preservation to serve our "aesthetic and moral sense."[23] He does not disdain as artificial the restoration ecology that applies the mind of a gardener to the recreation of lost natural systems such as midwestern prairies.[24] He believes human desires will and, by implication, should affect the evolution of nature. That belief puts Botkin at odds with green reactionaries, who despise human influence. He bluntly acknowledges, "Nature in the twenty-first century will be a nature that we make; the question is the degree to which this molding will be intentional or unintentional, desirable or undesirable."[25]

Botkin is a scientist, and he dodges the contentious political issues of whose definition of "desirable or undesirable" will get applied in what situation. In most of the examples he cites, where he himself has done applied research, the affected parties agree on the desirable outcome. The Hutcheson Forest was privately purchased in 1954; its owners want a forest of hickory and oak—the forest the first European settlers would have discovered. Similarly, most people want to protect Northwest salmon, if only to preserve the fishing stocks, and African elephants; the main issue is how to do so most effectively, with the least disruption of other human goals. (In many such cases, political economists using equally dynamic analysis have been independently working to square public goods with private incentives.[26]) At least at their current stage of development these questions are matters more of knowledge and technology than of power and coercion.

To reactionaries, however, Botkin's problem-solving approach is deeply political—and deeply offensive. In addressing such problems, Botkin relishes technology and believes it can help us understand and protect nature: "Having altered nature with our technology, we must depend on technology to see us through to solutions."[27] He sees nature not as something pristine, to be protected from human interference, but as something valuable, to be preserved through human action.

Reactionaries, by contrast, need nature as a moral absolute, exemplified by its perfect balance. "The ecological perspective begins with a view of the whole, an understanding of how the various parts of nature interact in patterns that tend toward balance and persist over time," writes Al Gore in his best-selling book called, not coincidentally, *Earth in the Balance*.[28] Botkin's research topples this entire worldview. His work declares that nature has no single goal—that there is no static standard for "the natural." If nature doesn't define its own purposes, and if even "natural" states may incorporate human artifice, then nature is no guide even to its own proper destiny, much less to human life.

This idea is deeply troubling to reactionary greens. "On the first Earth Day, it seemed that the great coming struggle would be between what was left of pristine nature, delicately balanced in [climax-ecology pioneer] Eugene Odum's beautifully rational ecosystems, and a human race bent on mindless, greedy destruction," the environmental historian Donald Worster writes nostalgically. "Two decades later, however, ecology had lost any clear notion of what pristine meant."[29]

Worster is a pioneer in his academic specialty and holds an endowed chair at the University of Kansas; his history of ecological ideas is a standard text. He cannot simply ignore the change that has swept through the science without sacrificing his own scholarly credibility.

But Worster clearly prefers the era in which "nature" appeared to back his own social vision. So he treats the new ecologists' meticulous work as mere invention, backed by a "hidden agenda" of supporting modern life.[30] Real ecology, *good ecology*, he implies, would come to different conclusions. Dynamic portrayals of nature, he charges, "constitute what I would call a new permissiveness in ecology. . . . This new ecology makes human wants and desires the primary test of what should be done with the earth. It denies that there is to be found in nature, past or present, any standard for, or even much of a limitation on, those desires."[31]

On this point, Worster is more or less correct. Botkin and his new ecologist colleagues do say that nature will be what we make it, that it has no "true" state. Humans do indeed have to choose, and, in that choice, human wants and desires will be what matters. That is the way the world is. Of course, those wants and desires include the pleasures of beautiful places and "unspoiled" nature, however defined. But if people like Worster, or Botkin himself, want to preserve "wild" areas, they will have to convince others to share their desire. And to get the nature they want, they will have to do much more than simply keep out humans. They will have to exercise artifice—to set fires, to favor some species over others, to act as active gardeners, not passive guardians.

Nature does, of course, impose some constraints on human actions: We cannot, as far as we know, go faster than the speed of light or be in two places at the same time. Chemicals bond in some ways and not in others. Certain plants require bright sunlight, others shade. Salmon will spawn only under certain, quite complicated, conditions. Any gardener knows, with Sir Francis Bacon, that to be commanded, nature must be obeyed. Nature tells us that if we want X, we must do Y and cannot do Z. It does not tell us whether to want, or not to want, X. It does not dictate that wilderness areas must remain "untrammeled by man,"[32] that logging, automobiles, wheat fields, and Disneyland are inherently evil, or that every species of beetle should be preserved.[33] Turbulent nature does not decree the one best state for each part of the globe. It cannot tell us what to want.

Worster emphatically knows what he himself wants, and he surely knows that his vision of the good life is unpopular—as a poverty-stricken reality, if not as a romantic fantasy. He recites the litany of peasant virtues, familiar from the writings of other green reactionaries, with its limits on risk taking, innovation, and imagination: "A stable, enduring rural society in equilibrium with the processes of nature cannot allow much freedom or self-assertiveness to the individual. . . . A farmer acts within a severely constraining network of duties and obligations that allow little personal initiative. That is the best way, people all over the world have understood, to avoid too much risk and preserve the rural community in harmony with the soil."[34] Worster wants human beings to sacrifice their tool-making instincts, their inquisitiveness, their desire for comfort, and their freedom. If he can convince us that nature is static, then he can claim a moral, *natural* imperative to maintain static human societies.

But nature does not provide the moral imperatives Worster and other reactionaries would like, the arguments that would silence the claims of freedom, exploration, and material progress. About the proper way for humans to live, nature is silent. Nature is too diverse and too dynamic to offer absolutes.

Sam, tow-headed and full of energy, zips across the lawn with the back-and-forth gait that gives toddlers that name. He is a year and a half old and joyfully exploring new territory. Tired, he sacks out on the grass, shaded by his mother and by my husband, conversing at a college reunion. The biggest threat to this good-natured little boy appears to be that I will inadvertently step on him. (I miss, barely.)

But the wristband on Sam's arm, a name tag from the reunion's kids' program, contains a warning: As healthy as he looks, Sam has cystic fibrosis. Only three months earlier, he spent nine days in the hospital with pneumonia. A steady stream of antibiotics accounts for his apparent health, and twice a day his parents must pop their cupped hands against his chest in "percussive therapy" to loosen the mucus that would otherwise clog his lungs.

About thirty thousand Americans have CF, which until a few decades ago killed its victims by the time they reached their teens. Better drugs and other therapies have extended life spans and freed people with the disease from frequent hospitalization. When Suzanne Thomlinson was diagnosed in 1964, her parents were told she might not live long enough to attend kindergarten. She is now a law school graduate who works as a bioethics counselor for the Biotechnology Industry Organization, supporting the research to which she feels she owes her life.[35] Sam's mother tells me about a sixty-year-old man active in Internet CF groups, a role model and inspiration. Still, cystic fibrosis remains a painful and ultimately deadly disease, killing most of its victims by their thirties.

Sam has better chances. Time is on his side. Scientists are pushing hard to find a way to deliver corrective genes to respiratory system cells. The idea is to reprogram enough of those cells that the body will stop overproducing mucus. The research has gone more slowly than people hoped when the CF gene was isolated in 1989, but it is progressing steadily, spurred by biotech's usual combination of idealism, ambition, curiosity, and greed. Eventually, researchers hope to do more than fix individual cells, which die and are replaced by other cells that also need reprogramming. They envision gene therapy that will correct the problem at its source, making cells reproduce and grow without the defect.[36] "This is an art," as Shakespeare said, "which does mend Nature, change it rather."

The very idea makes Bill McKibben sick. If the greenhouse effect doesn't end nature, he suggests, then genetic engineering will—and, worse yet, it will do so on purpose. Even if biotechnology works as well as advertised, which McKibben concedes "seems probable," it will make the world thoroughly phony, "a shopping mall, where every feature is designed for our delectation." That prospect is intolerable. "The end of nature sours all my material pleasures." he writes. "The prospect of living in a genetically engineered world sickens me."[37]

Rearranging genes—treating them as components that can be recombined to meet human wants—is hardly humanity's first venture in defying our given bodily natures. But genetic engineering extends artifice to a more fundamental level than did circumcision or cesarean sections, hair coloring or artificial hips, contact lenses or heart transplants. It fiddles with the generic As and Bs that control (in extremely complicated ways) how we turn out. To alter Sam's genes so that he did not have cystic fibrosis would be to make every cell in his body artificial, every cell directed to conscious human purposes. This art would not eliminate natural processes, but it would dramatically recreate them, as Renaissance gardeners changed the nature of tulips.

And it would open up a new infinite series. We can imagine not a single standard of biological perfection, but many different desirable possibilities, depending on our tastes and goals. (Given the complex ways that genes appear to interact, it's unlikely that we can make combinations without trade-offs.) And we aren't likely to ever be fully satisfied. Each improvement generates ideas for others.

Stasist critics warn that rather than face this weird-sounding biological future, we should just say no to *all* genetic engineering. Jeremy Rifkin, whose books on the subject McKibben praises, cautions against using gene therapy even to cure children like Sam. "Once we decide to begin the process of human genetic engineering," he writes in *Algeny,* "there is really no logical place to stop. If diabetes, sickle cell anemia, and cancer are to be cured by altering the genetic makeup of an individual, why not proceed to other 'disorders': myopia, color blindness, left-handedness? Indeed, what is to preclude a society from deciding that a certain skin color is a disorder?"[38] People see health as a continuum with no obvious stopping point; once a condition they dislike is medically correctable, they want to do something about it. To avoid this infinite series, therefore, Rifkin demands a bright line: no genetic engineering of any kind.

Other biotech critics take a seemingly more moderate approach. The influential conservative bioethicist Leon Kass tries to draw the line at curing diseases, citing a "natural norm" of health.[39] But this idea, like the notion of a single "natural" ecological state, falls apart on examination. Human beings in different times, places, and circumstances suggest different definitions of health; many of our biological characteristics evolved in environments in which we no longer live; and what's good for the species may not be good for a particular person.

The sickle cell trait offers protection against malaria, a benefit to the species and in that sense a norm, but at the cost of giving lethal sickle cell anemia to people who inherit traits from both parents.[40] A marathon runner and a boxer may be in peak condition, but what is healthy for each will be different. Barring technologies such as vitamin D supplements or sunscreen, the wrong skin color may indeed be a "disorder" in certain latitudes: Dark-skinned people face vitamin deficiencies in Scandinavia, while the pale risk serious sun damage in the tropics. Because of her low body fat, a top female marathon runner probably will not menstruate, a serious deviation from the natural standard of health; yet she may be, by other standards and her own goals, among the healthiest women on the planet. And fertility, which surely must be the "norm" for premenopausal adult females, is something many women seek medical intervention to avoid. So, for that matter, are the normal symptoms of menopause.[41]

Contrary to Kass's notion of a "natural norm," health is not a static standard but a condition defined by the lives people want to lead. Some things are clearly unhealthy—heart attacks, for instance—but that is because they interfere with just about any imaginable human goal. Aside from such extreme cases, different goals will produce different choices about trade-offs and standards. There is no reason to think that biotechnology, however powerful, will make it possible for someone with a sumo wrestler's physique to run the marathon efficiently. What makes a condition "unhealthy" is not that it is "unnatural" but that it interferes with human purposes.

Kass's "natural norm," however, deems only a very narrow range of biological limitations worthy of medical intervention. He accepts infertility, treats the extension of life expectancy by even twenty years as perverse, and condemns the "desire to prolong youthfulness." He issues a blanket condemnation of "our dissection of cadavers, organ transplantation, cosmetic surgery, body shops, laboratory fertilization, surrogate wombs, gender-change surgery, 'wanted' children, 'rights over our bodies,' sexual liberation, and other practices and beliefs that insist on our independence and autonomy."[42] Kass's "natural norm" of health accepts a lot of conditions that many, many people would like to avoid.

In this sense, Rifkin's assessment is basically correct. On a theoretical basis anyway, "there really is no logical place to stop" genetic interventions. At least some individuals will always be able to imagine a body better suited to their purposes. And Kass admits that the general public does not honor his notion of health as a static, natural standard. "One feels that people are finding the natural boundaries of life unacceptable," he told *The New York Times* when a sixty-three-year-old woman had a baby with the help of in vitro fertilization and embryo transfer, adding that "once you go that route, there's absolutely no limit."[43] His comment was less about the specific case at hand than about the general, open-ended drive to let individuals shape their biological destinies.

If health is not a static norm, then Rifkin is right about the line between nature and artifice. The only way to protect "natural" genetics is to prohibit *all* interference with human genes, even if that means letting children suffer genetic diseases. We can't pick and choose our purposes, calling some "natural" and some "artificial." Whether we like it or not, genetic engineering is unnatural. It turns our basic genetic components into human artifice.

While ecology raises questions about what nature is really like, undercutting the idea of a single natural standard, biotechnology thus forces us to confront a more basic question: Suppose that we do have a standard of the natural. Does that make what's natural right and what's unnatural wrong? Does nature draw lines we are morally bound to respect? Is "the natural" an ethical trump?

Much of the stasist opposition to biotechnology stems from the idea that such interventions in human biology are unnatural and hence immoral. As Kass told the *Times:* "Nobody wants to stand around and point a finger at this woman and say, 'You're immoral.' But generalize the practice and ask yourself, What does it really mean that we don't accept the life cycle or the life course? That's one of the big problems of the contemporary scene. You've got all kinds of people who make a living and support themselves but who psychologically are not grown up. We have a culture of functional immaturity."[44] Defying nature, in this assessment, is both immoral and immature. Virtue and wisdom lie in accepting what nature gives us—a life course of three score years and ten, a life pattern determined by evolution and luck, not by human action.

Kass's reaction is what pediatrician and bioethicist Norman Fost has called the "I was like—whoa" argument, after an expression his teenage daughter frequently used to describe her shock and disgust with this or that friend's actions.[45] Kass's disdain turns a subjective distaste for artifice into a philosophical principle, creating a high-brow version of McKibben's declaration that the prospect of genetic engineering "sickens" him. Indeed, Kass makes a positive virtue of interpreting aesthetic reaction as moral principle, writing elsewhere that "in this age in which everything is held to be permissible so long as it is freely done, in which our given human nature no longer commands respect, in which our bodies are regarded as mere instruments of our autonomous rational wills, repugnance may be the only voice left that speaks up to defend the central core of our humanity."[46]

The real problem for Kass's "natural science," it seems, may be the *un*revolutionary nature of biotechnology—our ability to integrate once-inconceivable new technologies into the mundane conventions of bourgeois existence. We don't grab onto high-tech medicine because it's new and different but because it offers to solve practical problems. As a result, we draw even the most extraordinary technologies into a broader cultural context that is far more resilient than reactionary wise men like to think. In a world where it's no big deal to take hormone therapy, Viagra, or Prozac, to have a face lift, or to know a child's sex before birth, a world in which even such radical interventions as sex-change operations and heart transplants have failed to turn society upside down, it is extremely difficult to argue that medical innovations are dangerous simply because they fool Mother Nature. It's hard to maintain the "like—whoa" attitude for very long.

Kass's repugnance argument also begs the question of what is central to our humanity. Why is it defined by a biological form or reproductive process, rather than the quest to learn and improve our condition? Many dynamist thinkers argue that, paradoxically, change and self-transformation are among the truest expressions of our enduring human nature.

"If human nature, on whatever basis, is seen as encompassing at least some forms of self-creation or self-transformation, then change is an aspect of a continuing (and unchanging?) capacity or predisposition for change," writes Michael H. Shapiro, a legal scholar concerned with the philosophical implications of "performance enhancement" technologies. "Changing in some ways is thus remaining the same in another way: we continue the process of realizing one's potential—and perhaps even raising it."[47] If, as Kass suggests, our wills are not autonomous of our bodies—as indeed they are not—the answer is not to subordinate the will to the body, the romantic choice. The answer is to allow mind and body to work together so that individuals can better accomplish their purposes.[48]

There may, of course, be specific moral arguments against particular biotech interventions, especially genetic changes to shape the not-yet-born, because those actions could cause suffering to the people they affect. But such arguments would be based on our moral sympathy and respect for individual lives and on particular knowledge of the specific application, not on a general reverence for natural forms. By contrast, revering nature means sacrificing the purposes of individuals to preserve the world as given. It requires that we force people to live with biological conditions that trouble them, whether diseases such as cystic fibrosis or schizophrenia, disabilities such as myopia or crooked teeth, or simply less beauty, intelligence, happiness, or grace than could be achieved through artifice.

Turning nature into the source of morality has always been philosophically problematic. At its best, ethical naturalism provides useful heuristics based on highly stylized ideas of nature. By imagining individuals as possessing natural rights, for example, we curb the destructive impulse to intrude on their personal autonomy. Using a different model of nature, however, we could just as easily justify a contrary idea—the organic holism of the ethnic group or the dominance of the strong. Nature itself remains amoral and out of control, giving us only if-then statements, not telling us what to want or do. We cannot fob off our moral choices on nature. It offers not norms but only the "permissiveness" that Donald Worster scorns in the new ecology. And in our "biological century," nature has become a dangerous place to look for moral standards.[49]

We live, after all, in an era in which evolutionary psychology explains that sexual promiscuity and often-violent sexual jealousy are only natural for human males, an outcome of reproductive imperatives.[50] Psychopharmacology demonstrates that changing brain chemistry can change personality.[51] Traits ranging from happiness to violent tendencies to sexual orientation appear to be at least partially "hardwired," the product of our natural physical makeup. These ideas have zoomed out of the labs, academic conferences, and psychiatrists' offices to permeate popular culture. They are the stuff of best-selling books, newsweekly cover stories, and talk show discussions. They are inescapable.

There are several possible reactions to these biological insights into the physical origins of the self. One, suggested by the writer Tom Wolfe, is that

> the notion of a self—a self who exercises self-discipline, postpones gratification, curbs the sexual appetite, stops short of aggression and criminal behavior—a self who can become more intelligent and lift itself to the very peaks of life by its own bootstraps through study, practice, perseverance, and refusal to give up in the face of great odds—this old-fashioned notion (what's a *boot*strap, for God's sake?) of success through enterprise and true grit is already slipping away. . . . The peculiarly American faith in the power of the individual to transform him-

self from a helpless cypher into a giant among men . . . is now as moribund as the god for whom Nietzsche wrote an obituary in 1882.

The result, Wolfe fears, will be a "lurid carnival that . . . may make the phrase 'the total eclipse of all values' seem tame."[52] If we see ourselves as biological beings, whose nature arises from the interplay of purely physical forces, he predicts, all hell will break loose.

Clinging to ethical naturalism makes Wolfe's scenario all the more likely. Establishing amoral nature as a moral exemplar leaves us with no way, short of divine revelation, to judge actions that have identifiable natural causes.[53] Rather than teach us to live well in the world as it is, ethical naturalism can only imagine a different world and then tell us that this imagined nature dictates good behavior. That "noble lie" will not hold up for long, especially in a culture where every halfbaked implication of every scientific discovery is instantly the subject of media chatter. No wonder Wolfe is scared.

Wolfe's is a plausible scenario, but not a necessary one. Equally plausible is Shapiro's suggestion that a greater understanding of our biological nature will simply give us more tools with which to shape our selves—more ways to "become more intelligent and lift [ourselves] to the very peaks of life," more ways to transform ourselves from helpless cyphers into giants. Those techniques won't necessarily make us more diligent, but they will certainly make us responsible for our fates.

If we understand biological nature as morally neutral, rather than a source of standards and justifications, there is no reason not to evaluate actions by their consequences rather than their causes. That a serial killer acted out of genetic and biochemical influences does not make his murders less terrible. That biology encourages a mother to protect her children does not make her nurturing less admirable. That the will summoned through some neurons can endure the pain or resist the anger signaled by others does not mean self-control is meaningless. David Hume was right: Reason has always been the slave of the passions. That makes the cultivation of life-enhancing moral sentiments, like the cultivation of better crops, both an exercise of artifice and an essential goal of civilization.

We have learned through sometimes bitter trial-and-error history that some behavior is compatible with human life, with peace and prosperity, and with increasing happiness and knowledge, and some is not. The source is less important than the result: We are well served to tolerate diverse personal goals, to respect the limits of centralized knowledge, to avoid hurting people who hurt no one themselves, and to respect the bonds of life not because natural forms tell us to do so but because we have learned through long and difficult cultural evolution that these rules will, more often than not, improve the human condition. The rules that permit dynamism and learning—that curb our instincts to distrust strangers, cling to the familiar, and impose our will on others—are among our most valuable of artifacts and, at the same time, the creators of new, evolving natural systems.

That our minds, our personalities, our selves are not separate from our bodies, that they are also natural systems, emerging from the complex interactions of their component physical parts, does not make them less precious or less important. It makes them all the more amazing. Nor does grounding our selves in physical substance make those selves less real—to the contrary. That understanding gives us greater opportunity to cultivate the selves we will become. To the traditional and enduring arts of "study, practice, perseverance, and refusal to give up," we add the tools of genetics and biochemistry.

The only question, then, is whether we will make those tools the province of individual self-fashioning or technocratic tyranny. When stasists invoke *Brave New World* to assail biotechnology, they forget that its world, too, is a static model: a technocratic nightmare controlled by a central authority, a completely artificial world molded to a single vision. It is the central control, not the technology, that makes that world artificial.

Aldous Huxley's imagined society in fact follows Pat Buchanan's maxim, offered as an attack on cloning, that "mankind's got to control science, not the other way around."[54] That society has taken up Rifkin's challenge to conduct a "rich and robust conversation over the kind of future we'd like for ourselves" and then imposed that single vision.[55]

Huxley's dystopia has heeded the advice of our technocratic bioethicists and editorialists—of all the people who solemnly intone that "society" must adopt an official, uniform attitude toward each new biological technique, rather than allow decentralized, trial-and-error choice. These technocrats argue, as one columnist puts it, that "because of the emotional investment of family members, society's dispassionate heads must set policy."[56] Following that pat prescription is the only way to get *Brave New World*. The novel's horror comes less from the mere presence of exotic technologies than from the uniformity and complacency of life in its world. It is a technocratic dystopia that has banished dynamism and cancelled the infinite series.

Contrary to Buchanan's personification of them, neither "mankind" nor "science" is a unitary actor. Both are complex, natural systems, composed of diverse individual human beings. Neither is under central control. The same is true of the "society" that Rifkin warns might "decid[e] that a certain skin color is a disorder." In a dynamist society, there can be no such decision, because there is no single authority to make it.

Yet time and again, stasists warn against biological dynamism for the very reason that they assume someone will be in charge, enforcing a homogeneous model of humanity. Kass attacks in vitro fertilization and cloning on the grounds that "to lay one's hands on human generation is to take a major step toward making man himself simply another one of the man-made things. . . . Thus, human nature becomes simply the last part of nature that is to succumb to the modern technological project, a project that has already turned all the rest of nature into raw material at human disposal, to be homogenized by our rationalized technique according to the artistic conventions of the day."[57] Kass's fear of "rationalized" homogenization assumes a technocratic world.

How, Rifkin muses, "is it possible for people to be leery of trusting anyone with authority over genetic technology and at the same time be in favor of the development of the technology itself?"[58] The answer is simple. People want genetic technology to develop because they expect to use it *for themselves,* to help themselves and their children, to work and to keep their own humanity. They see the new biological arts, like the rest of medical science, from the point of view of customers, not the perspective of rulers. In a dynamic, decentralized system of individual choice and responsibility, people do not have to trust any authority but their own. The stasists who frighten us with visions of bioengineered conformity forget that art is a way not just of controlling nature but of expressing and recreating the self. Only rarely will that self-expression lead to dull uniformity.

Our very selves, then, are part of the garden, simultaneously artificial and natural, within our control and beyond it. We need choose neither destruction nor quarantine: Nature and artifice are not antitheses but complements. "The wilderness is not just something you look at; it's something you are part of. You live inside a body made of wilderness material. I think that the intimacy of this arrangement is the origin of beauty. The wilderness is beautiful because you are part of it," writes architect Paul Shepheard. "Cultivation—the work of humans—has a different sort of beauty. There is nothing else under the sun than what there has always been. Cultivation is the human reordering of the material of the wilderness. If it is successful, the beauty of it lies in the warmth of your empathy for another human's effort."[59]

To reorder the material of the wilderness is the work of humans. But it is also our play, an activity pursued for its own sake. Through it, we not only create and explore nature but enjoy it. The sources of dynamism—of creativity and cultivation—lie not just in discipline but in delight.

CHAPTER SEVEN

FIELDS OF PLAY

Beach volleyball is a technocrat's nightmare. Like personal computers, chaos theory, and the motion picture industry, it was created by people fooling around in the California sun. It grew spontaneously, through the cooperative efforts of its players and fans. It had no goal, no final purpose, no plan. Beach volleyball was an end in itself. Its developers weren't even pretending to work. On the beaches of Santa Monica, Santa Barbara, and San Diego, they took a game originally designed for businessmen too out of shape for basketball and reinvented it: two players on a side, sand thick beneath their bare feet; a party atmosphere combined with the intense conditioning needed to jump, run, and maneuver on a shifting surface, with court temperatures reaching over 100 degrees and too few teammates to hide errors. The athletes' famously sculpted bodies and skimpy clothes are not just marketing gimmicks but a direct result of the sport's demands.

Fifty years after its first match, beach volleyball is a big business, drawing millions of dollars in corporate sponsorships and media deals. Its tournaments attract thousands of fans and offer tennis-level prize money. Some 12.6 million Americans played beach volleyball in 1996, up 22 percent from 1989. In 1996, it became an Olympic medal sport for both men and women—and was one of the first events to sell out.[1] Despite its iron discipline, beach volleyball is fun.

Which is why it got Newt Gingrich in so much trouble.

Every now and then, Gingrich's dynamist impulses peek out from his technocratic determination to mold American civilization to his carefully numbered plans. The 1996 Republican convention was one of those instances. There he was, a congressman from Atlanta, the host city of the 1996 Olympic Games, addressing a convention in San Diego, home to beach volleyball tournaments since the 1950s. Gold medalist Kent Steffes was there too—a Republican, a Gingrich fan, a UCLA economics graduate, the only C-SPAN devotee ever described by *People* magazine as "bronzed, brash, and built like a Greek statue."[2] How could Gingrich resist? He pulled Steffes up on stage and sang the praises of a civilization that could create such a sport. He celebrated the process, impossible to predict, that had given the world beach volleyball.

"A mere 40 years ago, beach volleyball was just beginning. Now it is not only a sport in the Olympics, but there are over 30 countries that have a competition internationally.... And there's a whole new world of opportunity opening up that didn't exist 30 or 40 years ago—and no bureaucrat would have invented it," said the Speaker of the House. "And that's what freedom is all about."[3]

Spontaneous, unpredictable opportunity; wild, unexpected paths to wealth; a worldwide phenomenon sprung from the frolicking of American enthusiasts; passion and vision creating whole new fields of play— "that's what freedom is all about." The convention crowd cheered.

The pundits howled—those on the left with laughter, those on the right with pain.

Gingrich had broken their codes of conduct. He had introduced something *trivial* into the solemn ceremonies of a political convention. Into the parade of children with AIDS and former welfare mothers who had gotten religion, he had brought a brash, bronzed reminder of fun. He had reached out into the plenitude of American life and snatched, as a metaphor for progress and inventiveness, *beach volleyball*. Like the Czech dissidents who had once embraced the nonconformist music of Frank Zappa, he had treated the dynamism of American popular culture as though it represented something precious. He had praised an endeavor on which Washington had no policy—and praised it for that very reason.

"Sink the man however far you try, and his irrepressible weirdness will insist on shining bright from the depths full fathom five," said *Newsday*'s Murray Kempton.[4] Walter Shapiro of *USA Today* concurred: "My heart soared at the transcendent weirdness of Newt's imagery."[5]

Gingrich had thought he was wrapping Republicanism in the Olympic flag, tying the Grand Old Party to youth, achievement, creativity, and freedom. In that dynamist moment, he had seen in beach volleyball a symbol of all the marvels that spontaneous, unregulated processes can produce. And by the standards of normal, technocratic politics, that vision made him irrepressibly, transcendentally *weird*. Unknowingly, he had crossed one of the chasms that divide the parties of dynamism and stasis. He had declared play a good thing: productive, valuable, a cherished quality of American civilization.

For his conservative allies, the speech was an occasion not of humor but of horror. "No More Beach Volleyball, Please," begged the lead editorial in *The Weekly Standard's* convention edition. Gingrich, said the editors, gave "the worst and most embarrassing speech of his career, locating the spirit of American freedom in Olympic beach volleyball."[6]

The horror was understandable. The conservative version of technocracy, after all, locates the spirit of American freedom in "national greatness"—bold, federal projects; grand monuments; a strong national defense; and a stable, dignified, unified culture.[7] Conservative technocracy is, above all, determined to reestablish the Puritan ethic as a governing ideal. Neo-Victorians do not play beach volleyball. They do not celebrate spontaneous invention, especially when it involves the brash and the bronzed.

Gingrich surely did not realize it, but his convention speech was not only weird. It was heretical. It represented a direct attack on one of the sacred texts of contemporary stasists, Daniel Bell's *The Cultural Contradictions of Capitalism*. In that work, Bell argued that by encouraging the spirit of play, capitalism would destroy itself. We were, he said, well on the way to that fate:

> In America, the old Protestant heavenly virtues are largely gone, and the mundane rewards have begun to run riot. The basic [old] American value pattern emphasized the virtue of achievement, defined as doing and making, and a man displayed his character in the quality of his work.... Despite some continuing use of the language of the Protestant ethic, the fact was that by the 1950s American culture had become primarily hedonistic, concerned with play, fun, display, and pleasure.... The world of hedonism is the world of fashion, photography, advertising, television, travel. It is a world of make-believe in which one lives for expectations, for what will come rather than what is. And it must come without effort.... Nothing epitomized the hedonism of the United States better than the State of California.[8]

Although Bell himself is politically eclectic, his ideas are common enough in conservative circles—his argument debuted in *The Public*

Interest, which he cofounded with neoconservative "godfather" Irving Kristol—to make praising beach volleyball tantamount to Republican blasphemy.

Bell's analysis is based on a series of dichotomies: work versus play, achievement versus pleasure, effort versus fun, reality versus the future, "doing and making" versus imagination. In a world ruled by those stark choices, it is the job of technocratic leaders—whether in political, intellectual, corporate, or religious life—to force or entice the undisciplined masses to perform their necessary but unpleasant roles. Without such leadership, our civilization will collapse, undone by its inherent contradictions.

For Bell and his technocratic allies, play is a dangerous impulse that must be contained. To reap the benefits of science, technology, and markets, we must deny ourselves fun. This repression theory of progress, which can be traced to the turn-of-the-century sociologist Max Weber, is shared by reactionaries who celebrate play and thus come to the exact opposite conclusion: Modernity is bad. "Risk, daring, and uncertainty—important components of play—have no place in industry or in activities infiltrated by industrial standards, which seek precisely to predict and control the future and to eliminate risk. . . . The degradation of play originates in the degradation of work," writes Christopher Lasch in *The Culture of Narcissism.*[9] Kirkpatrick Sale, a far less sophisticated thinker or careful historian than Lasch, lauds "the tribal mode of existence"—despite a life expectancy he pegs at 32.5 years—in part because it demanded only "maybe four hours a day per person on tasks of hunting and gathering and cultivating, the rest of the time devoted to song and dance and ritual and sex and eating and stories and games."[10] Since progress requires repression, such reactionaries want nothing to do with it.

Dynamists reject the repression theory. To the contrary, they see in play the source of progress and plenitude, the essential creator of variation in civilization's evolution. They celebrate the pleasures of achievement, the all-absorbing work that is its own reward. Dynamists understand that rules and discipline are inherent to play, not opposed to it. They appreciate imagination, creativity, and intangible goods. They do not equate the pursuit of beauty with hedonism, or splinter "what will come" from its source in "what is." And dynamists accept the psychological need for novelty as a fundamental characteristic of the human species, fostering resilience in an unstable environment. When Hayek writes that "it is in the process of learning, and in the effects of having learned something new, that man enjoys the gift of his intelligence," he is celebrating play.[11]

Play is not, then, simply a matter of games. It is the stuff of beach volleyball, yes, but also of art, science, and ritual; it is not the opposite of work or seriousness, for it may encompass either. Psychologists, anthropologists, ethologists, and other scholars have devoted many pages to defining this slippery, we-know-it-when-we-see-it concept. The closest definition may be one of the oldest: Johan Huizinga's, in the 1938 book *Homo Ludens,* or Man the Player. Writing as tyrannies inimical to the spirit of play were roiling Europe, the Dutch historian described play as "a voluntary activity or occupation executed within certain fixed limits of time and place, according to rules freely accepted but absolutely binding, having its aim in itself and accompanied by a feeling of tension, joy and the consciousness that it is 'different' from 'ordinary life.' "[12] Play, Huizinga argued, is the source of all culture; it is both freedom and order.[13] "True play knows no propaganda; its aim is in itself, and its familiar spirit is happy inspiration."[14] Play is what we do for its own sake. It is how we try new things, how we learn, and how we create new combinations.

Like the understanding of nature and artifice, the appreciation for play reached a pinnacle in the Renaissance, a period both deeply serious and deliberately playful. Writes Huizinga:

> We can scarcely conceive of minds more serious than Leonardo and Michelangelo. And yet the whole mental attitude of the Renaissance was one of play. This striving, at once sophisticated and spontaneous, for beauty and nobility of form is an instance of culture at play. The splendours of the Renaissance are nothing but a gorgeous and solemn masquerade in the accoutrements of an idealized past. The mythological figures, allegories and emblems, fetched from God knows where and all loaded with a weight of historical and astrological significance, move like the pieces on a chess-board.[15]

All of Bell's sins infused Renaissance culture—"play, fun, display, and pleasure"—and out of them came fantastic creations. Renaissance artists invented new rules by which to bind themselves and new games to play: tricks of perspective and light, structures of rhythm and rhyme, conventions of drama and metaphor. They brought the past into their present, and transformed it. They mingled myths, adopted alchemical symbology, turned the exotic discoveries of Asia and the Americas into imaginary continents. The Renaissance was a time—as Bell disapprovingly says of modern art—of "*syncretism* . . . defined by this extraordinary freedom to ransack the world storehouse and to engorge any and every style it comes upon."[16]

That extraordinary freedom is an essential aspect of play, a product of its push toward inventiveness. It is what makes play "subversive," and is the source of its creative destruction. Finding the perfect word, image, chess move, football maneuver, or musical sequence defies arbitrary limits. Play is an end in itself, bound by its own rules, and we grasp its tools wherever in the world's storehouse they may be. The spirit of play leads us to experiment, to try new combinations, and to take risks—sometimes with spectacular results. Shakespeare's inventive analogies surprise their audience with powerful associations, sensory memories, and emotional resonances. Consider the rich lines from *Macbeth*:

> *Sleep that knits up the ravelled sleave of care,*
> *The death of each day's life, sore labour's bath,*
> *Balm of hurt minds, great nature's second course,*
> *Chief nourisher in life's feast.*[17]

These utterly unexpected, yet utterly appropriate, comparisons require that the audience, too, enter into the spirit of play, to conjure up complex combinations in their own minds. Notes the psychologist Margaret Boden: "To compare sleep with human beings [knitters], death, hot baths, ointment and the main course of a meal (not to mention 'hurt minds' and 'life's feast')—all within a single sentence, expressed in a few lines of blank verse—is to awaken so many of the ideas latent in our minds that we experience a glorious explosion of newly recognized meanings."[18] Similarly, Shakespeare's vocabulary is plenitude itself—some seventeen thousand words, ransacked from every corner of his culture, then enriched by elaborate punning.[19]

Creative geniuses are those rare individuals who have, among other qualities, the discipline and gifts to master the large domains of knowledge that allow them to come up with such surprising combinations.

They play in larger fields than most other people: more athletic moves, more musical memories, more images and words, a deeper knowledge of mathematics, of history, of art. They mentally map their fields in ways that allow them to access the right combinations at the right time. Along the way, they may make new maps for others to follow—the periodic table or Samuel Johnson's *Dictionary*—or so thoroughly explore their own domain that they in effect create it anew, as Shakespeare recreated English. "Mental geography is changeable," writes Boden, "whereas terrestrial geography is not. . . . The 'journey through musical space' whose travellers included Bach, Brahms, Debussy and Schoenberg was a journey which not only explored the relevant space but created it, too."[20] Some creators rearrange the borders of their domains, drawing territories together to create whole new fields, from nuclear medicine to rock music.

However fantastic the innovation, creativity depends on the underlying structures and accumulated knowledge of the domains on which the creator builds. These inheritances provide the raw materials and the rules that make play possible. There is no scratch, even for the most inventive of minds. We do not create "what will come" except from what is and what has gone before, and that creation requires effort as well as joy.

When stasists worry about play, all they see is unruliness. Lasch fears that the order of modern industry will crush playfulness, while Bell warns of the boundlessness of the avant-garde, "a self-conscious search for future forms and sensations."[21] But rules are as much a part of play as freedom. Play, as Renaissance creators understood, is a garden, balanced between stability and novelty, between enabling structure and out-of-control creation. It is not a wilderness, not chaos. To play is not simply to emote, nor does it provide pleasure without effort. Play defies the romantic–rationalist dichotomy. It does not divorce reason from imagination.

Indeed, it is in play that the young, both human children and animals, learn the rules that govern the natural and social worlds: A square peg cannot fit in a round hole. When Mama puts her hands over her face, she does not really disappear. It is silly for adults to crawl—an action that makes babies laugh—because crawling is for babies, not parents.[22] Apes signal a desire to play with special gaits and faces, while children say, "Let's pretend." Such conventions are themselves a way of learning about conventions.[23]

And, of course, all games have their own rules, rules that extend not just to organized sports but to Bell's dreaded "make-believe." Huizinga tells the story of a four-year-old boy who has lined up a series of chairs, pretending they are train cars, and is sitting at their head. "Don't kiss the engine, Daddy," he says when his father comes in and hugs him, "or the carriages won't think it's real."[24] The child knows he is not an engine and the chairs are not carriages, but the rules of the game require that he act his part.

Rules are, in fact, one of the delights of play, for they require us to stretch our bodies and our minds. It is no fun to "play tennis with the net down," to undertake tasks that are too easy. Play requires not anarchy but challenge. As a child, the poet W. H. Auden constructed an elaborate fantasy world based on, of all things, lead mining. Much of the joy of creating this world lay in learning and applying its rules:

> It was . . . a purely private world of which I was the only human inhabitant. . . . However I needed the help of others in procuring me the raw materials for its construction. Others, principally my parents, had to provide me with maps, guide-books, text-books on geology and mining machinery, and when occasion offered, take me down real mines. Since it was a purely private world, theoretically, I suppose, I should have been free to imagine anything I liked, but in practice, I found it was not so. I felt instinctly, without knowing why, that I was bound to obey certain rules. I could choose, for example, between two kinds of winding engines, but they had to be real ones I could find in my books; I was not free to invent one. I could choose whether a mine should be drained by a pump or an adit, but magical means were forbidden.[25]

To turn his imagined landscape into an "anything goes" world would have been to destroy it, for the fun of its creation lay in finding originality within constraints. Young Auden was free to choose the raw material of his make-believe world—to indulge his fascination with lead mining—but having been "freely accepted," its rules became, in Huizinga's words, "absolutely binding."

So accustomed are we to the false dichotomy between play and order that even people who appreciate play's complexities sometimes forget that it cannot exist without rules. The psychologist David

Cohen, while cognizant of the importance of rules in his children's made-up games, loses that insight when confronted with a commercial product: fantasy role-playing games.

> They are sold on the basis that they give free rein to the imagination. In fact, they do no such thing. The authors have provided a very skilful set of building blocks—with enchanted forests, living corpses, relics of Tolkien, manacled monsters, etc.—which players can assemble in different ways. There is no way you can create a new set of characters within a game. You have to stick to certain rules. The games are only imaginative in a very limited sense, though players tend not to accept this. Reuben [Cohen's ten-year-old son] told me that he liked "to form my own world" and then, when I asked about rules, set characters and the importance of chance, conceded that you couldn't really be that omnipotent within the game. Still, he battled back, you used your imagination much more than in reading a book.[26]

In fact, Cohen's son is wiser than he. The games do allow Reuben to form his own world—subject to the constraints of its imaginary universe. Just as the real world is governed by material laws, which can be probed and tested, so the combinations available in a role-playing game are not limitless. But a good role-playing game does allow many different approaches; it is an open-ended, dynamic system. Its designers don't try to anticipate or dictate the players' every action. Rather, the value that game makers provide—the reason people like Reuben pay money for their products—lies in rules that make for varied, interesting play.

What makes the world Reuben's own is not that he is omnipotent, for he isn't, but that the rules do not determine in advance what his world will look like or how it will develop. That depends on the choices he makes. And, as Habitat showed on a larger scale, once released into the world of play, good games have a way of developing in unanticipated ways. The journalist Douglas Rushkoff, a close observer of role-playing gamer culture, notes: "The fantasy world around the players is as malleable as their individual strategies, and it changes as the players adopt different tactics. If players decide to solve problems through violence, the world becomes violent; if they choose to use magic or technology, then those skills become more valuable over the course of the game."[27]

Even the rules of chess, which can be shown mathematically to have a single best "solution," provide far too much variety—far too many branching choices—for even the most powerful computer. Chess-playing computers can use brute force only so far; they cannot see down all the branches to the game's end, so, like human players (though to a lesser extent), they have to use heuristics to evaluate positions. The beauty and fun of games arise from the many different combinations their rules make possible, the many different orders that emerge without prior design. A good game is different every time you play it.

In this sense, play teaches us something important about rules: Their mere existence does not make the world deterministic. We do not choose between a playful world with no rules and an orderly world with no play. We may, of course, make up new rules: write plays in blank verse instead of rhymes; play volleyball with two on a side instead of six; or invent role-playing games that combine high-tech weapons and elfin magic. But, whether with new rules or old, play depends on some kind of underlying order.

What confuses the critics both of play and of order is that play is unpredictable and open-ended. Although governed by rules, it is incompatible with determinism or stasis. "Play," writes Huizinga, "only becomes possible, thinkable and understandable when an influx of *mind* breaks down the absolute determinism of the cosmos."[28]

That influx of mind is what gives us fashion's X-factor, Eugen Fick's contact lens experiments, and 1,001 uses for Post-it notes. It creates the infinite series. If combinations explain the near-infinite supply of new ideas, play explains where those combinations come from. In Bell's view, among others,' capitalism and technology are driven by obvious, inescapable laws. Their results are inevitable: "The nature of change in the techno-economic order is linear in that the principles of utility and efficiency provide clear rules for innovation, displacement, and substitution."[29] Progress operates as a machine, requiring no human agency. No influx of mind is necessary.

But innovations don't in fact appear by some deterministic process. They are neither as predictable nor as predestined as technocrats imagine. They have to come from somewhere. Without variation, there can be no evolution. Selection—the weighing of utility and efficiency (hardly simple, unitary concepts themselves)—happens later. First, you have to have the ideas. You have to let people play.

*   *   *

It was 1973, and Dan Lynch had just started a new job as manager of the computer laboratory for the Artificial Intelligence Group at SRI, then a collection of fifty research labs. Lynch was charged with getting all kinds of weird peripherals—robots, lasers, oddball equipment—to talk to each other and to the lab's computers. One day, he recalls, "I found myself in my office looking at Shakey the Robot (the first robot) firmly blocking my exit. One of the researchers had programmed it to do that, and sat smirking outside my door. I had to figure out how to control Shakey right then and there to get it to move aside (and not take a wall out!). That was fun."[30]

Fun is a word you hear a lot from Lynch, an effusive Internet pioneer who is now the chairman of CyberCash, a company developing digital money for online transactions. Majoring in math was "fun." Helping a friend debug TCP/IP, the Internet's underlying programming rules, without pay was "fun." Coordinating two hundred programmers—none of whom worked for him or got paid to do the job (neither did he)—to turn the old Arpanet into the Internet was "fun." "I believe in fun," says Lynch. "I believe in vitality."[31]

This zest for play is common in Silicon Valley, even among people less personally exuberant than Lynch. By encouraging people to invest time without getting paid, play has provided nonfinancial "start-up capital" for many a budding enterprise. The Web directory Yahoo! was never intended to become a company. Its founders were graduate students who were just fooling around. "We began to index all of the information we were finding on the Web just for fun," recalls cofounder Jerry Yang.

> You could call it a hobby, you could call it a passion. Call it instinct. But it wasn't really business. We weren't making money doing it, and we were actually forsaking our schoolwork to do it. In the end it was sort of just the purity of the Internet, and its ability to influence tens of millions of people very rapidly, that got us really, really jazzed about doing what we were doing.

As Internet start-ups like Netscape began to attract attention and funding, Yahoo!'s founders actually wrote business plans for all sorts of other possible Internet ventures—but not for Yahoo!. Says Yang, "We didn't realize the thing that we were doing for fun was going to be the one that succeeded." It was only by thinking about how many Web users would be bereft of their service if they quit that they realized that, without knowing it, their play had created a vast market.[32]

Contrary to Bell's imaginings, this pursuit of play, while very Californian, is far from hedonistic. To the contrary, the environment's intense demands are part of the Valley's appeal. "I rowed at Princeton. [My work] is the closest corollary I can come to rowing in this world," says Tom Henry, who has been an executive in several high-tech startups. "It's relentless and you can never perfect it, and the computers just never get tired of challenging you." Henry says he does what he does because of "the chance to learn and the constant challenge. . . . For me, it's, yes, playing, innovating, risk taking. It's an adventure game."[33]

Though it flourishes there, playful work was not born in modern California. It does not depend on electronics, or sunshine, or even prosperity. It is as old as civilization. Five thousand years ago, unimaginably poor Stone Age women living in Swiss swamps were weaving intricate, multicolored patterns into their textiles and using fruit pits to create beaded cloth; archaeologists have found remnants of this ingenious, impractical production preserved in the alkaline mud.[34] Even in the most difficult of subsistence economies, mere utility—in this case, plain, undecorated cloth—does not satisfy human imaginations. We need to learn, to challenge ourselves, to invent new patterns. The fun of creating and using beautiful textiles goes back to some of humanity's oldest (and most taken-for-granted) technologies: the needle, the spindle, and the loom.

Creating such embellishment, which is also found in pottery, basketry, cosmetics, hairstyling, and jewelry, is the traditional play of women. It offers the challenge of innovation within established patterns, allowing an "influx of mind" that turns practical necessities into ingenious luxuries. This creativity is the ancestor of "the world of fashion" that Bell obsessively condemns as "illusions, the persuasions of the witches' craft."[35] In damning the decorative arts, Bell damns the search for beauty and satisfaction that inspires them.

He also would deprive us of their practical offspring: the modern chemical industry built on synthetic dyes, the glass created to make beads, the exploration in search of gold. The late metallurgist and historian of science Cyril Stanley Smith argued that

historically the first discovery of useful materials, machines, or processes has almost always been in the decorative arts, and was not done for a perceived practical purpose. Necessity is *not* the mother of invention—only of improvement. A man desperately in search of a weapon or food is in no mood for discovery; he can only exploit what is already known to exist. Discovery requires aesthetically-motivated curiosity, not logic, for new things can acquire validity only by interaction in an environment that has yet to be. Their origin is unpredictable.[36]

By examining art objects, Smith found the origins of metallurgy: casting molds to make statuettes, welding to join parts of sculptures, alloys to create interesting color patterns. Play is the impractical drive from which such practical discoveries are born. "Paradoxically man's capacity for aesthetic enjoyment may have been his most practical characteristic," writes Smith, "for it is at the root of his discovery of the world about him, and it makes him want to live."[37]

It is a delightful paradox: Play is what we do for its own sake, yet it is a spur to our most creative, most significant work. Athletes play, but so do scientists and surgeons. "It's fun," says the biochemist Bruce Ames, who studies the causes of cancer and aging. "I can't imagine a more enjoyable career. If you gave me $10 million tomorrow, I'd go on doing just what I'm doing. . . . It's always a challenge. It's always new problems. I'm 69 years old and I look forward to coming to work every morning."[38] The fun of constantly solving problems, of building and testing skills—the feeling of "tension and joy" that Huizinga identified as essential to play—is as necessary to progress as Henry Petroski's "form follows failure."

Indeed, notes the psychologist Mihaly Csikszentmihalyi, "philosophy and science were invented and flourished because thinking is pleasurable. If thinkers did not enjoy the sense of order that the use of syllogisms and numbers creates in consciousness, it is very unlikely that now we would have the disciplines of mathematics and physics."[39] Csikszentmihalyi's own work, inspired in part by his experiences playing chess, examines the pursuit of play's "tension and joy," which he calls "optimal experience," "enjoyment," or, most famously, "flow."

Through interviews and studies in which people record their activities and feelings when they are randomly paged, Csikszentmihalyi has found consistent patterns. People say they are happiest when they are completely absorbed by some activity that challenges their skills, provides feedback, has rules, and gives them a sense of control—when, in short, they are at play. With remarkable consistency across wildly varied endeavors, Csikszentmihalyi's research subjects compare flow-producing activities to problem solving, discovery, and exploration.[40] Whether or not people are literally discovering anything new, all these experiences offer a kind of novelty. A tennis player facing a competitor's moves or a sailor responding to shifting winds is solving that particular problem for the first time. Each game, each day on the ocean is different from all that have gone before. So, too, someone absorbed in a crossword puzzle or in tending a garden can see that work steadily grow into something new. The same is true, even more intensely, for raising a child.

Csikszentmihalyi's research program began with people whose pursuits were obviously absorbing—chess players, rock climbers, basketball players, dancers, composers—but over time he has discovered that people strive for, and find, such challenges in all sorts of activities. Although some endeavors are more conducive to play than others, achieving flow is a matter as much of personality as of occupation or environment. Some people simply have a knack for creating challenges that keep them eternally interested. Even in unlikely circumstances, they find the happy zone between boredom and anxiety, testing themselves neither too little nor too much. They find opportunities to play.

Maintaining that balance means constantly looking for harder tasks, because, as we learn and improve, the old challenges become too easy, even boring. The drive to play—to find enjoyment or flow—is one source of what business managers call "the learning curve," the pattern by which organizations and individuals get more productive over time. That pattern of ever-increasing competence, against ever-more-difficult challenges, is why Tom Henry compares his job to rowing in races. Because solving problems is interesting, people strive to find better ways to work. In this sense, play does mean living for "what will come rather than what is," in Bell's words, but such a life is hardly "without effort."

Csikszentmihalyi tells the story of Rico Medellin, an assembly line worker who does the same task almost six hundred times a day:

> Rico has been at this job for over five years, and he still enjoys it. The reason is that he approaches his task in the same way an Olympic athlete approaches his event: How can I beat my record? . . . With the painstak-

ing care of a surgeon, he has worked out a private routine for how to use his tools, how to do his moves. . . . When he is working at top performance the experience is so enthralling that it is almost painful for him to slow down. "It's better than anything else," Rico says.[41]

It is neither Bell's inexorable logic of "utility and efficiency" nor some external pressure to be virtuous that makes Rico Medellin increasingly good at his job. It is an influx of mind—Medellin's desire to play. His achievement is not just a matter of working hard, of doing his duty, or of effort without enjoyment. It is "better than anything else." It is fun. Certainly, Medellin is a responsible, disciplined employee, not someone who just follows his whims. But responsibility and discipline are not what make him special. To satisfy his bosses and the Puritan ethic, Medellin need only show up for eight hours a day and do each assigned task in forty-three seconds. To satisfy himself, he must do much more: better his record, an average of twenty-eight seconds per unit.

Medellin is obviously an unusual assembly line worker. But the progress of a dynamic civilization depends on the special people who make play out of work. In their all-absorbing passion, they create the variations that, through trial and error, become the source of progress. They make the discoveries that drive the infinite series. A dynamic society will nurture and celebrate such people.

A static, technocratic order, by contrast, requires a very different sort of personality: Bell's Puritan ideal, "a highly restrictive character structure whose energies were channeled into the production of goods and into a set of attitudes toward work that feared instinct, spontaneity, and vagrant impulse."[42] In short, a drone—someone who does what he is told and shuns novelty. Someone who avoids facing, or posing, challenges.[43] For a long time, American business did in fact reward Bell's drones: the line worker content to conform to "one best way," even if he could discover something better; the middle manager happy (in Tom Peters's words) to "sit on the 37th floor of the General Motors Tower passing memorandums from the left side of the desk to the right side of the desk for 43 years."[44]

But those reward systems have been overturned, in part because competitive pressure demands that more knowledge be applied to every job and in part because in an affluent society more people expect to get enjoyment as well as money from their work.[45] The American workplace is experiencing a tremendous influx of mind. These changes disorient reactionaries and appall technocrats. David Brooks, of the conservative *Weekly Standard*, recoils from "Cosmic Capitalists [who] practice Playfulness With a Purpose" and executives who "soar into a realm of unfettered imagination."[46] To suggest that productivity, responsibility, and resilience might flow from play, rather than from dutiful drudge work, threatens the foundations of technocracy.

Unlike stasist alternatives, however, a dynamic society does not demand that playful, creative people become rebels against the social order—for it imposes no single order, beyond basic rules that themselves allow for plenitude and experimentation. It permits niches for Bell's drones but does not require that Dan Lynch and Rico Medellin satisfy their creative impulses by becoming revolutionaries. Dynamism encourages people who want to play to find productive ways to do so. This openness to playful work not only promotes creativity and innovation; it makes the social order resilient. Just because businesspeople collect yo-yos or wear khakis instead of blue suits—or just because they enjoy their work—does not in fact mean, as Brooks would have it, that they must share "the same perspectives as the French revolutionaries of 1789."[47]

Here, then, is the reason play is such an important dividing line between stasists and dynamists: A playful society is, of necessity, dynamic, and a dynamic society rewards, or at least tolerates, people who play. Among its many goods are ever more fields of play, from beach volleyball to cancer research to assembly lines that encourage workers to solve problems themselves. For all its beneficial side effects, after all, play is an end in itself—a source of joy, satisfaction, and purpose. To satisfy our thirst for absorbing, enjoyable experiences, a dynamic society will, over time, learn new ways to play. It may go through periods of intense or regimented work, in order to reap some other reward, but it will not be satisfied with drudgery for long.

The playfulness that scares stasists is not only both a product and a source of dynamism, it is a vital adaptation to a dynamic world. That, indeed, appears to be why we play. The psychic rewards we get from solving problems and satisfying our curiosity make the human species more likely to survive in turbulent, or wildly divergent, environments. Many mammals play, but playfulness and curiosity are generally characteristics of the young, fading with maturity. Even chimpanzees, among the most curious of creatures, are far less inventive as adults than as juveniles. The ape "inventions" documented by ethologists, such as washing sweet potatoes in sea water and using sticks to catch termites, originated with juveniles who spread them to adults. Humans, by contrast, play all our lives, and adults do most of the inventing. For a human being not to be creative and curious is a sign of senility, not maturity.[48]

In a stable environment, in which all necessary skills can be mastered during childhood, adults do not need to play in order to survive. But the world sometimes demands new patterns. The environment, natural as well as human, is not stable. The evolutionary advantage of play, then, seems to be that it fosters resilience. One possibility is that play, in animals or humans, simply allows an individual to accumulate lots of different experiences on which to draw when faced with a challenge. It pulls more alternatives into the realm of the familiar. An animal that played as a child will therefore be more adaptable as an adult.[49]

But—the human advantage—an adult who continues to play will be more adaptable still, able to draw not only on old experiences but on the desire for new ones. Csikszentmihalyi suggests a thought experiment:

> Suppose that you want to build an organism, an artificial life form, that will have the best chance of surviving in a complex and unpredictable environment, such as that on Earth. You want to build into this organism some mechanism that will prepare it to confront as many of the sudden dangers and to take advantage of as many of the opportunities that arise as possible. How would you go about doing this? Certainly you would want to design an organism that is basically conservative, one that learns the best solutions from the past and keeps repeating them, trying to save energy, to be cautious and go with the tried-and-true patterns of behavior.
>
> But the best solution would also include a relay system in a few organisms that would give a positive reinforcement every time they discovered something new or came up with a novel idea or behavior, whether or not it was immediately useful. It is especially important to make sure that the organism was not rewarded only for useful discoveries, otherwise it would be severely handicapped in meeting the future. For no earthly builder could anticipate the kind of situations the species of new organisms might encounter tomorrow, next year, or in the next

decade. So the best program is one that makes the organism feel good whenever something new is discovered, regardless of its present usefulness. And this is what seems to have happened with our race through evolution.[50]

This drive to discover new things is what Tom Henry, the high-tech entreprenuer, means when he calls his work "an adventure game"—a world where surprises abound, where "players" thrive on "knowing that just around the corner is something new that you're going to have to learn and to react to."[51] Human beings can flourish from the tropics to the Arctic, through earthquakes and hurricanes, plagues and droughts, because we have developed the resilience that comes from play.

Once established, this resilience is not just good for meeting threats. It extends to everyday habits. Play nurtures a supple mind, a willingness to think in new categories, and an ability to make unexpected associations. The spirit of play not only encourages problem solving but, through novel analogies, fosters originality and clarity. "You can't do serious economics unless you are willing to be playful," writes the economist Paul Krugman, using a seemingly silly thought experiment about hot dogs and buns to skewer a journalist's solemn screed.[52]

By teaching us to nimbly switch mental categories, play encourages syncretism and serendipity, and they, in turn, create the combinations on which progress and plenitude depend. Nineteenth-century chemist Friedrich von Kekulé's insight into the ring structure of benzene—a dream of snakelike molecules twisting until one grabbed its own tail—was a playful leap over the scientific categories of the day, which deemed that structure impossible.[53]

Similarly, when Bruce Ames developed the famous Ames Test, a way of detecting mutagens by testing chemicals on bacteria rather than mice, he took cancer researchers by surprise: "The idea that you could do something in bacteria that was relevant to human cancer just didn't fit with people's thinking."[54] Like the developers of Yahoo!, whose hobby grew into a major enterprise, Ames wasn't even doing his primary work when he started work on the test. His official research was on the genetics of bacteria, particularly *salmonella*. The mutagen test was just a sideline, a way of playing around.[55]

By uniting two fields, the Ames Test gave researchers a powerful new way of exploring the causes of cancer. That effect is not just a matter of recombination, which often happens within a single field, but of creative encounters, of one discipline fertilizing another. Much innovation in fact occurs where worlds collide: The Renaissance came from the mingling of classical and medieval, the Old World and the New. Asked why the London School of Economics was such an exciting, productive place in the 1930s, Nobel laureate Ronald Coase attributes its creativity to an open environment that brought together economists from Europe, England, and the United States. "You just took whatever ideas were good and used them," he says, without worrying about what country or school of thought had originated the concept you needed.[56]

Where different disciplines, different cultures, different geographic regions come together, new combinations are particularly likely to form, simply because—like atoms in a boiling solution—ideas are more likely to run into each other. Our times are marked by the frequency of such encounters, and by the dynamism, the progress, and the stresses they generate. We are living on what the historian Daniel Boorstin calls the "Fertile Verge."[57]

CHAPTER EIGHT

ON THE VERGE

1771: "The different departments of life are jumbled together—The hod-carrier, the low mechanic, the tapster, the publican, the shop-keeper, the pettifogger, the citizen, the courtier, *all tread upon the [heels] of one another:* actuated by the demons of profligacy and licentiousness, they are seen every where, rambling, riding, rolling, rushing, justling, mixing, bouncing, cracking and crashing, in one vile ferment of stupidity and corruption—All is tumult and hurry: one would imagine they were impelled by some disorder of the brain, that will not suffer them to be at rest."[1]

1891: "The cultured Old South had no place in ribald, young and rushing Atlanter. . . . Jones was brother of an Atlanta livery-stable keeper and he, himself, was a sort of 'chambermaid' to horses, otherwise an ostler. In common with so many young fellows in their late teens in Atlanta, he had no family background, but that didn't matter with the girls of 'society.'. . . Atlanta, as is to be expected, was the worst human-hash in the whole South."[2]

1993: "Loss of rural employment and migration from the country-side to the cities causes a fundamental and irreversible shift. It has contributed throughout the world to the destabilization of rural society and to the growth of vast urban concentrations. In the urban slums congregate uprooted individuals whose families have been splintered, whose cultural traditions have been extinguished."[3]

London in the late eighteenth century. Atlanta in the late nine-teenth. Los Angeles, Tijuana, Bangkok in the late twentieth. Cities on the verge, topsy-turvy, a "human-hash." Symbols of upheaval and disorder, of settled ways overthrown and disparate people tossed together. In such metropolitan jumbles, we find E. F. Schumacher's dreaded

191

"footloose" society: "a big cargo ship in which the load is in no way secured."[4] Stasists recoil from these "young and rushing" places, fearing that squalid conditions will endure indefinitely—or, worse, that social dynamism and economic growth are themselves permanent. To avoid what John Gray calls "the overdevelopment of the city, its deformation as a megalopolis,"[5] reactionaries would forever yoke the world's peasants behind a water buffalo. In the name of order, technocrats limit building and restrict growth.

No one celebrates slums. But in the "mixing, bouncing, cracking and crashing" of cities on the make, dynamists find vitality, creativity, humor, and hope. Amid the tastelessness and excess emerge extraordinary things. Such places teem with new ideas and possibilities. As Samuel Johnson said of the jumble that produced political economy and the English novel, "When a man is tired of London, he is tired of life."

With benefit of hindsight, we find the ferment of Johnson's London not in "stupidity and corruption" but in the city's rich intellectual and artistic life. That life was as dependent on London's "rushing, justling, mixing" culture as were the prostitutes and publicans. The city, writes historian John Brewer, "drew Scottish authors and publishers like Tobias Smollett, David Hume and William Strahan; Irish essayists, orators and actors like Dean [Jonathan] Swift, Oliver Goldsmith, Edmund Burke and the Sheridans, father and son; Welsh poets and painters like Evan Lloyd and Richard Wilson; and English provincials, none more distinguished than Johnson and [actor David] Garrick, who walked from Lichfield together in 1737."[6] Boom towns break down barriers; they mix together talent from everywhere; they challenge complacency and overturn assumptions. They are sometimes ugly and almost always stressful, but they foster invention, progress, and learning. They let people chase their dreams.

The richness of such special places lies not in a specific urban form but in the cross-fertilization and new combinations they encourage. They exemplify what the historian Daniel Boorstin calls "the Fertile Verge": "a place of encounter between something and something else." Boorstin sees "verges" as the secret to American creativity:

America was a land of verges—all sorts of verges, between kinds of landscapes or seascapes, between stages of civilization, between ways of thought and ways of life. During our first centuries we experienced more different kinds of verges, and more extensive and more vivid verges, than any other great modern nation. . . .

In ancient, more settled nations, uniformity was idealized. . . . Grandeur and vitality came somehow from within, from purity, from a refusal to fulfill any other people's destiny. The American situation was different. The creativity—the hope—of the nation was in its verges, in its new mixtures and new confusions.[7]

A verge is not a sharp border but a frontier region: where the forest meets the prairie or the mountains meet the flatlands, where ecosystems or ideas mingle. Verges between land and sea, between civilization and wilderness, between black and white, between immigrants and natives (and between immigrants from different lands), between state and national governments, between city and countryside—all mark the American experience. From those verges came inventions like the Pennsylvania rifle, a blend of German gunsmithing and frontier necessity.[8] Immigrants, and the children of immigrants, created the movie industry on the verges between art and commerce, between New York and Los Angeles, between technology and craft.[9] Pentecostal Christianity grew on the verges between rural and urban, South and West, black and white, male and female.[10]

The historian Frederick Jackson Turner's famous "frontier hypothesis," Boorstin argues, captures only one fertile verge among many; the closing of the frontier was not the end it seemed. The encounters continue to this day, shaping American character and culture. "When a New England Brahmin, proud of his *Mayflower* ancestry, objects to *kibitzing*," says Boorstin, "I hear what happens on the Fertile Verges of language."[11]

We live in a time marked by its many verges: between formerly segregated economies, nations, and cultures; between home and work, male and female, East and West, children and adults. The causes are many and, in many cases, familiar to the point of cliché: instantaneous communications and easy transportation; tumbling trade barriers and international capital flows; immigration and the Internet. But their products disperse in unpredictable ways. International trade explains the spread of "Toyotaism" to Western factories—though even that diffusion is hardly as simple as just buying and selling cars—but what about meditation and *feng shui*? In such a world, it's no wonder that postmodernists imagine the dissolution of all boundaries while nationalist reactionaries demand the reinforcement of sovereignty. Boundaries that we took for granted seem a lot less certain.

But boundaries are not disappearing. They are just getting blurry—turning into verges. Such regions of encounter assume that real differences exist. Forests are not the same as prairies. Gospel music is not bluegrass. Yiddish is not English. But verges create new realities. Yiddish is the product of the verge between Hebrew and German; English of the verge between Anglo-Saxon and Anglo-Norman, a French dialect. These tongues further evolved on later verges, absorbing words, phrases, and diction from other languages their speakers encountered. Languages of the verge, Yiddish and English are nonetheless distinct in themselves.

This balance between real difference and genuine combination confuses stasists. They imagine only segregation or homogeneity, either fiercely guarded enclaves or utter sameness—in Benjamin Barber's apocalyptic terms, "Jihad vs. McWorld."[12] But that stark choice is not the only way life works. In a dynamic system, differences persist, but they also enrich one another. Verges do not extinguish variety; they create plenitude. They make new combinations not only possible, but likely.

Consider popular music. It has long been a stasist truism that the cultural imperialism of Western pop would wipe out the diversity of world music, as surely as McDonald's is supposed to crush local cuisines. Once imported via mass communication, critics predicted, Anglo-American music would roll over local cultural forms, displacing them with what the ethnomusicologist Alan Lomax called a global "grey-out."[13] This vision, which has faded among specialists but still crops up in the writings of social critics such as Barber, neatly fits a technocratic model of culture, in which art is dictated rather than evolving. But it misses how cultural processes actually operate.

American popular music itself undercuts the logic of the grey-out scenario; even ignoring significant influences from abroad, it is the ever-evolving product of many cultural verges, with each new musical genre creating opportunities for still more verges. Far from producing homogeneity, global communication has multiplied the verges on which musical forms can evolve, trading influences and sharing traditions. The sociologist Orlando Patterson observes:

> It is simply not true that the diffusion of Western culture, especially at the popular level, leads to the homogenization of the culture of the

world. Indeed, my research, and that of the best scholars working in this area, suggests that just the opposite is the case. Western-American cultural influence has generated enormous cultural production, in some cases amounting to near hypercreativity in the popular cultures of the world . . .

Not homogenization, then, but the revitalization and generation of new musical forms has been the effect of the global exchange process. Some of these forms remain local, providing greater choice and stimulus to the local culture. Examples of such revitalization include the modernization of the traditional Camerounian *makassi* style with the introduction of the acoustic rhythm guitar; the development of the *highlife* music of Ghana, which fused traditional forms with jazz, rock, and Trinidadian calypso rhythms; the vibrant local modernization of traditional Afro-Arab music in Kenya. Elsewhere, musical forms under Western impact have broken out of their provincial boundaries to become regional currency, as, for example, the Trinidadian and American pop influenced *kru-krio* music of Sierra Leone, which swept West Africa during the sixties and seventies.[14]

Patterson's crowning example is reggae. In the late 1950s, working-class Jamaicans bored with native *mento* music (itself a merging of the folk music of the island's British settlers and West African slaves) began listening to rhythm-and-blues records and bluegrass "cowboy music" from the United States. As they imitated these foreign forms, Jamaicans blended them with their own distinct cadences and with the African music of Afro-Jamaican religious sects. In the process, they invented a whole series of new genres: ska, rock-steady, and finally reggae. And, contrary to the stasist fable of one-way cultural imperialism, the reggae carried by Jamaican immigrants became popular music in Britain and later in the United States, where it mutated into rap.[15] The process continues. In recent years, ska has been one of the hottest rhythms in alternative rock.

For those who genuinely fear boring homogeneity, seeing the plenitude produced by dynamic cultural processes should be a comfort. But many critics are at least as worried about maintaining static cultural purity—avoiding competition, integration, reinvention, or mutation—as they are about a global grey-out; Lomax himself wanted cultures to preserve "the unified folkways of their forefathers." In stasist rhetoric, *homogenization* is a code word for change, for disturbing *existing* uniformity. The problem with Western music isn't, then, that it eliminates traditional forms but that it encourages them to evolve in new directions.

Similarly, French regulators periodically try to stamp out foreign words, on the grounds that the French language must be defended against invasion and obliteration. This justification, too, disguises the fear of cultural evolution. There is no danger that "Franglais" will become English. But absorbing English words and American slang does alter French, and that evolutionary process defies both reactionary yearnings and technocratic standards. "This Franglais, this mixture of English and French, is a completely artificial language," charges Daniel Oster, the professor heading the team to update the official French dictionary. "It's made by disc jockeys, journalists, and all sorts of media."[16] The use of the term *artificial* to describe an evolving, uncontrolled language rather than one carefully crafted by experts is odd; *natural* would be more appropriate.

The stasist criticism of rock and English, mass communications and commercial culture, contains this element of truth: As they spread worldwide, these systems accelerate change. They are, in poet and critic Frederick Turner's apt phrase, "universal solvents." They make mixing easier. Turner writes of rock:

> Originating in a fertile combination of the sophisticated African musical tradition with European and Latin American elements, a new musical medium emerged in the Sixties which is perhaps the most potent, because the most fundamental, of all forces for change. . . . Essentially what happened was that a very simple, pan-human rhythmic beat was discovered, of no musical merit in itself, to which the music of all world cultures could be set and which served as a liquid medium that would enable musical syncretism to take place. . . . Rock has been like alcohol, which can serve as the base for the most exquisite blends of perfume, the most delicate liqueurs.[17]

Just as a chemical solvent, such as alcohol or water, enables molecules to break apart and recombine in new ways, so does the basic rhythm of rock encourage musical traditions to exchange patterns, creating new forms. It fosters new combinations.

Similarly, English provides a linguistic solvent, a verge between nationalities. Along with mathematics and accounting, it carries the international work of science, of finance, of commerce and transportation. And in many cosmopolitan cities, English is the lingua franca of everyday life: How else, in Los Angeles, is the Cambodian doughnut maker to communicate with his Salvadoran customers, the Vietnamese manicurist with her Persian clients, the Russian tailor with her Mexican seamstress? The same is true in multilingual countries like India or South Africa. Another language would do—everyone could speak Spanish, Arabic, or Mandarin—but some sort of solvent is essential. Even if it is no one's mother tongue, a common language, like a common musical rhythm, allows true exchange rather than mere coexistence. Such universal solvents permit the fusion that Turner calls "interculturalism," as opposed to the "pluralism" that locks people and cultures into neat boxes and "requires no change in one's own or one's neighbor's perspective."[18]

Here we find ourselves, once again, searching for the bonds of life, considering not just abstract systems—languages, music—but the person-to-person connections that produce them. After all, the fundamental verge is where individuals meet, the encounter between someone and someone else. A marriage is a verge, as is a business partnership or the relationship between teacher and student. From such verges, larger ones arise: families, religious congregations, educational institutions, industries and commercial districts, professions and civic associations. The amazing hodgepodge of Johnson's London drew its creativity not simply from the brilliance of its component members but from their interaction. They created clubs and gathered in coffee houses, debating politics and art. They broke the status bonds of patronage to invent a new contract-driven publishing industry.

Stasist critics, who ignore the complex creativity of verges, often scorn the places and legal institutions that make such new associations possible. Above all, they detest commercial bonds. Against both evidence and theory to the contrary, they insist that commerce is atomistic rather than social, that contracts break rather than forge bonds. "Markets are contractual," writes Barber, "rather than communitarian, which means they stroke our solitary egos but leave unsatisfied our yearning for community, offering durable goods and fleeting dreams but not a common identity or collective membership—something the blood communities spawned by Jihad, reinforced by the thinness of market relations, do rather too well."[19] A technocrat opposing his vision to dynamists and reactionaries, Barber prefers "deliberative" processes that put a premium on centralized articulation and promise carefully engineered results. He sees "community" emerging less from shared interests, experiences, or beliefs than from politics. In this view, markets and contracts by their very nature serve only to destroy community.

Yet Barber himself reports on the use of markets to reinforce community; he just does not recognize what he's telling us. He complains that teenagers in rural Nebraska yearn for MTV and "see the shopping mall as the great hangout of the rest of the nation, and [lament that] they don't have one." What Barber denounces as "the videology of a McWorld utterly indifferent to diversity or democracy," these young people interpret very differently. They imagine verges where teenage community can flourish—a common territory for hanging out and a common language of music and imagery. They are seeking not strokes for their solitary egos but settings and art that will foster interaction, that will allow them to create their own "little corner of the universe" out of the adult world.

Echoing the old complaint that you can't keep them down on the farm, Barber frets that in pursuit of such communities, teenagers will leave their home towns for the big cities, abandoning Nebraska for L.A. or Smolensk for St. Petersburg, and thus casting aside "whatever distinct culture . . . may have attached to their youth."[20] Like the snobs who scorned London's "vile ferment" and Atlanta's "human-hash," he wants to maintain the purity of the old, unmixed world. Unlike those unabashed aristocrats, however, Barber aims his fire not at the new verges themselves but at the technology, media, and commerce that produce them. We can easily imagine that if dropped in the eighteenth century, he would rail against newspapers, coffee houses, and the lure they exerted on impressionable country lads like Samuel Johnson. Transported to the nineteenth, he would denounce railroads, telegraphs, and the Sears catalog.

The turbulence of places on the verge can, of course, be quite unnerving. Traveling the South while researching his 1981 book, *The Nine Nations of North America*, Joel Garreau was struck by the way people in other places—even very small places—worried about becoming "like Atlanta." What, Garreau wondered, do southerners have against

Atlanta? The crime there is bad, he knew, but not as bad as in Houston or New Orleans, which don't evoke the same fears. The traffic, while congested, is typical for any city. The neighborhoods are nice, the housing relatively inexpensive, the universities good, race relations decent. Observing the culture shock of recent immigrants from the southern countryside—including a teenage girl who had never seen an escalator and a young woman from the Tennessee mountains who complained that Atlanta men were unfriendly—Garreau concluded that what people feared about Atlanta was its insecurity. In that human-hash of a city, a place of strangers and new experiences, no one could be sure who they were or where they fit in. With great opportunity came turbulence and uncertainty.[21]

Dynamic systems are not merely turbulent, however. They respond to the desire for security; they just don't do it by stopping experimentation. Rather, they enable people to create their own corners of the universe, their own "artificial" pockets of stability within the broader dynamic world. In some cases, stressed-out city dwellers simply move to smaller, less tumultuous places, a step made much easier by the same communications and transportation technologies that make people "footloose." While metropolitan areas (including suburbs) still account for 80 percent of the U.S. population, some "micropolitan" areas—small towns outside metro areas—are growing even faster than booming cities like Atlanta. These are places like St. George, Utah; Elko, Nevada; and Columbia, Tennessee, that offer what demographer Kevin Heubusch describes as "'city' benefits on a manageable scale—community without the crush, services without the stress."[22] Garreau notes that the fairly even economic growth across much of the South has been driven by the appeal of smaller, more manageable communities, the sorts of places that dot the region: "Small cities and towns are where people want to live, and small cities and towns are where industries want to go."[23]

Despite their advantages, however, small, friendly towns cannot offer the creative verges and wide-ranging opportunities of the mixed-up metro areas in which most people live. Getting away from it all cannot be the only way to cope with turbulence. And dynamic social systems are in fact continually inventing ways to provide personal stability amid change. Just as the coffee houses and clubs of Johnson's London created havens for friendship and camaraderie, today's commercial institutions often serve the human need for community. Once open to the public, they take on roles beyond the purely profit-making purposes of their creators.

In recent years, Garreau has become an expert on "edge cities," the new urban form of office parks, malls, and suburban-style neighborhoods. What he has found in his reporting is what anyone who actually lives or works in such a place can see from experience. Life, in all its variety, continues. And so does community. A mall, says Garreau, is "not just a retail place. You go there at 10 o'clock in the morning and you see all these old people doing their t'ai chi, like in a Chinese village square. . . . You hang out there at 4:30 or 5 in the afternoon, and you see all these young people flirting with the opposite sex, just like in a Mexican village square. This has all the functions that a city has always had."[24]

Or consider the proliferation of coffee houses in the 1990s. Until recently, many U.S. social critics made much of the lack of "third places," neither home nor work, where people could hang out and chat. Unlike Europeans, they complained, Americans have no café culture; shopping malls, suburbia, and commerce in general, they charged, have destroyed the democratic conversation of bars and social clubs.[25] Such criticism was overstated, ignoring the many informal interactions that occur in such places as malls, restaurants, and doughnut shops. But the "third place" critique did identify a real source of discontent—as Starbucks discovered when its stores took off in ways the company never expected.

The original idea, writes CEO Howard Schultz, "was to provide a quick, stand-up, to-go service in downtown office locations." Instead, the fastest-growing Starbucks stores turned out to be those near where people lived—the ones that functioned as neighborhood watering holes. The young adults who had grown up hanging out in shopping malls were looking for safe, friendly places to be with other people, places where, in Schultz's words, "No one is carded and no one is drunk." In focus groups, Los Angeles customers said they went to Starbucks because the place felt social. The company adjusted its strategy accordingly, building more and larger neighborhood stores, with more tables to sit around. It now deliberately seeks to foster a social, European-style café environment.

Like 3M with its Scotch tape and Post-it notes, Starbucks had addressed not only a need it could identify but many others it didn't realize were there. It prospered by tapping both the knowledge of its founders and the unarticulated desires of its customers. Starbucks discovered an X-factor. Schultz writes:

> Back in 1987, none of us could foresee these social trends, and how our stores could accommodate them. What we did, though, was to appeal to the sophistication and wisdom and better nature of our potential customers, providing them the kind of music and atmosphere that we liked for ourselves.
>
> People didn't know they needed a safe, comfortable, neighborhood gathering place. They didn't know they would like Italian espresso drinks. But when we gave it to them, the fervor of their response overwhelmed us.[26]

The book superstores that so distress advocates of traditional independent booksellers fill a similar niche. They create interesting, safe, comfortable gathering spots for people who love books. They, too, have become important "third places." Combining all these trends, my husband spends Sunday afternoons playing chess—a classic third-place activity—at a coffee-selling book superstore in a mall.

For many other people, of course, Sunday fellowship takes a different form. Among the most important sources of stability amid dynamism are some of the oldest: religious congregations. The forms of religious practice are as subject to experiment and feedback as any other social institutions; they too adapt to the particular needs of time, place, and circumstance. In turbulent times and places, religious communities provide secure havens of faith and fellowship. No L.A. parking lot is complete without numerous cars carrying that most ancient of Christian symbols: a fish, marking the verge between the fisherfolk of Galilee and the language of the Greeks.[27] In this seemingly secular city, evangelical Christian communities flourish.

And on the verge between Protestant America and newly urbanized immigrants has grown many a small evangelical church. Essayist Richard Rodriguez, a Catholic and a keen observer of California life, writes:

> The other day I was jogging up the street past the Filipino evangelical church in my neighborhood. Every day they come from other parts of the city, pissing off the neighborhood by taking up all the parking places. They have predawn services, and evening prayer services, and they are in

church on Sundays from dawn till dusk. . . . The small Protestant church revives the Catholic memory of the countryside. In the small evangelical church, people who are demoralized by the city turn to the assurance of community. In the small church, each soul has a first name again. One hand grips another's hand against anonymity. Hymns resound over the city, wild with grace, and the world becomes certain and small."[28]

Left free to innovate and to learn, people find ways to create security for themselves. Those creations, too, are part of dynamic systems. They provide personal and social resilience.

Like other innovations, these social institutions are threatened by the intolerant plans and formidable powers of technocrats. When Starbucks wanted to establish stores in San Francisco, it discovered that many neighborhoods flatly prohibited third places. The city had banned the conversion of retail shops into restaurants. Starbucks could only sell coffee and pastries to go; it couldn't encourage customers to linger and converse, because the law forbade chairs. Sure that stores, not restaurants, were what their neighborhoods needed, and were all those neighborhoods would need far into the future, technocratic planners had stifled the vitality and adaptability of San Francisco's communities.

Starbucks by then was rich and famous, not a little upstart enterprise, so it was able to get away with less desirable locations. Instead of building the neighborhood shops it knew would be most successful— stores on the verge between home and commercial life—it opened in busy shopping districts. And it eventually got the law changed. The city council agreed to a new zoning category, "beverage houses," solving the problem until the next innovator comes along with something the zoning code hasn't considered. "Once the code was changed," writes Schultz, "many cafés opened, reenergizing the neighborhood street life in several communities in the city of San Francisco."[29]

Small churches face similar problems, with far fewer resources. New congregations are usually bootstrap operations, meeting first in homes, then in storefronts or office buildings, and only then in specially designed religious buildings. At every step in their evolution, they confront official plans that can block their own. In 1997, the city of Garden Grove, California, shut down five Korean churches because they were operating in commercial zones, which is against local regulations. "When we bought [the building], we assumed that everything was legal, that we would just move into the building, renovate it and worship and pray," said the pastor of a seventy-five–member church that had paid $500,000 for a small building amid auto repair garages and fast food restaurants. "That was obviously our mistake because we didn't check. But we didn't know."[30]

In Los Angeles, the city council refused to let a small Orthodox Jewish congregation conduct services in a rented house.[31] Old Tappan, New Jersey, blocked a Korean Catholic congregation that wanted to turn an abandoned Chinese restaurant into a church. In Sayreville, New Jersey, a Hindu group had to sue the city to get permission to convert a YMCA into a temple.[32] The city of Corinth, Texas, refused to give the Harvest Metropolitan Community Church, a gay and lesbian congregation, a permit to build on a site zoned for light-industrial use.[33] Neighbors in San Jose, California, are suing to block construction of a large Sikh temple, even though the property is in an area whose zoning permits churches.[34]

Over the past two decades, churches have gone from obvious neighborhood amenities to targets of zoning bans. That can keep established congregations from adapting to their members' changing needs; in northeastern suburbs, for instance, many synagogues have had great difficulty getting approval to follow their members to new locations.[35] And rigid zoning hits new congregations and minority groups particularly hard. "Churches no longer carry the cachet that they once did, that they sweep away for all citizens all opposition," says Marc Stern, a lawyer with the American Jewish Congress, "and that's particularly true when it comes to smaller or less established churches—which means new immigrant groups or smaller denominations."[36] The very groups most likely to need havens of support and stability, and least likely to have the political or financial clout to cope with technocratic rigidities, are the ones who face the greatest barriers. To their "yearning for community," Barber's "deliberative democracy" just says no.

When religious congregations run into political opposition, the people trying to keep them out usually deny any prejudice—against Koreans or Jews, Hindus or Sikhs, evangelicals or gays. You can never tell for sure, of course, and sometimes things do get ugly, but in most cases the opponents are telling the truth. "I'm sure there are people who would prefer the whole community be white Anglo-Saxon, but I think the concerns of the community are traditional zoning concerns," says a lawyer who represented an Iranian-Jewish congregation seeking permission to build in a Long Island town. "It generally boils down to 'Are you going to affect the way I live?' "[37] The problem isn't bias; it's change. "I don't want to live next to a landmark," says a San Jose resident opposed to the Sikhs' elaborate plans for a temple. "Why should I be called a bigot and a racist because I like my neighborhood the way it is?"[38]

I like my neighborhood the way it is. That is the all-too-understandable sentiment that motivates stasist policy. Much as we may want some things to get better, we want others to stay exactly the same. We like our neighborhoods, our jobs, our industries, our cities, our social customs, our art or music, our scientific theories, our general worldviews *just the way they are.* We don't want them challenged by competition or altered by other people's ideas of progress. Form may follow failure, as Henry Petroski suggests, but "failure" is in the eye of the beholder. If improving your world means changing mine, I may do everything possible to thwart you—not out of hatred toward you and yours, but because I like my world the way it is. Richard Rodriguez's neighbors, angry about competing for parking spaces, would understand.

But if every voluntary experiment must answer the question, "Are you going to affect the way I live?" with a no, there can be no experiments, no new communities, no realized dreams. A city, an economy, or a culture is, despite the best efforts of stasists, fundamentally a "natural" system. As a whole, it is beyond anyone's control. Any individual effort at improvement changes not just its particular target but the broader system. In that process, there may be progress, but there will also be disruptions, adjustments, and losers.

When Vidal Sassoon's precision haircuts became popular, traditional barbers and beauty parlor owners lost business. Desktop publishing gave graphic designers far more control over their work, but the new technology also forced them to acquire new skills—and it put paste-up artists out of work. One of my college professors recounted how, in the 1960s, the first Mars missions had ruined one of his own professors' work. That scientist had perfected the art of creating "Mars jars"—containers that simulated the Martian atmosphere according to the best available astronomical information. Once probes orbited Mars, the jars became obsolete. They offered only educated guesses, while the Mars missions gave definitive answers.

Competition in the telephone business brought enormous benefits to most people: more choice in equipment and services; lower prices; much more rapid innovation; and many new jobs at upstart telecom companies, their suppliers, and customers. But competition disrupted the once-secure world of people who had devoted their careers to Ma Bell. "It's like being a battered spouse," an AT&T middle manager said when the company announced in January 1996 that it would lay off forty thousand employees (a number it later reduced). "You feel so dependent. You can't leave because you want the security, but you have no self-esteem. . . . When I joined the company I believed that if I worked hard and applied myself, I'd be recognized for that contribution. The company welcomed you, made you feel valuable. They don't value me now."[39] Confronted with the prospect of such personal angst, people quite naturally resist new ideas, inventions, or institutions, regardless of how much those innovations might help others improve their own lives or realize their dreams. And visible losers attract far more sympathy than invisible, often still-hypothetical, winners.

From such practical, personal objections springs most support for stasis. Here, too, is a verge: between ideological stasists and self-interested parties opposed to specific changes. But this verge is anything but fertile. To the contrary, it represents a potent combination for stifling creativity. The sterile verge between stasists and interest groups provides a host of shifting arguments and techniques for opposing change. Each side gives the other cover. The ideologues keep the interest groups from sounding crass and selfish, while the interest groups keep the ideologues from sounding mean, elitist, or just plain nuts. Stasists bring the idealism, while interest groups offer anecdotes, money, and political clout.

It isn't terribly appealing to argue, for instance, that you want everyone else to be worse off so that your company can charge high prices, run inefficiently, and not worry about coming up with new and better products. Far better to invoke reactionary ideals of loyalty and stability, to suggest that turbulence is evil and competition suspect—or to offer technocratic promises of predictability and order against the messiness of experimentation. If you can also suggest that uncontrolled "technology" is plowing over "people," so much the better. The people inventing and using new technology don't count much in stasist calculations—and, chances are, they haven't yet gotten organized into an interest group.

But while stasist ideology sounds good when reduced to evocative buzzwords, it doesn't sell as a package. In contemporary America at least, it is hard to persuade people that the open-ended future is, in general, a bad idea, that experiments are inherently evil, or that progress is a myth. It is very easy, however, to encourage people to ask, "Are you going to affect the way I live?" and to refuse to take yes for an answer. It is easy to make change sound scary—A temple as big as a Costco! Thousands of people out of work! Smut on the Internet! Brave New World!—and, by doing so, to veto every new idea before it can even be tried. Interest-group politics allows stasists to camouflage their ideals under "pragmatic" concerns.

As with any other verge, of course, the categories eventually begin to blur. Many of the plaintiff attorneys whose lawsuits crush medical technologies and dog high-tech growth companies may honestly believe that the world would be better off without silicone-gel breast implants, Bendectin morning-sickness medicine, Norplant contraceptives, high-risk stocks, or risks in general. Many appear to be genuine Naderite stasists. But they also reap millions of dollars in fees, putting them among the highest-paid lawyers in the country.[40] Conversely, when the president of the local home owners' lobby becomes a fanatic opposed to nearly all growth—and expects to exercise veto power over each prospective restaurant that wants to open in a commercial block—she may think she is simply protecting her property values. But she has abandoned economic calculations, becoming indistinguishable from an ideological reactionary wielding technocratic authority.

The sterile verge between stasist ideologues and status quo interest groups is made possible by the powerful legal institutions that translate stasist theory into vehicles for blocking change. The technocratic zeal for neat, carefully controlled cities produced the planning processes that make small churches—or small construction projects—prohibitively expensive or too complicated to pursue. The San Jose Sikhs must fight for their temple in court because no-growth reactionaries have made any change in "the environment" subject to legal challenge. Stasist institutions shift the burden of proof from the people who want to block new ideas to those who want to experiment. Such institutions seek not simply to compensate for or mitigate extreme side effects but, rather, to treat any change as suspect. They assume that the best state of the world is stability: *I like my neighborhood the way it is.*

Thanks to alliances between antichange ideologues and established interests, writes the economic historian Joel Mokyr, "technological creativity has proved rare and ephemeral," a quality marking golden ages that pass all too quickly.[41] Mokyr is a pessimist, arguing that no society when left on its own will remain creative for long:

> Sooner or later the forces of conservatism, the "if-it-ain't-broke-don't-fix-it," the "if-God-had-wanted-us-to-fly-He-would-have-given-us-wings," and the "not-invented-here-so-it-can't-possibly-work" people take over and manage through a variety of legal and institutional channels to slow down and if possible stop technological creativity altogether. Technological leaders like 17th-century Holland or early 19th-century Britain lost their edge and eventually became followers. . . . It is as if technological creativity is like youthful vitality: As time passes, the creative juices gradually dry up, and sclerosis sets in. Societies become increasingly risk-averse and conservative, and creative innovators are regarded as deviants and rebels.[42]

The primary check on this phenomenon is competition. When one country becomes inhospitable to innovation, invention occurs elsewhere. And where there is international rivalry, whether military or commercial, governments are less likely to adopt stasist policies in the first place, lest they fall behind their rivals. (The same is true, to a lesser degree, of interstate or even intercity competition within federalist systems like the United States.)

Our interconnected world thus offers both promise and dangers. Its many verges promote creativity. At the same time, however, the end of the Cold War has reduced the competition among nations, not only bringing the benefits of peace, of course, but also making technological and economic stagnation less hazardous. Meanwhile, there is a drive toward policy "harmonization." Although policies can in theory be harmonized to maintain openness and competition, in many cases the goal is to protect detailed regulations from international challengers.

The European Union's "social charter," for instance, seeks to dictate employment terms for all European companies. Nationalist opponents of free trade treaties have, as a compromise, attempted to attach provisions requiring uniform labor or environmental laws. Efforts are under way to ban human cloning worldwide. The Internet has made questions about how best to protect intellectual property without stifling new ideas particularly tricky. But instead of allowing experimentation and competition in intellectual property law, Western governments that once offered different approaches are now determined to adopt a single standard. "All the lines are being drawn in favor of increased protection," says the legal scholar David Post, who would like to see competing alternatives, including systems with looser rules about copying, that would allow better institutions to evolve through trial and error.[43]

Harmonization can stamp out the competition that protects innovators from the tyranny of the status quo. Rather than nested rules that compete within a broader dynamic system, these policies enforce statist dictates that offer no escape. Such a "level playing field" not only disregards local knowledge, it discourages new ideas. The enclosed, uniform legal world of the Roman Empire, notes Mokyr, "was surprisingly uncreative technologically and was rescued from complete stasis only by non-citizens living outside it."[44]

Even more striking is the history of China, for centuries the most innovative society on earth. In nearly every area of human endeavor, the Chinese developed technologies far ahead of their European counterparts: metallurgy, chemistry, spinning and weaving, mining, navigation and ship building, paper, porcelain, the wheelbarrow, the horse collar, clocks, gunpowder—in some cases, such as iron casting, more than a millennium before Europe. They copiously documented many inventions in handbooks, treatises, and encyclopedias, often illustrated by diagrams. During these centuries of creativity, China had many cities on the verge: commercial centers where travelers brought not only products but also ideas from abroad, enriching Chinese learning with Arabic, Persian, and Buddhist science, philosophy, and technology—and, in turn, taking Chinese learning home.[45]

Then in the fifteenth century it all stopped. Even the books disappeared.[46] Voyages of exploration were forbidden, and the records of earlier voyages burned. By 1500, building a seagoing junk with more than two masts was punishable by death; a half-century later, going to sea to trade was considered a form of treason.[47] Long-established technologies for mining, silk reeling, and telling time were forgotten. The state took over some foreign trades and shut down others, eliminating the unpredictable verges of the merchant cities. "By the time Europeans came to China in some numbers in the sixteenth century," writes the historian David Landes, "two hundred years of indigenous rule by the Ming had screwed the bureaucratic lid on tight."⁴⁸ Even after contact with Europe, the Chinese ignored European advances— neither adopting them nor treating them as competition. With a unified, geographically contiguous empire, Chinese officials could assume their nation was self-sufficient. They had no use for verges.

The details of how and why China abandoned its heritage of technological dynamism are murky. What is clear, however, is that reactionary ideals, technocratic administration, and monopoly power converged to enforce stability at the cost of stagnation. Even in its creative period, China's dynamism was primarily technological, not social, economic, or political; the government was both highly bureaucratic and absolutist. The only people allowed to study astronomy or time keeping, for instance, were the court astronomers.⁴⁹ The very openness of the mandarin bureaucracy—which could be entered, regardless of birth, by any man who performed well on civil service examinations—pulled many of China's best minds away from other, more creative pursuits. The exam system was based entirely on the mastery of a handful of neo-Confucian classics, encouraging neither intellectual variety nor curiosity and new ideas.⁵⁰ The governing philosophy was one of order, subordination, and stasis. And like most bureaucracies, the mandarinate developed a strong interest in protecting the status quo. The system became reinforcing—a sterile verge between interests and ideology.

"Rigid etiquette and complete obedience and conformism became the hallmark of the Chinese government under the Ming emperors [1368–1644]," writes Mokyr. "At the same time the Chinese civil service became a major force in preserving the status quo. The two great enlightened Manchu despots, K'an Chi (1662–1722) and Ch'ien Lung (1736–1795), whose rules are invariably described as peaceful and prosperous, were interested in pacification, order, and administration. In their search for stability, their interests and those of the bureaucracy converged. The absolutist rule of an all-powerful monarch whose preference was for stability above all discouraged the kind of dynamism that was throbbing throughout Europe at the time."⁵¹

More important than the regime's hostility to innovation was its monopoly power. Would-be Chinese innovators had no outlet. Unlike the fragmented states of Europe, the Chinese empire encompassed the equivalent of a continent, leaving no havens of creativity nearby. And because Chinese invention had always been done under state auspices, there were no private enterprises to provide money and encouragement once the government stopped supporting innovation. State support and, hence, progress itself could be turned off like a faucet.

China's story raises the specter of the end of progress, the death of dynamism even in its limited, technological form. Social, economic, scientific, and cultural vitality—and the accumulation and transmission of knowledge—are not conditions we can take for granted. They are fragile and often fleeting, vulnerable to both attacks and neglect. They require the right environment.

The enemies of dynamism are forever arguing that we must destroy dynamic processes in order to save them. The open society, they assert, is its own greatest enemy and should therefore be closed. Dynamism, in this analysis, survives only as a moral parasite, sucking off the inherited virtue of stasist eras; over time, it depletes that virtue and is destined to wither and die. This position is extremely disingenuous. Either dynamism is worth preserving for as long as possible, or it is not. Claiming that dynamic processes should be curbed now, because they're doomed anyway, hardly suggests concern for their well-being. It is just one more justification for abandoning the open future in favor of something engineered to stasist specifications.

Hence, Daniel Bell writes of the cultural contradictions of capitalism, warning that the system will self-destruct. His views echo through the writings and speeches of countless technocrats and reactionaries. Combining Bell's repression theory of progress with Barberian notions of evil consumerism versus civic virtue, Hillary Clinton frets that American popular culture is "turning people away from being citizens into being consumers." She complains that the First Amendment, by protecting media from technocratic direction, allows "a relentless, unstopping, message of consumer, materialistic pleasure." Neatly summarizing Bell's thesis (without attribution), she tells global movers and shakers meeting in Davos, Switzerland, "There is no doubt that we are creating a consumer-driven culture that promotes values and ethics that undermine both capitalism and democracy. In fact, I think you could argue that the kind of work ethic, postponement of gratification, and other attributes that are historically associated with capitalism, are being undermined by consumer capitalism."[52]

Always in such assessments, there is the notion that dynamism depends on stasist virtues: that goodness, morality, ethics, and peace are attributes not of the evolving future but of the unchanging past, not of decentralized, out-of-control competition but of top-down authority—that the openness of dynamism, its trial-and-error skepticism, and its challenging nature mean it can survive only by living off the habits and attitudes of less turbulent times.[53] This argument is not simply a brief for the wisdom inherited from previous generations, which like all cumulative knowledge is a product of dynamic processes; rather, it is a claim that there is something suspect about the open-ended future—and about the discontent that leads to experiments, improvements, and progress. It is another assertion that dynamism is too dangerous, even to itself, to be left unchecked.

Meanwhile, some otherwise sympathetic thinkers argue that dynamic processes inevitably undermine the virtues and institutions on which they depend. Mokyr's pessimism suggests this position. No society, in his assessment, can permanently resist the sterile verge. Dynamism is, if nothing else, too exhausting to be maintained. The late political economist Mancur Olson similarly stressed the paralysis that interest groups and bureaucracies create over time.[54] And Joseph Schumpeter, who coined the term "creative destruction" to describe economic competition, argued that the progress and prosperity created by markets would eventually doom them. Capitalism's success, he predicted, would support more and more intellectuals, who would then intensify and channel the popular discontent with economic turbulence and, in the process, destroy entrepreneurial freedom.[55] Sympathetic though these pessimists may be to dynamism, they do not see any way—except possibly the checks of international competition—to preserve trial-and-error experimentation. The sterile verge is too powerful. Over time, it chokes off new ideas.

If, as Mokyr suggests, dynamism and creativity are "like youthful vitality," the question for dynamists is whether there is any way to keep a society young. Identifying the sterile verge is the first step to countering it. But maintaining dynamism also depends on cultivating certain public virtues: the behaviors and habits of mind that allow dynamic societies to flourish over time.

These vital qualities cannot be plucked from stasist catechisms. Contrary to technocratic and reactionary preaching, dynamist virtues are most threatened not by dynamic processes but by stasist habits, attitudes, and expectations—the habits, attitudes, and expectations that currently dominate our public discourse. There are indeed, as Hillary Clinton suggests, "values and ethics that undermine capitalism and democracy," but they are not nearly so crass or simple as the desire for more consumer goods. Olson's interest groups are not slackers lusting after Nintendo games; they are hard-working, highly organized lobbies seeking political power: the power to end other people's experiments and guarantee their own security. It is by following stasist impulses, not "consumerist" desires, that they suck the life from capitalism and democracy.

One possible protection against such socially enervating behavior is institutional. Much to Mrs. Clinton's apparent chagrin, for instance, the First Amendment protects most American media experiments from political overrides. With its checks and balances, not only between government branches but between what its framers called "factions," the U.S. constitutional system erected many such barriers to federal action. These barriers have, however, greatly eroded. While institutional constraints can curb passing political whims, they alone cannot protect dynamism over the long term. Once the rulers of a society—in a democracy, the citizenry—become hostile to decentralized, trial-and-error processes, legal institutions will change accordingly. The sclerosis Mokyr fears comes not because dynamism destroys itself but because people abandon it, either because they do not understand what is at stake or because they do not care.

Dynamists, then, need a deeper understanding of their own public virtues, in part as a defense against the stasist charge that they have none and, more important, because only by cultivating these qualities can we hope to guard against sclerosis. While dynamism requires many private virtues, including the curiosity, risk taking, and playfulness that drive trial-and-error progress, its primary public virtues are those of *forbearance:* of inaction, of not demanding a public ruling on every new development. These traits include tolerance, toughness, patience, and good humor. Here we find a different sort of self-control from the Puritan denial lauded by Bell's repression theory: the self-restraint not to impose your own idea of the one best way on others, not to use political power to short-circuit trial-and-error learning.

Stasists reflexively respond to any experiment or proposal by seeking centralized, usually political, action. They simply assume, as a matter of course, that each new development demands official activity to stop, control, or, occasionally, endorse it. Sometimes the response borders on panic, especially if the idea is genuinely novel. New technologies, such as genetic engineering or financial derivatives, produce rushed, nearly hysterical reactions. But so do far less exotic experiments—corporate restructuring, managed care health plans, Madonna videos, even break-fast cereal price increases[56]—that clearly are subject to all sorts of competitive checks. By contrast, dynamist forbearance patiently lets trial-and-error evolution take its course. It certainly does not demand an end to criticism—managed care is far better when patients raise a ruckus about unresponsive bureaucracy—but neither does it insist on immediate, official, top-down, once-and-for-all action.

Tolerance is foremost among the virtues of forbearance—not the tolerance that makes no judgments, but the tolerance that permits peaceful differences. This attitude contrasts sharply with the stasist expectation that no one should be disrupted by other people's enterprise, that altering the status quo should require permission. A dynamist, too, may prefer his neighborhood just the way it is; he may not like his neighbor's new house or the temple proposed down the block. But he does not expect to exercise veto power over other people's improvements or to cancel other people's dreams. He does not argue, as one radio host suggested, that "mansionization" is a public "problem," because people who build large houses in modest neighborhoods make the old timers feel uncomfortable.[57] Discomfort does not justify stamping out differences.

Tolerance demands toughness. It means accepting that we cannot always have things our own way and that we must not limit our neighbors' experiments, aspirations, or ideas just because they might make us feel bad. As Jonathan Rauch notes in *Kindly Inquisitors,* those who believe in the dynamic process of intellectual inquiry, which he calls "liberal science," must endure the discomfort that comes along with criticism. Inquiry is a competitive, trial-and-error system that requires not only experiments but sometimes brutally frank feedback: "Those of us who hold sacred the right to err and the duty to check need to understand that our defense of liberal science must preach not only toleration but discipline: the hard self-discipline which requires us to live with offense."[58] Maintaining society's "youthful vitality" requires both tolerance and a thick skin.

It also requires patience. Dynamists avoid panic in the face of new ideas. They realize that people get used to new developments, that they adjust—the two-story house next door turns out to be no big deal—and that they often reject bad ideas without any centralized, official response. The critic Martha Bayles, whose writings on popular music reflect fairly conservative tastes, takes a dynamist approach to culture, including cultural developments she dislikes. She believes in informed criticism, and plenty of it. But she is patient. Criticism, she suggests, should not be a prelude to censorship but part of an ongoing, dynamic process. "Built into the wise use of cultural authority is an appreciation of the process of learning," she says. "It is vital to remember that learning, and self-correction, are constantly occurring within popular culture. . . . In the end, it is this patient work of criticism, self-correction, and teaching that is most imperiled by censorship." Bayles's approach is not just a matter of policy—censorship versus free speech—but of process. Rather than looking for short-cuts that will make art turn out exactly the way she envisions it, she values the give and take that deepens cultural understanding.

By contrast, the urge to make grand, public, quasi-official pronouncements often backfires. It overrides the gradual, informed feedback from markets and critics. And by raising the specter of censorship, even implicitly, it turns cultural losers into artistic heroes. Until Bill Bennett and Bob Dole made rap music a political issue, says Bayles, "gangsta rap and other offensive styles were getting dissed by many of their own fans. Snoop Doggy Dogg's second album had not sold half as well as his first. And a low-budget film, *Fear of a Black Hat*, had subjected rap to the most relentless kind of criticism: insider satire. But thanks to Bennett's and Dole's campaign, offensive rap got a new lease on life."[59]

Patient forbearance is made easier by a generous spirit and a healthy sense of humor. These often-undervalued qualities not only discourage the crisis mentality that demands immediate action but also counteract the aesthetic revulsion that drives many stasist prescriptions. The "Yuk factor"—as the bioethicist Tom Wilkie terms the inevitable, usually temporary, reaction to new biomedical techniques—applies in many other realms as well.[60] For many stasists, bad taste, or taste different from their own, is a public "problem," demanding immediate action. Rarely do they acknowledge that lousy aesthetics may simply be a matter of poverty or transition, much less that aesthetic tolerance, like religious tolerance or free speech, is a quality essential to maintaining a peaceful and dynamic society. To the contrary, their conviction that the future must be molded to a single standard makes aesthetics all the more important, a guide to the one best way.

So, for instance, the antiautomobile zealot James Howard Kuntsler justifies his attacks on cars and suburbs—and supports technocratic plans to impose his reactionary preferences—by citing "the ubiquitous panorama of eight-lane highways, strip malls, parking lagoons, fry pits, muffler shops, jive-plastic garden apartments, housing subdivisions, office 'parks,' and all the other familiar furnishings of the National Automobile slum."[61] In other words, *Yuk*. Identifying a similar theme, one reviewer aptly observes of *Jihad vs. McWorld* that "one note can be heard throughout Barber's discussion: a distaste for 'McWorld' in all its manifestations. Barber clearly abhors McDonald's, the evil empire itself, with its day-glo arches, plastic decor, factory food and tacky advertising. . . . I like many of the things that Barber likes—neighborhood stores, bistros, good food, good wine—but I try not to confuse my tastes with my politics."[62]

Dynamists maintain a sense of proportion about "jive-plastic garden apartments" and "day-glo arches." Some revel in variety and enjoy contemplating the niches such things fill, while others simply stick to bistros and boutiques. Either way, dynamists do not get hysterical over bad taste, or see impending doom in the "rambling, riding, rolling, rushing, justling, mixing, bouncing, cracking and crashing" of tumultuous times. They appreciate the comic side of life. "There's a lot of kitsch going in the world," says the trade lawyer Brink Lindsey, reflecting on his travels in Asia's cities on the verge. "When nobody's in control, the human comedy bursts forth in all kinds of tasteless and goofy directions. But it is *comic*. If you can loosen up and have any kind of sense of humor or irony about it—be it junk TV or *Beavis and Butt-head* or people walking around with completely inane English slogans on their T-shirts in Asia—it's humorous."[63] A dose of humor helps keep changes in perspective.

The party of life, the party that fears no "abyss" in the unfolding future, is itself the product of many verges. Dynamists are not like environmentalists, feminists, or countless other "-ists." They are not a self-conscious group united by a single identity or value, but, rather, an emergent cultural coalition, springing from many different interests and experiences. Every dynamic system—from evolving cities to the global economy, from social plenitude to scientific knowledge, from the Internet to the arts—provides a model in which instinctive dynamists can see general patterns. To create a dynamist alternative to the sterile stasist verge, then, means drawing together this wide array of passions and interests into a powerful fertile verge.

It is better, Machiavelli famously said, to be feared than loved. And stasists claim fear as an ally: fear of change, fear of the unknown, fear of comfortable routines thrown into confusion. They promise to make the world safe and predictable, if only we will trust them to design the future, if only they can impose their uniform plans. Those promises may be false, but they are also appealing. The open-ended future can be genuinely scary, the turmoil it creates genuinely painful.

Dynamists too have fear on their side: fear of stagnation, of poverty, of pain. Stasist prescriptions, we can say with conviction, stifle the very processes through which people improve their lives—from the invention of new medical treatments to the creation of art. In their quest for stability, stasists make society brittle, vulnerable to all sorts of disasters. They disregard and disrespect important knowledge, the specific knowledge through which we each shape our lives. They scorn pleasures not their own, improvements they did not conceive. They lock individuals into narrow status boundaries, blocking opportunity and self-definition. They are frighteningly intolerant.

As a political matter, then, dynamists rally not to guarantee themselves security or to impose their ideas on others, but to defend their own ventures from being wiped out. On this verge between dynamist principle and self-interested enterprise, we find the high-tech managers who want to hire skilled immigrants, the musicians who fear censorship, the home schoolers who want to teach their own children, the scientists who oppose bans on embryo research, the importers who support free trade, the Internet activists who seek to protect encryption, the builders who want to build. Their piecemeal efforts can be effective in the short term. Concentrated interest groups, as Mancur Olson observed, exercise enormous political clout on their specific issues.

But such efforts cannot reverse stasist assumptions. They cannot change the political–intellectual culture that demands that creators ask permission to create, that every experiment get approval in advance, that we choose the one best way. As long as that culture remains dominant, defensive efforts, motivated by the fear of stasist plans, must be repeated again and again, dissipating energies that would otherwise go into productive enterprises. While necessary, these piecemeal fights are too specific and too immediate to create a permanent fertile verge.

Fear, then, is not enough. Neither is self-interest. The dynamist verge must be bound by love: love of knowledge, love of exploration, love of adventure, and, just as much, love of small dreams, of the textures of life. These passions are broad enough to bring dynamists together across interests and disciplines, professional affiliations and cultural associations. Only then will the dynamist verge become truly fertile.

Some dynamists believe that the future must lie in bold ventures, private endeavors too grand to be contained in technocratic schemes: the terraforming and settlement of Mars, the doubling of human life span. Such big dreams, they argue, are important not only for their own sakes but to keep sclerosis at bay, to demonstrate that great things can still be done, that the sterile verge has not extinguished enterprise. The spirit of Tennyson's Ulysses—"to strive, to seek, to find, and not to yield"—is, they believe, the great tonic for a youthful culture.[64]

A verge, however, arises when two *different* things meet. The dynamist verge draws as much power from the love of the particular as from sweeping visions of adventure. While dramatic ventures can be invigorating, they can also make us lose sight of the amazing achievements that occur bit by bit: the contact lenses and credit card systems; the ever-lighter soda cans, ever-more-productive farms, ever-faster memory chips, ever-sharper printing; the painstaking advancement of techniques for surgery, for manufacturing, for distribution, for laboratory science, for hairstyling.

The dynamist verge cherishes these things too. It cares about intensive progress. And it perceives what stasists miss—the spectacular creativity and cumulative knowledge embedded in the things we take for granted: in the making of movies, the fabrics and shapes of our clothes, the subtle combinations of fine cuisine, the emotional impact of religious rituals, the arrangements of supermarkets, and the catalogs of libraries; in beach volleyball and bread machines, pianos and Post-it notes; in the inexpensive, portable, and varied music that permeates contemporary life. We live in an enchanted world, a world suffused with intelligence, a world of our making. In such plenitude, too, lies an adventurous future.

"It is in the process of learning," Hayek reminds us, "in the effects of having learned something new, that man enjoys the gift of his intelligence."[65] It is in curiosity, problem solving, and play that we discover who we are. These are the very qualities and activities that make the future unknown, and unknowable. On the verge between centuries, the dynamist promise is not of a particular, carefully outlined future. The future will be as grand, and as particular, as we are. We cannot build a single bridge from here to there, for neither here nor there is a single point. And there is no abyss to cross.

NOTES

In the notes that follow, I have provided URLs only for those sources that exist primarily or exclusively on the World Wide Web. Many other sources, including most of the articles from *Reason,* are also available online. Links to them and to other background material are available at www.dynamist.com.

INTRODUCTION:
THE SEARCH FOR TOMORROW

1. Tony Baxter, press conference and tour, Disneyland, Anaheim, California, April 24, 1998.
2. Jerry Hirsch, "Almost Time to Go Back to the Future," *The Register* (Orange County), February 10, 1998, p. A-1.
3. James Sterngold, "Is This Tomorrow? Nah. Yesterday," *The New York Times,* May 10, 1998, Sec. 4, p. 16.
4. Tim Appelo, "The Future Isn't What It Used to Be," *Los Angeles Times,* January 4, 1998, Calendar section, pp. 6, 77. Judith Adams strangely attributes the vision of technology as a "killing thing" to the popular comic strip *Dilbert,* which actually takes the exact opposite view. "Dilbert and I love technology on an emotional level," says Scott Adams, the strip's creator. One of the rules in the *Dilbert* licensing "bible" is that technology is good; licensees aren't allowed to portray it as bad. Scott Adams, e-mail to the author, March 8, 1998.
5. John M. Findlay, *Magic Lands: Western Cityscapes and American Culture After 1940* (Berkeley: University of California Press, 1992), pp. 52–116.
6. Steven Watts, *The Magic Kingdom: Walt Disney and the American Way of Life* (Boston: Houghton Mifflin, 1997), pp. 388, 402.
7. M. Mitchell Waldrop, *Complexity* (New York: Simon & Schuster, 1992), p. 334.
8. The phrase is from Frederick Turner, *Tempest, Flute, and Oz* (New York: Persea Books, 1991), pp. 6–33: "What universal solvents will ensure the liquidity and translatability of cultural value?" He suggests global telecommunications, international financial markets, global environmental problems, and "the rhythm of contemporary popular music."

CHAPTER ONE
THE ONE BEST WAY

1. "Through the Looking Glass," *Crossfire*, CNN, January 2, 1995.
2. Patrick J. Buchanan, *The Great Betrayal: How American Sovereignty and Social Justice Are Sacrificed to the Gods of the Global Economy* (New York: Little, Brown, 1998).
3. "Broadest Range of American Political Spectrum Ever to Jointly Petition a President Call [*sic*] for GATT Vote Postponement," news release, August 8, 1994; "Statement by Ralph Nader on the Proposed World Trade Organization and the Letter to President Clinton," August 8, 1994; letter to President Bill Clinton, August 8, 1994.
4. Sara Catania, "Zealots Target Sierra Club," *L.A. Weekly*, February 20–26, 1998, p. 17.
5. Patrick J. McDonnell and Paul Jacobs, "FAIR at Forefront of Push to Reduce Immigration," *Los Angeles Times*, November 29, 1993, p. A-1; Linda Chavez, "What to Do About Immigration," *Commentary* (March 1995): 34–35; Marla Cone, "Sierra Club to Remain Neutral on Immigration," *Los Angeles Times*, April 26, 1998, p. A-1; John H. Cushman, Jr., "Sierra Club Rejects Move to Oppose Immigration," *The New York Times*, April 26, 1998, p. 14; Al Martinez, "And All the Trees Were Singing," *Los Angeles Times*, May 1, 1998, p. B-1; "Population Ballot Question," at tamalpais.sierraclub.org/sc%5Felections/1998/pop.htm.
6. Neil Postman, "Science and the Story That We Need," *First Things* (January 1997): 29.
7. Larry B. Stammer and Robert Lee Hotz, "Faiths United to Oppose Patents on Life Forms," *Los Angeles Times*, May 18, 1995, p. A-1; "Statement of Dr. Richard D. Land, Executive Director, The Christian Life Commission of the Southern Baptist Convention," National Press Club, May 18, 1995; "Statement by Jeremy Rifkin, President, Foundation of Economic Trends," Joint Appeal Against Human and Animal Patenting press conference, May 18, 1995.
8. Bob Ickes, "Die, Computer, Die!" *New York*, July 24, 1995, pp. 22–26.
9. *The Weekly Standard*, October 30, 1995.
10. Brian Murray, "The Rebel in the Gray Flannel Suit," *The Weekly Standard*, January 19, 1998, p. 37.
11. Thomas Frank, "Just Break the Rules: Business and Bad Values," *The Washington Post*, June 11, 1995, p. C-1.
12. Paul Starobin, "Rethinking Capitalism," *National Journal*, January 18, 1997, p. 106.
13. Gary Chapman, "When High Technology Stoops Low," *Los Angeles Times*, February 9, 1998, p. D-6.
14. "Turn for Better in Fuel Crisis," *U.S. News & World Report*, January 28, 1974, pp. 13–14.
15. John Kenneth Galbraith, *The New Industrial State* (Boston: Houghton Mifflin, 1967), pp. 11–34, 71.
16. Historically, there have also been important radical utopian futurists—notably

Marx, Saint-Simon, and their intellectual progeny—who prescribed or foretold a transformation of humanity on the way to a teleologically determined future. They do not, however, play a significant role today. Both their teleology and their utopianism have been largely discredited. While their remaining followers theoretically constitute a third party of stasis, which imagines an eventual and inevitable shift to a hence-unchanging state of the world, nowadays they tend to ally with either reactionaries or technocrats.

17. Patrick J. Buchanan, "On the Altar of 'Global Trade,'" syndicated column, Tribune Media Services, October 4, 1994.

18. Edward Goldsmith, *The Way: An Ecological World-View*, rev. and enl. ed. (Athens, Ga.: University of Georgia Press, 1998), p. 13.

19. "Industrial Society and Its Future," a supplement to *The Washington Post*, September 19, 1995, pp. 2, 6.

20. Arthur Schlesinger, Jr., "Has Democracy a Future?" *Foreign Affairs* (September–October 1997): 7–8.

21. Jacques Attali, "The Crash of Western Civilization: The Limits of the Market and Democracy," *Foreign Policy* (Summer 1997): 60–61.

22. E. F. Schumacher, *Small Is Beautiful: Economics As If People Mattered* (New York: Harper & Row, 1973), p. 33.

23. Christopher Lasch, *The True and Only Heaven: Progress and Its Critics* (New York: Norton, 1991), p. 39.

24. Fred Charles Iklé, "Growth Without End, Amen?" *National Review* March 7, 1994, pp. 36–44. Fred C. Iklé, "The Perils of Xenophilia," *The National Interest* (Summer 1995): 94–96.

25. Iklé, "Perils of Xenophilia," p. 95.

26. *Gemeinschaft* and *Gesellschaft* are rich sociological terms that distinguish traditional premodern societies from capitalistic ones. One short definition is "tight communal bonding versus cosmopolitan liberty"; see Charles Heckscher, *White-Collar Blues: Management Loyalties in an Age of Corporate Restructuring* (New York: Basic Books, 1995), p. 33. Others emphasize the importance of physical proximity to *Gemeinschaft* and implicit or explicit contracts to *Gesellschaft*.

27. "The National Prospect," *Commentary* (November 1995): 80. Edward Luttwak, "Turbo-Charged Capitalism and Its Consequences," *London Review of Books*, November 2, 1995, p. 7.

28. Charlotte Allen, "Why Don't Republicans Hate Disney's America?" *The Washington Monthly* (May 1994): 11, 13. Lack of hyphenation of Wal-Mart is in the original.

29. Twelve Southerners, *I'll Take My Stand: The South and the Agrarian Tradition* (New York: Harper & Row, 1930, 1962 ed.) pp. xxvi–xxvii.

30. Ibid., p. 4.

31. Sally Bedell Smith, "Billionaire with a Cause," *Vanity Fair* (May 1997): 134–144, 195–199. With a lifestyle that included five lavish homes in four countries, to which he traveled in his own Boeing 757, James Goldsmith clearly did not prescribe the peasant life for himself, only for others.

32. Sir James Goldsmith, *The Trap* (New York: Carroll & Graf Publishers, 1994), p. 39.

33. John Gray, *Beyond the New Right: Markets, Government and the Common Environment* (London: Routledge, 1993), pp. 124–177. Goldsmith thanks Gray on the acknowledgments page of *The Trap*, p. 5.

34. Donald Worster, *The Wealth of Nature: Environmental History and the Ecological Imagination* (New York: Oxford University Press, 1993), pp. 66, 179. Worster's work is discussed in greater depth in Chapter 6.

35. Goldsmith, *The Way*, pp. 137–138.

36. Kirkpatrick Sale, *Human Scale* (New York: Coward, McCann, 1980), p. 392.

37. "Currents," *Utne Reader* (July–August 1995): 37.

38. Sale, *Human Scale*, p. 396.

39. Jeremy Rifkin with Ted Howard, *Entropy: A New World View* (New York: Bantam Books, 1980), pp. 214, 216.

40. Adam Werbach, *Act Now, Apologize Later* (New York: HarperCollins, 1997), pp. 235–237.

41. Schumacher, *Small Is Beautiful*, pp. 58, 68.

42. Eugene D. Genovese, *The Southern Tradition: The Achievement and Limitations of an American Conservatism* (Cambridge: Harvard University Press, 1994), pp. 1–2, 23.

43. Lasch, *The True and Only Heaven*, pp. 487–488. It is important to note that Lasch does not simply sympathize with working-class people in their struggles against high-handed treatment by political elites. Rather, he endorses their values and cultural attitudes.

44. Tom Carson, "Buchanan's Ride: On the Campaign Trail with the Happiest Man in America," *The Village Voice*, August 29, 1995, p. 18.

45. Peter Beinart, "The Nationalist Revolt," *The New Republic*, December 1, 1997, pp. 24–26.

46. Theodore Roosevelt is quoted in John Morton Blum, *The Progressive Presidents: Roosevelt, Wilson, Roosevelt, Johnson,* (New York: Norton, 1980), p. 45.

47. Herbert Croly, *The Promise of American Life*, introduction by John William Ward (Indianapolis: Bobbs-Merrill, 1965), p. 5.

48. John M. Jordan, *Machine-Age Ideology: Social Engineering and American Liberalism, 1911–1939* (Chapel Hill: University of North Carolina Press, 1994), p. 66.

49. The quote is from Judsen Culbreth, editor of *Working Mother*, on *CNN Early Prime*, October 23, 1997.

50. Bill Clinton, State of the Union Address, January 27, 1998, available at www.whitehouse.gov/WH/SOTU98/address.html.

51. Phil Frame, spokesman for the National Highway Traffic Safety Administration, quoted in Matthew L. Wald, "Hard Line on Air Bags," *The New York Times*, October 31, 1997, p. F-1. NHTSA subsequently relaxed its rules somewhat, but it still grants permits for air bag shutoff switches only to people whose heights, medical conditions, or number of children constitute "valid" reasons for deactivating the bags. Warren Brown and Cindy Skrzycki, "U.S. to Allow Air Bag Cutoff Switches," *The Washington Post*, November 18, 1997, p. A-1.

52. White House Domestic Policy Council, *The President's Health Security Plan*, introduction by Erik Eckholm (New York: Times Books, 1993).

53. Jordan, *Machine-Age Ideology*, p. 106.
54. Newt Gingrich with David Drake and Marianne Gingrich, *Window of Opportunity: A Blueprint for the Future* (New York: Tor Books, 1984), pp. 74–79.
55. Julie Pitta, "Laissez-faire Not Spoken Here," *Forbes*, December 1, 1997, p. 58; Amy Harmon, "Why the French Hate the Internet," *Los Angeles Times*, January 27, 1997, p. A-1. Jay McCormick, "Language of Love Is Left on the Lurch on the Net," *USA Today*, January 9, 1997, p. 9A. Kim Thomas, "Keyed Up and Ready for Battle," *Financial Times*, August 20, 1996, p. 9.
56. Newt Gingrich, *To Renew America* (New York: HarperCollins, 1995), pp. 191–192, and *Window of Opportunity*, pp. 40–67.
57. *20/20*, ABC, May 29, 1992.
58. Joe Klein, "Who Are These People?" *Newsweek*, August 21, 1995, p. 31; Beinart, "The Nationalist Revolt," p. 26.
59. Robert Guskind, "Border Backlash," *National Journal*, June 4, 1994, p. 1299.
60. Tom Hayden, *Reunion: A Memoir* (New York: Random House, 1988), p. 97.
61. Richard Sclove and Jeffrey Scheuer, "On the Road Again? If Information Highways Are Anything Like Interstate Highways—Watch Out!," in Rob Kling, ed., *Computerization and Controversy: Value Conflict and Social Choices*, 2d ed. (San Diego: Academic Press, 1996), pp. 606–612. For a dynamist critique of Sclove and Scheuer, see Sara Baase, "Impacts on Communities: Comments on Sclove and Scheuer," *Computers and Society* (December 1997): 15–17.
62. "Summary of The 21st Century Project," directed by Gary Chapman, www.utexas.edu/lbj/21cp/summary.html.
63. Gary Chapman, testimony before the House Committee on Science, Space, and Technology, Subcommittee on Science, September 7, 1994, available at www.utexas.edu/lbj/21cp/testimony.html.
64. Clara Jeffery and David M. Noer, "Does America Still Work?" *Harper's Magazine* (May 1996): 35; Edward Luttwak, "Buchanan Has It Right," *London Review of Books*, May 9, 1996, pp. 6–8.
65. Joseph Nocera writes in *Fortune:* "In a less litigious society, a government official would be able to say out loud that a medical device needed further study, and that's what would happen: There would be further study. Instead, Kessler's call for an implant moratorium became the spark that finally lit the blaze. Within weeks, 100 lawsuits had become 1,000 lawsuits. The stampede had begun." Joseph Nocera, "Fatal Litigation," *Fortune*, October 16, 1995, p. 74. See also Michael Fumento, "A Confederacy of Boobs," *Reason* (October 1995): 36–43.
66. David A. Kessler, "The Basis of the FDA's Decision on Breast Implants," *New England Journal of Medicine*, June 18, 1992, pp. 1713–1715.
67. Marcia Angell, *Science on Trial: The Clash of Medical Evidence and the Law in the Breast Implant Case* (New York: Norton, 1996), p. 63.
68. Curtis J. Sitomer, "Genetic Engineering," *The Christian Science Monitor*, September 25, 1986, p. 16.
69. Jeremy Rifkin, *Algeny* (New York: Viking Press, 1983), cover blurb on 1984 Penguin paperback edition.
70. Al Gore, *Earth in the Balance: Ecology and the Human Spirit* (Boston: Houghton Mifflin, 1992), pp. 269, 274.

CHAPTER TWO
THE PARTY OF LIFE

1. Jim Dowe, speech at Third Annual Bionomics Conference, Redwood City, California, October 20, 1995.
2. Paul Krugman, "The Power of Biobabble," *Slate,* October 23, 1997, www.slate.com/Dismal/97-10-23/Dismal.asp.
3. William Gruber, "Rollback Urged on Depression-Era Finance Laws; Competition, Innovation Are Treasury Themes," *Chicago Tribune,* November 18, 1997, Business section, p. 3.
4. David Ignatius, "The Marx Mistake," *The Washington Monthly* (April 1997): 42–45. Ignatius has since quit as a business editor and become a columnist.
5. Michael Hirsch, "The Evils of Markets," *Newsweek,* February 10, 1997, p. 67.
6. Walter A. McDougall, "The Death of Technocracy," *The Wall Street Journal,* October 3, 1997, p. A10.
7. Madhusree Mukerjee, "Seeing the World in a Snowflake," *Scientific American* (March 1996): 36–42.
8. Tom Peters, interview with the author, May 15, 1997, published as "The Peters Principles," *Reason* (October 1997): 45–46. Peters attributes these metaphors to others: Henry Mintzberg, author of *The Rise and Fall of Strategic Planning,* and Arie de Geus, author of *The Living Company.*
9. Jane Jacobs, *The Death and Life of Great American Cities* (New York: Vintage Books, 1961) pp. 428–448.
10. Joel Garreau, *Edge City: Life on the New Frontier* (New York: Anchor Books, 1991) p. 9.
11. Kevin Kelly, *Out of Control: The Rise of Neo-Biological Civilization* (Reading, Mass.: Addison-Wesley, 1994).
12. Grant McCracken, *Plenitude* (Toronto: Periph.: Fluide, 1997), p. 18.
13. Jonathan Rauch, *The Outnation: A Search for the Soul of Japan* (Boston: Harvard Business School Press, 1992), *Kindly Inquisitors: The New Attacks on Free Thought* (Chicago: University of Chicago Press, 1993), and *Demosclerosis: The Silent Killer of American Government* (New York: Times Books, 1994).
14. Stewart Brand, *How Buildings Learn: What Happens After They're Built* (New York: Penguin, 1994), pp. 188–189.
15. Esther Dyson, interview with the author, February 24, 1996, published as "On the Frontier," *Reason* (October 1996): 28–34.
16. Friedrich A. Hayek, *The Constitution of Liberty* (Chicago: University of Chicago Press, 1960) p. 408.
17. Walter Truett Anderson, *Evolution Isn't What It Used to Be: The Augmented Animal and the Whole Wired World* (San Francisco: W. H. Freeman & Co., 1996), p. 33.
18. Brink Lindsey, interview with the author, April 12, 1996. At the time of the interview, Lindsey was an attorney with Wilkie Farr & Gallagher in Washington, D.C. He now directs trade policy studies at the Cato Institute.
19. Julian Simon, "The Five Greatest Years for Humanity," *Wired* (January 1998): 68.

20. Richard Barbook and Andy Cameron, "The Californian Ideology," *Science as Culture* 6, p. 1 (1996): 44–72. Barbook and Cameron fill their article with paeans to French technocracy and Saint-Simonist utopianism and conclude, "The developers of hypermedia must reassert the possibility of rational and conscious control over the shape of the digital future."

21. John Perry Barlow, in "What Are We Doing On-Line?" *Harper's Magazine* (August 1995): 36.

22. Tom Peters, interview with the author, p. 44.

23. Jim Belcher, interview with the author, October 21, 1997.

24. Kenneth Labich, "Kissing Off Corporate America," *Fortune*, February 20, 1995, pp. 44–62. The recruiter is Steve Brashear of Hewlett-Packard.

25. Daniel H. Pink, "Free Agent Nation," *Fast Company* (December–January 1998): 131–146; speech at "Workforce Challenges: Employment Policy for a Dynamic World," Center for Market Processes Legislative Staff Retreat, Annapolis, Maryland, February 18, 1998; interview with the author, March 21, 1998.

26. Tom Peters, *Liberation Management: Necessary Disorganization for the Nanosecond Nineties* (New York: Knopf, 1992), p. 497.

27. Frederick Turner, interview with the author, March 16, 1996.

28. Martha S. Siegel, "Anarchy, Chaos on the Internet Must End," *San Francisco Chronicle*, January 2, 1995, p. A19. The absence of "firm direction" does not mean an absence of rules, nor does it imply an "anything goes" culture. Indeed, Siegel's discontent with the Internet's lack of central authority probably stems from her experiences after violating its mores; she and her husband "spammed," or mass e-mailed, advertising for their legal services and were ostracized for breaking Internet custom prohibiting such mass commercial mailings.

29. Mike Godwin, interview with the author, October 29, 1996.

30. Mitchel Resnick, "Changing the Centralized Mind," *Technology Review* (July 1994): 33–34.

31. Herbert A. Simon, *The Sciences of the Artificial*, 2d ed. (Cambridge: MIT Press, 1981), p. 40.

32. Glenn Garvin, "Reaping the Whirlwind," *Reason* (January 1993): 26–31.

33. Arian Ward, "Reengineering and Its Discontents," letter to the editor, *Fast Company* (April–May 1996): 18.

34. Arian Ward, interview with the author, April 3, 1996.

35. James K. Glassman, "A Credo, Not a Contract," *The Washington Post*, April 2, 1996, p. A13.

36. James Glassman, interview with the author, November 15, 1995.

37. Hayek, *The Constitution of Liberty*, p. 400.

38. Garreau, *Edge City*, p. 9.

39. Aaron Wildavsky, "Progress and Public Policy," in *Progress and Its Discontents*, ed. Gabriel A. Almond, Marvin Chodorow, and Roy Harvey Pearce (Berkeley: University of California Press, 1982), p. 366.

40. Richard Cohen, "A Man with a Wallet," *The Washington Post*, February 6, 1996, p. A15.

41. Steve Forbes press conference, Irvine, California, January 10, 1996.
42. *Inside Politics,* CNN, March 14, 1996.
43. "Indecency" is a legal category, distinct from "obscenity," that includes speech that is constitutionally protected in print but has been prohibited in broadcasting on the grounds that it is unfit for children. Radio shock jock Howard Stern is the most famous recent violator of indecency regulations; George Carlin's "Seven Dirty Words" routine is the most famous historical example.
44. Congressmen Christopher Cox and Ron Wyden, press release, June 30, 1995, p. 2.
45. Lynn Scarlett, interview with the author, December 21, 1997.
46. Godwin, interview with the author.
47. Randal O'Toole, interview with the author, December 12, 1997. During the 1980s, O'Toole studied the forest plans from more than half the national forests and came to the conclusion that the only way to explain the seemingly inexplicable behavior of the foresters was that they were responding to the incentives established by Congress and doing what maximized their budgets. In some cases, the response was ingenious. National forests are given no money for prescribed burning (which is necessary to allow sequoia seeds to germinate) unless the fire is part of a reforestation effort. So Sequoia National Forest clear-cut forty acres, leaving only one giant sequoia standing. It then did the burn, to allow the seeds from that tree to grow. Unfortunately, the shade from a single tree was insufficient to shelter the seedlings, and O'Toole could find only a single one surviving when he visited the forest.
48. Rauch, *Demosclerosis,* pp. 145, 178.
49. Mike Godwin, *Cyber Rights: Defending Free Speech in the Digital Age* (New York: Times Books, 1998), p. 300.
50. Thomas Sowell, *The Economics and Politics of Race: An International Perspective* (New York: Quill, 1983), pp. 243, 257.
51. Stephen Toulmin, *Cosmopolis: The Hidden Agenda of Modernity* (New York: Free Press, 1990) pp. 178–179.
52. Jonathan Kaufman, "How Cambodians Came to Control California Doughnuts," *The Wall Street Journal,* February 22, 1995, p. A-1.
53. Bob Secter, "Pol Pot Reprise. Who's Guarding the Guardians?" *Chicago Tribune,* August 3, 1997, Perspective section, p. 1. The Cambodian killing fields are a monument to what it really takes to turn even a less-developed modern society into the green-reactionary dream of a world without cities, trade, technology, or knowledge workers.
54. Jesse H. Ausubel, "Regularities in Technological Development: An Environmental View," *Technology and Environment,* eds. Jesse H. Ausubel and Hedy E. Sladovich (Washington, D.C.: National Academy Press, 1989), p. 72.
55. Robert H. Williams, Eric D. Larson, and Marc H. Ross, "Materials, Affluence, and Industrial Energy Use," *Annual Review of Energy* (1987), pp. 99–144.
56. John Tierney, "Betting on the Planet," *The New York Times Magazine,* December 2, 1990, pp. 52–53, 74–81: "In October 1980 the Ehrlich group bet $1,000 on five metals—chrome, copper, nickel, tin and tungsten—in quantities that each cost $200 in the current market. A futures contract was drawn up oblig-

ating Simon to sell [Ehrlich's group] these same quantities of the metals 10 years later, but at 1980 prices. If the 1990 combined prices turned out to be higher than $1,000, Simon would pay them the difference in cash. If prices fell, they would pay him. . . . The bet was settled this fall without ceremony. Ehrlich did not even bother to write a letter. He simply mailed Simon a sheet of calculations about metal prices—along with a check for $576.07. . . . Each of the five metals chosen by Ehrlich's group, when adjusted for inflation since 1980, had declined in price. The drop was so sharp, in fact, that Simon would have come out slightly ahead overall even without the inflation adjustment called for in the bet."

57. *Charlie Rose Show,* PBS, "America and the World Today," December 17, 1997.
58. Michael Cox, interview with the author, November 1995. Cox is vice president of the Federal Reserve Bank of Dallas. My experience growing up in Greenville, South Carolina, in the 1960s and 1970s mirrors Cox's. The coming of chains did not destroy the few locally originated restaurants; it merely added to the variety available to a growing and increasingly prosperous population.
59. Benjamin R. Barber, *Jihad vs. McWorld: How Globalism and Tribalism Are Reshaping the World* (New York: Times Books, 1996). Barber, who is deeply distressed by choice-driven processes that aren't controlled by articulate intellectuals, is striking in his ability to turn snob appeal into political philosophy. Unlike Friedman, who just worries about losing local color, Barber draws remarkable moral equivalences: "In East Berlin, tribal communism has yielded to capitalism. In Marx-Engelsplatz, the stolid, overbearing statues of Marx and Engels face east, as if seeking distant solace from Moscow: but now, circling them along the streets that surround the park that is their prison, are chain eateries like T.G.I. Friday's, international hotels like the Radisson, and a circle of neon billboards mocking them with brand names like Panasonic, Coke, and GoldStar. New gods, yes, but more liberty?" (p. 6).
60. Paul Frumkin, "Tomorrow's Customer: A Look at the Future," *Nation's Restaurant News,* October 27, 1997, p. 74. The quote is from Lonnie Schiller, president and co-owner of Schiller Del Grande Restaurant Group, speaking on a panel at the Multi-Unit Food Service Owners 1997 convention.
61. McCracken, *Plenitude,* p. 67.

Chapter Three
The Infinite Series

1. Associated Press, "Unabomber's Letter," *The Charleston Gazette,* April 27, 1995, p. P3A. Howard Kurtz and John Schwartz, "FBI Releases Letter in 'Unabom' Case; Message to Earlier Mail-Bomb Victim Decries 'Techno-Nerds,' " *The Washington Post.* April 27, 1995. Other material on Gelernter and the bomb is taken from Steven Levy, "The Unabomber and David Gelernter," *The New York Times Magazine,* May 21, 1995, p. 50, and David Gelernter, *Drawing Life: Surviving the Unabomber* (New York: Free Press, 1997).
2. David Gelernter, "Unplugged," *The New Republic,* September 19 and 26, 1994, p. 14.

3. David Gelernter, "Wiretaps for a Wireless Age," *The New York Times*, May 8, 1994, sec. 4, p. 17.
4. Gelernter, *Drawing Life*, p. 28.
5. David Gelernter, "The Immorality of Environmentalism," *City Journal* (Autumn 1996): p. 22.
6. David Gelernter, *1939: The Lost World of the Fair* (New York: Free Press, 1995), p. 273.
7. Kirkpatrick Sale, "Heed the Message, Not the Messenger," *Los Angeles Times*, September 20, 1995, p. B-9.
8. This phrase is from Stanley Lebergott, *Pursuing Happiness: American Consumers in the Twentieth Century* (Princeton: Princeton University Press, 1993), p. 35.
9. John Gray, *Beyond the New Right: Markets, Government and the Common Environment* (London: Routledge, 1993), p. 139.
10. Friedrich A. Hayek, *The Constitution of Liberty* (Chicago: University of Chicago Press, 1960), p. 41.
11. In later writings, Hayek himself suggested a stronger claim: that civilization is an evolutionary process, discovering by trial and error an "extended order" of institutions that allows larger populations to survive. F. A. Hayek, *The Fatal Conceit: The Errors of Socialism* (Chicago: University of Chicago Press, 1988).
12. Christopher Lasch, *The True and Only Heaven: Progress and Its Critics* (New York: Norton, 1991), pp. 47–48.
13. Joel Mokyr, *The Lever of Riches: Technological Creativity and Economic Progress* (New York: Oxford University Press, 1990), pp. 54, 71.
14. A. G. Sabell, "The History of Contact Lenses," in Anthony J. Phillips and Janet Stone, eds., *Contact Lenses: A Textbook for Practitioner and Student*, 3d ed. (London: Butterworths, 1989), pp. 1–31. Additional information taken from Contact Lens Council fact sheet, "Important Dates in Contact Lens History."
15. Another obsessed inventor's determination gave us soft contact lenses. The original polymer gel was developed by Czechoslovakian researchers looking for a general material compatible with living tissue. After six years of experiments to apply it to contact lenses, the Czechoslovakian Ministry of Health stopped the research. Sure that the idea had promise, chemist Otto Wichterle continued working on it in his kitchen, and after a year or so succeeded, "using a procedure which the specialists in optics regarded as absurd and unrealistic, that is, by polymerization in open rotating moulds." Using an improvised device, he and his wife produced 5,500 lenses, which were then successfully tested. The process was soon licensed to Bausch & Lomb. See Otto Wichterle, "The Beginning of the Soft Lens," in Montague Ruben, ed., *Soft Contact Lenses: Clinical and Applied Technology* (New York: Wiley, 1978), pp. 3–5. A major goal of soft lenses was to permit mass production in standard sizes, thereby allowing disposable lenses. Driving down manufacturing costs took decades of incremental improvements. Daily disposables became available in the United States in 1995, thirty-four years after Wichterle's kitchen success. See also Virginia Postrel, "The Spirit of Play," *Forbes* (September 21, 1998):102.
16. Henry Petroski, *The Evolution of Useful Things* (New York: Knopf, 1992), p. 22.
17. Ibid., pp. 84–86.

18. Ibid., p. 26. The man quoted is David Pye.
19. Harry E. Teasley, Jr., "Thriving in the Future," in Richard M. Ebeling, ed., *The Future of American Business* (Hillsdale, Mich.: Hillsdale College Press, 1996) pp. 118–119.
20. Scott Rawlins, "The Real Story on Pesticide Use," American Farm Bureau Federation, June 5, 1996, p. 3.
21. John Horgan, *The End of Science: Facing the Limits of Knowledge in the Twilight of the Scientific Age* (Reading, Mass.: Helix Books, Addison-Wesley, 1996).
22. Paul Romer, speech at Reason Weekend, Scottsdale, Arizona, March 22, 1996.
23. *Visions of Light*, American Film Institute documentary, 1994.
24. Christopher Marlowe is credited in the literary imagination with the invention of blank verse, because he was the first poet-playwright to demonstrate its power. It was, however, first used in drama by Thomas Sackville and Thomas Norton in *Gorboduc*, a mostly forgotten play written several decades before Marlowe's *Tamburlaine*. Russell A. Fraser and Norman Rabkin, eds., *Drama of the English Renaissance: The Tudor Period* (New York: Macmillan, 1976), p. 81.
25. Herbert A. Simon, *The Sciences of the Artificial*, 2d ed. (Cambridge: MIT Press, 1981), pp. 189–190.
26. Grant McCracken, *Plenitude* (Toronto: Periph.: Fluide, 1997), pp. 18, 22–26, 44, 53–54.
27. Gelernter, *1939*, p. 149.
28. Ibid., p. 262.
29. Ibid., p. 259.
30. Susan Jonas and Marilyn Nissenson, *Going, Going, Gone: Vanishing Americana* (San Francisco: Chronicle Books, 1994), pp. 128–129.
31. Carol J. Williams, "Russian Voters Are Aligned by Age, Gender," *Los Angeles Times*, June 16, 1996, pp. A-1, A-8.
32. Peter Passell, "Soviet Economy: Red Storm Ebbs," *The New York Times*, April 25, 1990, p. D-2. Robert Pear, "Evolution in Europe: Soviet Experts Say Their Economy Is Worse Than U.S. Has Estimated," *The New York Times*, April 24, 1990, p. A-14. Nicholas Eberstadt, *The Tyranny of Numbers: Mismeasurement and Misrule* (Washington, D.C.: AEI Press, 1995), pp. 136–149.
33. Advisory Commission to Study the Consumer Price Index, Michael J. Boskin, chairman, *Toward a More Accurate Measure of the Cost of Living: Final Report to the Senate Finance Committee*, December 4, 1996.
34. Dean Baker, "The Overstated CPI—Can It Really Be True?" *Challenge* (September–October 1996): 31. This article was based on a preliminary report, but Baker expressed similar sentiments about the final document as well.
35. Stephanie Mills, *Whatever Happened to Ecology?* (San Francisco: Sierra Club Books, 1989), p. 106.
36. N. Suresh, "Sustained Advertising Promoting Unsustainable Consumption," Consumer Unity and Trust Society Briefing Paper No. 2, April 1996. Toothbrushes and toothpaste come in for particular attack as indicators of creeping consumerism: "Till recently, in rural India, people used neem twigs as a pasteless tooth brush. And some use medicinal preparations as tooth powder. Today, the colour TV ads hardsell the healthy advantages of using angled, plas-

tic toothbrushes made from Du Pont bristles and mint-flavoured toothpastes [and] the virtues of using foaming, fluoride-based toothpastes. Some 250 million tooth brushes were sold in India in 1995. Toothpaste consumption increased from 39,610 tonnes in 1993 to 43,000 tonnes in 1994. The rural share of toothpaste is now 38 per cent—an increase of 10 percentage points in six years." These numbers are designed to be frightening indicators of "unsustainable consumption," not heartening indicators of progress.

37. Gray, *Beyond the New Right*, p. 127.
38. Daniel Bell, *The Cultural Contradictions of Capitalism* (New York: Basic Books, 1976), pp. 65–66, 70.
39. Theodore Roszak, "The Case Against Computers: A Systemic Critique," panel discussion, Computers, Freedom, and Privacy conference, San Francisco, March 28–31, 1995.
40. Gray, *Beyond the New Right*, pp. 137–138.
41. Joel Mokyr, "Progress and Inertia in Technological Change," in John A. James and Mark Thomas, eds., *Capitalism in Context: Essays on Economic Development and Cultural Change in Honor of R. M. Hartwell* (Chicago: University of Chicago Press, 1994), p. 234.
42. Isadore Rosenfeld, "Health Report," *Vogue*, June 1994, p. 122.
43. U.S. House of Representatives, *Unsolicited Bank Credit Cards: Hearings Before the Committee on Banking and Currency*, November 8–9, 1968, p. 8.
44. Phillip Brooke, "Bank Credit Cards Face Strong Pressure from Consumers, Legislators for Restrictions," *American Banker*, May 21, 1971, pp. 1, 27. My sometime research assistant, Nick Schulz, notes with amusement that he has a Visa card from the Wright Patman Congressional Federal Credit Union: "Every purchase I make must make him turn in his grave."
45. Joseph Nocera, *A Piece of the Action: How the Middle Class Joined the Money Class* (New York: Simon & Schuster, 1994), p. 54.
46. Aaron Wildavsky, *Searching for Safety* (New Brunswick, N.J.: Transaction Books, 1988), pp. 77–78.
47. For further exploration of this dichotomy, using the contrasting strategies of Silicon Valley and the Boston-area high-tech community as examples, see Virginia Postrel, "Resilience vs. Anticipation," *Forbes ASAP*, August 25, 1997, pp. 57–61.
48. Michael Oakes, "Shaky Recovery," *Reason* (January 1998): 31. The official quoted is Kiyoyuki Kanemitsu, director of the Kobe city government's international affairs division.
49. Leslie Helm, "Kobe Is Watched for Clues to Japanese Direction," *Los Angeles Times*, February 5, 1995, p. D-1; Teresa Watanabe, "Hammering Home a Point," *Los Angeles Times*, February 17, 1995, p. D-1.
50. Kirk Johnson, "Retail Competition Brings Service, and Smiles," *The New York Times*, May 27, 1996, p. A-1.
51. Freeman Dyson, *From Eros to Gaia* (New York: Pantheon Books, 1992), p. 56.
52. Ibid., pp. 54–56. Also, James Bennett and Phillip Salin, *Privatizing Space Transportation*, Reason Foundation Study #102, March 6, 1987.
53. Kevin Flynn, Lynn Bartels, Ann Imse, and John Rebchook, "What Was Said,

What Really Happened," *Rocky Mountain News,* February 25, 1996, p. 17A.
54. Arthur Hodges, "DIA: One Year Later," *The Denver Post,* February 25, 1996, p. A-1. Also, Kevin Flynn and Lynn Bartels, "Trying Its Wings," *Rocky Mountain News,* February 25, 1995, 1996, p. 16A.
55. David Frum, *Dead Right* (New York: Basic Books, 1994), pp. 190, 196–197.
56. Edward J. Kane, *The S&L Insurance Mess: How Did It Happen?* (Washington, D.C.: Urban Institute Press, 1989), pp. 5–6.
57. U.S. General Accounting Office, *Financial Audit: Resolution Trust Corporation's 1995 and 1994 Financial Statements* (July 1996), pp. 13, 19.
58. Robert A. Caro, *The Power Broker: Robert Moses and the Fall of New York* (New York: Vintage Books, 1974), pp. 508, 557.
59. Robert Moses, *Working for the People: Promise and Performance in Public Services* (New York: Harper & Brothers, 1956), p. 112.
60. Caro, *The Power Broker,* pp. 961–983.
61. Martin Anderson, *The Federal Bulldozer* (New York: McGraw-Hill Paperbacks, 1967), p. 52–54.
62. Chester W. Hartman, "Lessons for Urban Planners," in Sean M. Fisher and Carolyn Hughes, eds., *The Last Tenement: Confronting Community and Urban Renewal in Boston's West End* (Boston: Bostonian Society, 1992), p. 72. Hartman's survey of former West End residents found that more than a quarter were living in substandard housing two years after displacement and 86 percent were paying more for housing. Median rent had risen by 73 percent.
63. Anderson, *The Federal Bulldozer,* p. 2.
64. Ibid., p. x.
65. Sidney Plotkin, *Keep Out: The Struggle for Land Use Control* (Berkeley: University of California Press, 1987), p. 7.
66. Dyson, *From Eros to Gaia,* p. 243.

Chapter Four
The Tree of Knowledge

1. Steve Gibson, interview with the author, November 8, 1995. At the time of the interview, Gibson was the executive director of the Bionomics Institute. He is now vice president for finance at Maxager Technology Inc.
2. Amy M. Spindler, "Are Retail Consultants Missing Fashion's X-Factor?" *The New York Times,* June 13, 1996, p. B8.
3. Walter Olson, panel discussion on industrial policy, American Enterprise Institute policy conference, Washington, D.C., December 3, 1996.
4. "If They're So Smart, Why Aren't They Rich?" *Forbes* (Fall 1983, special issue): 228.
5. Charles H. Ferguson, "From the People Who Brought You Voodoo Economics," *Harvard Business Review* (May–June 1988): 55–62.
6. See Jane Jacobs, *The Death and Life of Great American Cities* (New York: Vintage Books, 1961). Martin Anderson, *The Federal Bulldozer* (New York: McGraw-Hill Paperbacks, 1967). Robert A. Caro, *The Power Broker: Robert Moses and the*

Fall of New York (New York: Vintage Books, 1974). Sean M. Fisher and Carolyn Hughes, eds. *The Last Tenement: Confronting Community and Urban Renewal in Boston's West End* (Boston: Bostonian Society, 1992). Robert Moses, *Working for the People: Promise and Performance in Public Services* (New York: Harper & Brothers, 1956).

7. Lynn Scarlett, chair of California's Inspection and Maintenance Review Committee, interviews with the author, October 1996. Also, Lynn Scarlett, "Smogged Down," *Reason* (December 1996): 67–70.

8. Freeman Dyson, *From Eros to Gaia* (New York: Pantheon Books, 1992), pp. 242–243.

9. Peter Drucker interview with Peter Schwartz and Kevin Kelly, "The Relentless Contrarian," *Wired* (August 1996): 182.

10. Michael Polanyi, *Personal Knowledge: Towards a Post-Critical Philosophy* (Chicago: University of Chicago Press, 1962), p. 31.

11. Wendell Berry, *The Unsettling of America: Culture and Agriculture* (San Francisco: Sierra Club Books, 1977), p. 21. This romantic contempt for specialized competence can be found even among people whose instincts make them at least borderline dynamists. The late science-fiction writer Robert A. Heinlein wrote, in the voice of a fictional character, that "a human being should be able to change a diaper, plan an invasion, butcher a hog, conn a ship, design a building, write a sonnet, balance accounts, build a wall, set a bone, comfort the dying, take orders, give orders, cooperate, act alone, solve equations, analyze a new problem, pitch manure, program a computer, cook a tasty meal, fight efficiently, die gallantly. Specialization is for insects." The character was, however, essentially immortal, a rare condition that makes specialization less necessary. Robert A. Heinlein, *Time Enough for Love* (New York: Berkeley Medallion/G. P. Putnam's Sons, 1973), p. 248.

12. David Gelernter, *Mirror Worlds: The Day Software Puts the Universe in a Shoebox. . . . How It Will Happen and What It Will Mean* (New York: Oxford University Press, 1992), pp. 52–53, 183. Gelernter is quite evocative on the human drive for topsight: "If *insight* is the illumination to be achieved by penetrating inner depths, *topsight* is what comes from a far-overhead vantagepoint, from a bird's eye view that reveals the *whole*—the big picture; how the parts fit together. . . . It is *the* quality that distinguishes genius in any field. (What Newton displayed when he saw planets reeling round the sun and teardrops falling as two pieces of one picture. . . .) It is the keystone of a beautifully transparent definition of *philosopher*: one who seeks 'to transcend the world of human thought and experience, in order to find some point of vantage from which it can be seen whole.' " Such "seeing whole," is, however, *not* seeing everything; it is the ability to abstract useful and relevant patterns. Confusing the ability to see patterns with a knowledge of the whole is a dangerous fallacy.

13. Ross Perot, speech at Reform Party Convention, Long Beach, California, August 11, 1996.

14. Rick White, speech at Progress and Freedom Foundation Aspen Summit, August 5, 1996. White was defeated for re-election in 1998.

15. Pat Buchanan, "Is America Becoming Two Nations?" *The Arizona Republic,*

October 17, 1994, p. B5.

16. In the 1970s the amount of carbon steel in an American car dropped by 35 percent, replaced by lighter-weight materials. Iddo K. Wernick, Robert Herman, Shekhar Govind, and Jesse H. Ausubel, "Materialization and Dematerialization: Measures and Trends," *Dædalus* (Summer 1996); 182.

17. Donald F. Barnett and Robert W. Crandall, *Up from the Ashes: The Rise of the Steel Minimill in the United States* (Washington, D.C.: Brookings Institution, 1986); Richard Preston, *American Steel: Hot Metal Men and the Resurrection of the Rust Belt* (New York: Prentice Hall, 1991).

18. Jon Casimir, "Battlestations in Cyberspace," *Sydney Morning Herald Spectrum*, July 29, 1995, p. 5.

19. John Perry Barlow, "A Declaration of the Independence of Cyberspace," February 8, 1996, available at www.eff.org/pub/Publications/John_Perry_Barlow/barlow_0296.declaration, among other locations.

20. Ibid.

21. Kirkpatrick Sale, "Principles of Bioregionalism," in Jerry Mander and Edward Goldsmith, eds., *The Case Against the Global Economy: And for a Turn Toward the Local* (San Francisco: Sierra Club Books, 1996) p. 483.

22. Eric von Hippel, "'Sticky Information' and the Locus of Problem Solving: Implications for Innovation," *Management Science* (April 1994): 429–439.

23. Ibid., p. 431. The quote is taken from an interviewee cited by H. M. Collins, "The Seven Sexes: A Study in the Sociology of a Phenomenon, or the Replication of Experiments in Physics," *Sociology* (May 1975); 205–224.

24. Polanyi, *Personal Knowledge,* p. 53.

25. Michael Lenehan, "The Quality of the Instrument," *The Atlantic Monthly* (August 1982): 46. Lenehan's article contains a wealth of examples of sticky local knowledge.

26. Michael Kass, conversation with the author, May 31, 1997, and e-mail to the author, January 6, 1998.

27. Preben Sander Kristensen, "Flying Prototypes: Production Departments' Direct Interaction with External Customers," *International Journal of Operations and Production Management* 12, nos. 7/8 (1992): 207.

28. Ikujiro Nonaka, "The Knowledge-Creating Company," *Harvard Business Review* (November–December 1991): 98.

29. Morris Berman, *The Reenchantment of the World* (Ithaca: Cornell University Press, 1981), p. 69.

30. Berry, *The Unsettling of America,* p. 20.

31. Sale, "Principles of Bioregionalism," in *The Case Against the Global Economy,* p. 482.

32. Berry, *The Unsettling of America,* p. 61.

33. Christopher Lasch, *The True and Only Heaven: Progress and Its Critics* (New York: Norton, 1991), p. 467.

34. Sale, "Principles of Bioregionalism," p. 481.

35. Lenehan, "The Quality of the Instrument," p. 43.

36. David Owen, *The Man Who Invented Saturday Morning: And Other Adventures in American Enterprise* (New York: Villard Books, 1988), p. 149.

37. David Gelernter, "Shaping American Society for the Digital Age" (panel, Progress and Freedom Foundation Aspen Summit, August 5, 1996), and e-mail to the author, September 5, 1996.

38. Friedrich A. Hayek, "The Use of Knowledge in Society," in *Individualism and Economic Order* (Chicago: University of Chicago Press, 1948, Midway Reprint 1980), pp. 78–80, 87–88. Originally published in *American Economic Review* (September 1945): 519–530.

39. This is a simplified version of actual events in the mid-1990s.

40. Henry Petroski, *The Evolution of Useful Things* (New York: Knopf, 1992), pp. 84–86.

41. Howard Rudnitsky, "How Sam Walton Does It," *Forbes*, August 16, 1982, p. 42. Pankaj Ghemawat, "Wal-Mart Stores' Discount Operations," Harvard Business School Case 9-387-018, revised July 1987.

42. Betty Friedan, *The Feminine Mystique* (New York: Penguin Books, 1963), pp. 9–10, 15–32. Friedan titled her first chapter, "The Problem That Has No Name," clearly establishing the book as an effort at articulation.

43. Virginia Huck, *Brand of the Tartan: The 3M Story* (New York: Appleton-Century-Crofts, 1955), pp. 143–147. The story of Scotch cellophane tape has become a business fable, whose details are almost always recounted inaccurately and made more dramatic than they actually were. Huck's book, an official corporate history whose research included access to such records as the bakery's original letter to 3M, is the authoritative source. Another interesting aspect to the story is how essential developing an easy-to-use dispenser with a built-in cutting edge was to the tape's success. Creating a good dispenser took a year and a half of experiments, but, says Huck, "many in 3M feel that without it, Scotch Brand cellophane tape might have quickly waned in popularity."

44. Peter F. Drucker, *Innovation and Entrepreneurship: Practice and Principles* (New York: Harper & Row, 1985), p. 192.

45. Gelernter, "Shaping American Society for the Digital Age."

46. Thomas K. McCraw, *Prophets of Regulation* (Cambridge, Mass.: Belknap Press of Harvard University Press, 1984), pp. 91–94.

47. John Tierney, "A Kick for the Economy," *The New York Times Magazine*, November 6, 1996, pp. 28–30.

48. Carole Sugarman, "Who's Minding the Store? The Seemingly Senseless Division of Federal Labeling Authority," *The Washington Post*, May 11, 1988, p. E1; Colman Andrews, "Restaurant Notebook," *Los Angeles Times*, November 29, 1987, Calendar section, p. 98. Andrews notes that the USDA "also made Puck change the designation of his 'Country Sausage' pizza—on the grounds that the sausage used wasn't made in the country." Under public pressure, the agency has more recently adopted "informal standards" that allow sauceless pizzas to be labeled as "white pizza." Associated Press, "As Menus Expand, Government May Order New Pizza Rules," *The New York Times*, December 1, 1996, p. 29.

49. Tama Starr, "The 7.63% Solution," *Reason* (February 1996): 31. The title of Starr's article is taken from the precise quota required for female iron workers.

50. Commission on the Skills of the American Workforce, *America's Choice: High*

Skills or Low Wages! (Rochester, N.Y.: National Center on Education and the Economy, June 1990), pp. 82–83. Hillary Rodham Clinton was a member of the National Center's board of trustees. The commission also included Laura D'Andrea Tyson, later head of Clinton's Council of Economic Advisors. Also Bill Clinton and Al Gore, *Putting People First: How We Can Change America* (New York: Times Books, 1992), p. 128; Virginia I. Postrel, "Training Wreck," *Reason* (December 1992): 4–5. Jonathan Rauch, "The Idea Merchant," *National Journal* (December 12, 1992): 2833, 2835–2836.

51. Sheila A. Moloney, "The Lady in Red Tape," *Policy Review* (September–October 1996): 51.

52. Virginia I. Postrel, "Who's Behind the Child Care Crisis?" *Reason* (June 1989): 25.

53. Rick Marin, "Blocking the Box," *Newsweek*, March 11, 1996, p. 60. The person quoted is University of Wisconsin professor Joanne Cantor.

54. John E. Yang, "Rep. Coburn Apologizes; Speech Complained of Movie's Sex, Violence," *The Washington Post*, February 27, 1997, p. B-2. Coburn in no way retracted his condemnation of the network. He simply apologized "for appearing insensitive to the worst atrocities known to man."

55. Ann W. O'Neill, "Actress Fired over Pregnancy Wins $5 Million," *Los Angeles Times*, December 23, 1997, p. A1.

56. Walter K. Olson, *The Excuse Factory* (New York: Free Press, 1997), p. 56.

57. Ibid., p. 274.

CHAPTER FIVE
THE BONDS OF LIFE

1. Rachel Inman, letter to the author, December 16, 1996.

2. Virginia I. Postrel, "How Bureaucratic Decrees Fuel the Nation's Rage," *The Washington Post*, February 5, 1995, p. C-3.

3. Marianne Lavelle, "Environment Vise: Law, Compliance," *The National Law Journal*, August 30, 1993, pp. S1–S2.

4. Peter H. Schuck, "Legal Complexity: Some Causes, Consequences, and Cures," *Duke Law Journal* (October 1992): 20, 22–23.

5. Judy Klemesrud, "Sassoon Refuses to Finger-Wave for State Test," *The New York Times*, September 20, 1966, p. 51.

6. Grant McCracken, *Big Hair: A Journey Into the Transformation of the Self* (Woodstock, N.Y.: Overlook Press, 1995) p. 55.

7. Claudine Williams, "Hair Wars: Underground on 125th Street," *The New York Times*, August 21, 1994, Section 13, p. 4; Pamela Reynolds, "Homespun Hair," *The Boston Globe*, October 25, 1996, p. 71; William H. Mellor, *Is New York City Killing Entrepreneurship?* report from the Institute for Justice, November 1996, pp. 18–21; "Challenging Barriers to Economic Opportunity: *Cornwell v. California Board of Barbering and Cosmetology*," Institute for Justice Litigation Backgrounder, January 28, 1997; *Joanne Cornwell and American Hairbraiders and Natural Hair Care Association v. California Board of Barbering and Cosmetology et al.*, complaint filed in U.S. District Court, Southern District of California, January 28, 1997.

8. JoAnne Cornwell, press conference, San Diego, January 28, 1997. In 1997, Cornwell and other African-style hairdressers, including the Braiderie's owners, sued the state of California, charging that its cosmetology regulations violated their economic liberties under the California and U.S. constitutions and had no relation to their work. The case was still in court when this book went to press.

9. McCracken, *Big Hair,* p. 50.

10. Released in September 1982, the Commodore 64 took its name from the computer's then-generous 64K random-access memory—about 1/200th of what the now-obsolete PowerBook Duo on which this book was written has. The standard modem ran at 300 baud (bits per second), compared to the common 28,800 baud that people today find aggravatingly slow for cruising the World Wide Web. Customers used their television sets as monitors. The computer did come with two joysticks, which were used for maneuvering around Habitat.

11. Chip Morningstar, "Settlements on The Electronic Frontier," transcript of a talk presented at IEEE CompCon '91, February 2, 1991, available at www.communities.com/paper/settlmnt.html. Further background on Habitat is taken from Chip Morningstar and F. Randall Farmer, "The Lessons of Lucasfilm's Habitat," in Michael Benedikt, ed., *Cyberspace: First Steps* (Cambridge: MIT Press, 1991), pp. 273–301 and also available at www.communities.com/paper/lessons.html; F. Randall Farmer, "Habitat Anecdotes," www.communities.com/paper/anecdotes.html.

12. Chip Morningstar, interview with the author, January 14, 1997.

13. Ibid.

14. Philip K. Howard, *The Death of Common Sense: How Law Is Suffocating America* (New York: Random House, 1994).

15. Vidal Sassoon, *Sorry I Kept You Waiting Madam* (London: Cassell, 1968), p. 172. This statement was originally reported by Priscilla Tucker in the *New York Herald Tribune.*

16. JoAnne Cornwell, press conference, San Diego, January 28, 1997.

17. David Zane Mairowitz, "Fascism à la Mode," *Harper's Magazine* (October 1997), 59–67.

18. Walter K. Olson, *The Litigation Explosion: What Happened When America Unleashed the Lawsuit* (New York: Truman Talley, 1991), p. 144.

19. Elinor Ostrom, *Governing the Commons: The Evolution of Institutions for Collective Action* (Cambridge: Cambridge University Press, 1990), pp. 18–21.

20. Katie Hafner and Matthew Lyon, *Where Wizards Stay Up Late: The Origins of the Internet* (New York: Simon & Schuster, 1996), p. 227.

21. Sharon Eisner Gillett and Mitchell Kapor, "The Self-Governing Internet: Coordination by Design," in Brian Kahin and James H. Keller, eds., *Coordinating the Internet* (Cambridge: MIT Press, 1997), pp. 3–38. Also available at ccs.mit.edu/CCSWP197.html. Gillett and Kapor note (pp. 10–12): "The modular design of the Internet affords the evolution and adaptability that have been so critical to its long-term survival . . . the Internet's designers didn't really know what the network would be used for; their best guess, that people

would use it to share compute cycles (remote login), was supplanted by the popularity of applications, such as email, that allow people to communicate with each other. Had they oriented the network toward remote login applications, the Internet would have turned out to be an interesting historical footnote. Instead, they created a general-purpose platform that enabled the emergence, nearly two decades later, of the graphical World Wide Web, catapulting the Internet into prime time."

22. Hafner and Lyon, *Where Wizards Stay Up Late*, pp. 147–148.

23. William Cronon, *Nature's Metropolis: Chicago and the Great West* (New York: Norton, 1991), pp. 114–116: "Formerly, the transportation network had assiduously maintained the bond of ownership between shippers and the physical grain they shipped. Farmer Smith's wheat from Iowa would never be mixed with Farmer Jones's wheat from Illinois until some final customer purchased both . . . as the scale of Chicago's grain trade grew, elevator operators began objecting to keeping small quantities of different owners' grains in separate bins that were only partially filled. . . . The only obstacle to achieving this greater efficiency was the small matter of a shipper's traditional legal ownership of physical grain. The organization that eventually solved this problem—albeit after several years of frustrated efforts and false starts—was the Chicago Board of Trade. . . . [It decided] to designate three categories of wheat in the city—white winter wheat, red winter wheat, and spring wheat—and to set standards of quality for each. In this seemingly trivial action lay the solution to the elevator operators' dilemma about mixing different owners' grain in single bins. . . . Farmers and shippers delivered grain to a warehouse and got in return a receipt that they or anyone else could redeem at will. Anyone who gave a receipt back to the elevator got in return not the *original* lot of grain but an equal quality of *equally graded* grain."

24. Stewart Brand, *How Buildings Learn: What Happens After They're Built* (New York: Penguin Books, 1994), p. 2.

25. Anne Vernez Moudon, *Built for Change: Neighborhood Architecture in San Francisco* (Cambridge: MIT Press, 1986), p. 75.

26. Ibid., p. 92.

27. Henry Sumner Maine, *Ancient Law* (Tucson: University of Arizona Press, 1986), p. 165.

28. Richard A. Epstein, *Simple Rules for a Complex World* (Cambridge: Harvard University Press, 1995), pp. 73–74.

29. John Gray, *Beyond the New Right: Markets, Government and the Common Environment* (London: Routledge, 1993), p. 125.

30. Charles Oliver, "The Ghost of Christmas Presents," *Reason* (January 1990): 38.

31. Max Vanzi and Carl Ingram, "Democrats Vow to Fight Changes in State Overtime Law," *Los Angeles Times,* January 28, 1997, p. A3.

32. Edward L. Ayers, *The Promise of the New South: Life After Reconstruction* (New York: Oxford University Press, 1992), pp. 136–146. Ayers notes that railroad segregation, with its orderliness and neat signs, "was not a throwback to old-fashioned racism; indeed, segregation became, to whites, a badge of sophisti-

cated, modern, managed race relations." It was, in many ways, a perfect technocratic scheme, seeking to shape the future of social relations despite the dynamism of technology, urbanization, and blacks' increasing prosperity.

33. Lawrence Wright, "One Drop of Blood," *The New Yorker,* July 25, 1994, pp. 46–47.

34. Elizabeth Bartholet, "Where Do Black Children Belong? The Politics of Race Matching in Adoption," *Reconstruction* (1992), 29.

35. Prior to the civil rights movement, of course, many states had outright bans on interracial adoption. Ironically, such bans were overturned by the U.S. Supreme Court in 1972, the same year as the NABSW's influential resolution.

36. Nina Shokraii, "Adopting Racism," *Reason* (November 1995): 50–51. Donna G. Matias, "Separate Is Not Equal: Striking Down State-Sanctioned Barriers to Interracial Adoption," Litigation Backgrounder, Institute for Justice, April 13, 1995.

37. Randall Kennedy, "Orphans of Separatism: The Painful Politics of Transracial Adoption," *American Prospect* (Spring 1994): 39–40.

38. Chip Morningstar, interview with the author, January 14, 1997.

39. Mark S. Miller, interview with the author, January 14, 1997.

40. Hernando de Soto, *The Other Path: The Invisible Revolution in the Third World,* trans. June Abbott (New York: Harper & Row, 1989), pp. 133–151.

41. Ibid., pp. 12–13.

42. In adjacent towns founded at the same time by people from the same Andean village, researchers from De Soto's institute found dramatic differences: "One had three-story buildings with television sets lit behind the curtains and Toyotas and Volkswagens downstairs. It had neatly trimmed lawns, and you could reasonably describe it as a middle-class neighborhood. Across the road was your typical shantytown: corrugated iron, cardboard walls, poor sanitation. . . . [The first town's informal mayor] had dedicated most of his time to obtaining property titles. . . . Ten years later, the value of the homes was 41 times greater than in the other town." Hernando de Soto, "What's Wrong with Latin American Economies," *Reason* (October 1989): 39–40.

43. Ibid., p. 40.

44. Douglass C. North, *Institutions, Institutional Change and Economic Performance* (Cambridge: Cambridge University Press, 1990), p. 54.

45. Paul Joskow, comments at the Inaugural Conference for the International Society for New Institutional Economics, Washington University, St. Louis, September 19, 1997.

46. Esther Dyson, interview with the author, March 27, 1998.

47. Epstein, *Simple Rules for a Complex World,* p. 39.

48. William H. Honan, "New Law Against Age Bias on Campus Clogs Academic Pipeline, Critics Say," *The New York Times,* June 15, 1994, p. B-9; Richard A. Epstein and Saunders MacLane, "Keep Mandatory Retirement for Tenured Faculty," *Regulation* (Spring 1991): 85–96.

49. In the 1991 case of *Cohen v. Cowles Media,* the U.S. Supreme Court ruled that journalists could be sued for breaking confidentiality promises to sources. But such suits are incredibly rare, almost unheard of.

50. Bruce Nolan, "Fallen Reporter's Quest Raises Ethical Questions," *The Times-Picayune*, May 18, 1996, p. B8.

51. Jacob Sullum, "Secrets for Sale," *Reason* (April 1992): 33.

52. Walter K. Olson, *The Excuse Factory: How Employment Law Is Paralyzing the American Workplace* (New York: Free Press, 1997), pp. 19–20, 199–200.

53. This happened to me when I called the *Wilkes-Barre Union Leader* in 1989. Although the employee in question had an exemplary record—as I found by talking with a former colleague working at another publication—the sweeping policy was presumably designed to prevent negative references that might trigger lawsuits.

54. Henry Petroski, *The Evolution of Useful Things* (New York: Knopf, 1992), p. 249.

55. Ali Rasheed, press conference, San Diego, January 28, 1997.

56. Nathan Rosenberg, *Exploring the Black Box: Technology, Economics, and History* (Cambridge: Cambridge University Press, 1994), p. 98.

57. David Brewster, "Let's Chuck Charter Schools and Get On with Our Lives," *The Seattle Times*, March 20, 1998, p. B4.

58. Shigeo Shingo, *A Study of the Toyota Production System from an Industrial Engineering Point of View*, trans. by Andrew P. Dillon (Portland, Ore. Productivity Press, 1989), pp. xxiv, 107–108.

59. Brian Lamb, interview with Thomas W. Hazlett and Rick Henderson, December 1995, published as "Changing Channels," *Reason* (March 1996): 42.

60. Robert M. McMath, "Throwing in the Towel," *American Demographics* (November 1996): 60, "When Cold Coffee Gets Iced," *American Demographics* (March 1997):60, and "What's in a Name?" *American Demographics* (December 1996): 60.

61. Tom Peters, interview with the author, May 15, 1997, published as "The Peters Principles," *Reason* (October 1997): 44.

62. Karl R. Popper, *Conjectures and Refutations: The Growth of Scientific Knowledge* (London: Routledge, 1989 ed.), pp. vii, ix. The second clause Popper added in his preface to the second edition. Popper's work tends to suggest that each individual scientist should seek to falsify his own theories, while other thinkers, including those inspired by Popper, tend to emphasize the way the scientific system as a whole tests theories through competition.

63. Jonathan Rauch, *Kindly Inquisitors: The New Attacks on Free Thought* (Chicago: University of Chicago Press, 1993), p. 64.

64. Ibid., p. 69.

65. Donald McCloskey, "Beyond the Margin," *Reason* (March 1991): 57. The article is a review of *The Lever of Riches: Technological Creativity and Economic Progress* by Joel Mokyr.

66. Brand, *How Buildings Learn*, pp. 12–23.

67. The Internet's layered protocols provide a similar model of nested rules. See Gillett and Kapor, "The Self-Governing Internet: Coordination by Design," p. 15: "IP is a basic building block, intended to be supplemented by higher-level protocols more oriented toward the needs of particular applications. Application developers do not interface directly to IP, but to the layers above

it. The higher the layer, the more specific the purpose of the protocol. For example, IP delivers packets with no reliability guarantees, and all Internet traffic uses it. TCP, which layers directly on top of IP, reliably delivers ordered streams of data; most, but not all, Internet traffic uses TCP. HTTP, which layers on top of TCP, delivers Web pages; all traffic between Web browsers and servers uses HTTP, but none of the traffic for non-Web services does.... The general-purpose nature of IP means that many different applications—including those not yet invented—can layer on top of it. The layering leaves application developers free to concentrate on their portion of the problem, such as publishing documents (e.g. the Web) or managing messages (e.g. e-mail and news). Lower layers—with interfaces that are openly-specified and freely available to all—take care of the rest."

68. Esther Dyson, "Labels and Disclosure Part II: Privacy," *Release 1.0*, February 19, 1997, p. 1. See also David R. Johnson and David G. Post, "Law and Borders," *Release 1.0*, June 19, 1996, and www.cli.org/X0025_LBFIN.html. Also David R. Johnson and David G. Post, "And How Shall the Net Be Governed? A Meditation on the Relative Virtues of Decentralized, Emergent Law," in Brian Kahin and James H. Keller, eds., *Coordinating the Internet* (Cambridge: MIT Press, 1997), pp. 62–91.

69. Roberta Romano, *The Genius of American Corporate Law* (Washington, D.C.: AEI Press, 1993), pp. 82–83.

70. Peter Huber, "Cyberpower," *Forbes,* December 2, 1996, p. 146.

71. Jerry Mander, "Technologies of Globalization," in Jerry Mander and Edward Goldsmith, eds., *The Case Against the Global Economy: And for a Turn Toward the Local* (San Francisco: Sierra Club Books, 1996), p. 358.

72. Jeremey Brecher, "Global Village or Global Pillage?" *The Nation,* December 6, 1993, p. 685.

CHAPTER SIX
CREATING NATURE

1. Plants are created before they can be planted and grow, because there is no rain and no one to work the land. Genesis 2:5. The mist that animates the land is parallel to the breath of life that animates man.

2. Genesis 2:15. To work and to keep: "l'avdah u'l'shamrah."

3. Bill McKibben, *The End of Nature* (New York: Anchor Books, 1989), p. 73.

4. John Gray, *Beyond the New Right: Markets, Government and the Common Environment* (London: Routledge, 1993), p. 138.

5. Herbert A. Simon. *The Sciences of the Artificial,* 2d ed. (Cambridge: MIT Press, 1981), pp. xi, 6.

6. The idea of defining the natural as out of control is developed in Kevin Kelly, *Out of Control: The Rise of Neo-Biological Civilization* (Reading, Mass.: Addison-Wesley, 1994).

7. Jared Diamond, "How to Tame a Wild Plant," *Discover* (September 1994), 102.

8. Stephen Toulmin, *Cosmopolis: The Hidden Agenda of Modernity* (New York: Free Press, 1990) p. 148.

9. McKibben, *The End of Nature*, p. 91.
10. See, for instance, Ronald Bailey, "Hi There, Bambi," *Forbes*, October 16, 1989, p. 46. John Hunt, "A Warning of Armageddon," *Financial Times*, January 17, 1990, p. 25. Julia Neuberger, "How Green Is His Folly," *The Sunday Times*, January 14, 1990, p. H4. For a positive view that makes much of the same line, see Ellen Goodman, "Altered Environment: In the World of Nature, We Are the Problem," *Chicago Tribune*, September 17; 1989, sec. 5, p. 8.
11. Andrew Marvell, "The Mower Against Gardens," in H. R. Woudhuysen, ed., *The Penguin Book of Renaissance Verse 1509–1659*, selected and with an introduction by David Norbrook, (London: Penguin Books, 1993), pp. 472–473.
12. Frederick Turner, "The Merchant of Avon," *Reason* (March 1997): 36.
13. William Shakespeare, *The Winter's Tale*, Act IV, scene iv, lines 89–97.
14. Kelly Loo tour taken by the author, July 1994. Jayne Clark, "Valley of Kings Lives Up to Its Name," *The Register* (Orange County) October 2, 1992, p. E-5; Steve Chapple, "Far Away from It All: Waipio Valley, on Hawaii's Big Island, Is a Lost Place Where Wilderness Thrives," *Audubon* (May 1994): 34; Barb and Ron Kroll, "Hawaiian Horsemen Live Simply," *The Toronto Star*, September 26, 1993, p. J-13; Greg Ward, *Big Island of Hawaii: The Rough Guide* (London: Rough Guides, 1995), pp. 102, 122–127.
15. William K. Stevens, "New Eye on Nature: The Real Constant Is Eternal Turmoil," *The New York Times*, July 31, 1990, p. C-1.
16. Ibid.
17. Daniel D. Botkin, *Our Natural History: The Lessons of Lewis and Clark* (New York: Grosset/Putnam, 1995), pp. 15–16.
18. Alston Chase, *In a Dark Wood: The Fight over Forests and the Rising Tyranny of Ecology* (Boston: Houghton Mifflin, 1995), p. 252.
19. J. T. Cuningham, "Woodland Treasure," *Audubon* (July–August 1954), quoted in Daniel B. Botkin, *Discordant Harmonies: A New Ecology for the Twenty-First Century* (New York: Oxford University Press, 1990), p. 52.
20. Daniel Botkin, "A Natural Myth," *Nature Conservancy* (May–June 1992): 38.
21. Daniel Botkin, speech at Duke University School of Law, April 18, 1996, reported in Monte Basgall, "A Call for New Environmental Policies," *Dialogue*, April 26, 1996, www.dukenews.duke.edu/Dialogue/eco426.html. See also Monte Basgall, "Defining a New Ecology," *Duke Magazine* (May–June 1996): 39–41.
22. Basgall, "A Call for New Environmental Policies."
23. Botkin, *Our Natural History*, pp. 22–38, 154–155, 269.
24. See William R. Jordan III, "'Sunflower Forest': Ecological Restoration as the Basis for a New Environmental Paradigm," in A. Dwight Baldwin, Jr., Judith De Luce, and Carl Pletsch, eds., *Beyond Preservation: Restoring and Inventing Landscapes* (Minneapolis: University of Minnesota Press, 1994), pp. 17–34.
25. Daniel B. Botkin, *Discordant Harmonies: A New Ecology for the Twenty-First Century* (New York: Oxford University Press, 1990), pp. 177, 193.
26. See, on preserving elephants, Karl Hess, Jr., "Wild Success," *Reason* (October 1997): 32–41.
27. Botkin, *Discordant Harmonies*, p. 191.

28. Al Gore, *Earth in the Balance: Ecology and the Human Spirit* (Boston: Houghton Mifflin, 1992), p. 2.
29. Donald Worster, *Nature's Economy: A History of Ecological Ideas,* 2d ed. (New York: Cambridge University Press, 1994), p. 389.
30. Ibid., p. 424: "Scientists have abandoned that equilibrium view of nature and invented a new one that looks remarkably like the human sphere in which we live." Donald Worster, *The Wealth of Nature: Environmental History and the Ecological Imagination* (New York: Oxford University Press, 1993), p. 39: "One suspects a hidden agenda. A world full of accidents and misfits . . . is a scientific paradigm with many current political uses."
31. Worster, *The Wealth of Nature,* p. 152.
32. The Wilderness Act of 1964 describes wilderness as a place "where the Earth and its community of life are untrammeled by man and where man himself is a visitor who does not remain." Many such protected areas were in fact shaped by the actions of their human residents and still require human intervention to maintain their desired "natural" state. Edwin Dobb, "Cultivating Nature," *The Sciences* (January–February 1992): 45.
33. Worster is genuinely worried that the new ecology might not sufficiently establish the moral ill of wheat fields and Disney: "On the contrary, historicism can lead either to a complete cynicism or to the acceptance of any set of ideas or any environment that humans have created as thoroughly legitimate. By the logic of historicism Disneyland must be as legitimate an environment as Yellowstone National Park, a wheat field as legitimate as a prairie, a megalopolis of thirty million people as legitimate as a village. Each has been the product of history and therefore each must stand equal to any other. Each offers unique dynamics to be probed and understood, but any set of historical dynamics, like any set of beliefs or institutions, must appear to the consistent historicist to be as good as any other." Worster, *Nature's Economy,* p. 428.
34. Worster, *The Wealth of Nature,* pp. 66–67.
35. Suzanne Thomlinson, testimony before National Bioethics Advisory Commission, October 4, 1996.
36. Charles Arthur, "Gene Therapy Offers Hope to Cystic Fibrosis," *The Independent,* March 4, 1997, p. 5; John Pope, "N.O. Research Alters Cystic Fibrosis Cells," *The Times-Picayune,* March 4, 1997, p. A-3; Natalie Angier, "Cystic Fibrosis Experiment Hits a Snag," *The New York Times,* September 22, 1993, p. C-12; Gina Kolata, "Cystic Fibrosis Surprise: Genetic Screening Falters," *The New York Times,* November 16, 1993, p. C-1.
37. McKibben, *The End of Nature,* pp. 167, 173.
38. Jeremy Rifkin, *Algeny* (New York: Viking Press, 1983), p. 231.
39. Leon R. Kass, *Toward a More Natural Science: Biology and Human Affairs* (New York: Free Press, 1985), p. 173: "Health is a natural standard or norm—not a moral norm, not a 'value' as opposed to a 'fact,' not an obligation—a state of being that reveals itself in activity as the standard of bodily excellence or fitness, relative to each species and to some extent to individuals, recognizable if not definable, and to some extent attainable."
40. Carrying the genetic "trait" for a disease means having one recessive gene,

where two are required to have the disease. The trait alone may manifest itself in milder ways, such as the positive antimalarial effects of sickle cell traits.

41. For development of this argument, see H. Tristram Engelhardt, Jr., "Ideology and Etiology," *The Journal of Medicine and Philosophy* (1976): 256–268, and *The Foundations of Bioethics* (New York: Oxford University Press, 1986), pp. 169–170.

42. Kass, *Toward a More Natural Science*, pp. 45, 305–309, 318, 297–298.

43. Gina Kolata, "Childbirth at 63 Says What About Life?" *The New York Times*, April 27, 1997, sec. 1, p. 20.

44. Ibid.

45. Norman Fost, "'I Was Like—Whoa': A Commentary on Shapiro's *Performance and the Enhancement and Control of Attributes*," *Southern California Law Review* (1991–1992): 115–120: "I share a general queasiness about performance-enhancing technologies, as I doubtless would have been queasy about the Copernican and Darwinian discoveries, and as I am about men in certain professions wearing earrings and ponytails. That is to say, 'I am like—whoa' about some of these things. But everything that makes us queasy does not involve a moral question. I believe it is necessary to say more than 'I am like—whoa' to justify interfering with a person's liberty. Or, at the least, I simply do not consider being 'like—whoa' to constitute an argument against these technologies."

46. Leon R. Kass, "The Wisdom of Repugnance," *The New Republic*, June 2, 1997, p. 20.

47. Michael H. Shapiro, "The Technology of Perfection: Performance Enhancement and the Control of Attributes," *Southern California Law Review* (1991–1992): 34–35.

48. Leon Kass does not write as a romantic but as an ancient, informed by Greek and selected Jewish thought. But he is nonetheless affected by the romantic sentiments with which contemporary discussions of nature are saturated. (See note 57 for a good example.) And his work leads, despite its intent, to a splitting of body from mind.

49. "The Biological Century" is physicist Greg Benford's term. See Gregory Benford, "Biology: 2001," *Reason* (November 1995): 22–29.

50. David M. Buss, "Evolutionary Psychology: A New Paradigm for Psychological Science," *Psychological Inquiry* (1995): 1–30. John Horgan, "The New Social Darwinists," *Scientific American* (October 1995): 174–181.

51. Although psychopharmacology for serious diseases such as schizophrenia and clinical depression is not new, treatments suitable for more mundane conditions have become refined and wider spread in recent years. The possible implications for how we think about personality and selfhood were influentially explored in Peter D. Kramer's best-selling book, *Listening to Prozac: A Psychiatrist Explores Antidepressant Drugs and the Remaking of the Self* (New York: Viking, 1993).

52. Tom Wolfe, "Sorry, But Your Soul Just Died," *Forbes ASAP*, December 2, 1996, pp. 220, 222.

53. Revelation has problems of its own, the most obvious practical difficulty being that different people disagree about its nature and message. But issues

of revelation are matters for another book. Our concern here is the interplay of ideas in a pluralist culture where even religious beliefs are affected, at least on the margin, by scientific discoveries and secular arguments.

54. *Crossfire*, CNN, March 6, 1997.
55. Jeremy Rifkin, *The Biotech Century: Harnessing the Gene and Remaking the World* (New York: Jeremy P. Tarcher/Putnam, 1998), p. 236.
56. Barbara Yost, "Medical Breakthroughs Offer Macabre Miracles," *The Phoenix Gazette*, May 26, 1995, p. B12.
57. Kass, *Toward a More Natural Science*, p. 73. See also the peculiar unnumbered footnote on p. 34: "Curiously, the implicit goal of biomedical technology—indeed, of the entire project for the conquest of nature—could well be said to be the reversal of the Fall, and a return of man to the hedonic and immortal existence of the Garden of Eden. Yet we can point to at least two difficulties. First, the new Garden of Eden will probably have no gardens; the received splendid world of nature will be buried beneath asphalt, concrete, and other human fabrications, a transformation that is already far along. (Recall that in Aldous Huxley's *Brave New World*, elaborate consumption-oriented, mechanical amusement parks—featuring, e.g., the centrifugal bumble-puppy—have supplanted wilderness and even ordinary gardens.) Second, the new inhabitant of the new 'Garden' will have to be a creature for whom we have no precedent, a creature as difficult to imagine as to bring into existence. He will have to be simultaneously an innocent like Adam and a technological wizard who keeps the Garden running." Having declared that Eden is the goal, he circularly reasons that an innocent Adam must dwell there. And, of course, he is as hostile to amusement parks as the Disney-hating Donald Worster.
58. Rifkin, *Algeny*, p. 236.
59. Paul Shepheard, *The Cultivated Wilderness: Or, What Is Landscape?* (Cambridge, Mass.: MIT Press, 1997) p. 233.

CHAPTER SEVEN
FIELDS OF PLAY

1. Sporting Goods Manufacturers Association, *Sports Participations Trends Report 1996: Statistical Highlights from American Sports Analysis* (North Palm Beach, Fla.: Sporting Goods Manufacturers Association, 1996); Christine Foster, "Have Sand, Will Travel," *Forbes*, September 8, 1997, p. 156; Michael Farber, "Fun in the Sun," *Sports Illustrated*, August 5, 1996, pp. 88–95; Richard Hoffer, "Day 8: Who Needs Water? Just Add Sand," *Sports Illustrated*, Commemorative Issue (August 1996): 58–64; Martha Brant and Mark Star, "Sand Blasters," *Newsweek*, June 3, 1996, pp. 76–78; Kurt Pitzer "The Sunshine Boys," *People*, June 26, 1995, pp. 42–47; Joanne Kaldy, "Volleyball: This Fast-Growing Sport Serves Up Fun and Profit," *Parks and Recreation* (April 1995): 54–58; Marcy Magiera, "Pro Volleyball Serves Up Brand Sponsorships," *Advertising Age*, June 11, 1990, pp. 3, 57; Matthew Grimm, "Miller Nets New V-Ball Pact," *Brandweek*, December 13, 1993, p. 33; Matthew Grimm, "Coke, Nestea Net $5M Pro Volleyball Deal," *Brandweek*, November 19, 1993, pp. 1, 8; Judith

Waldrop, "Beach Ball Bonanza," *American Demographics,* March 1994, p. 4; "History of Beach Volleyball," at www.volleyball.org/history_beach.html.

2. "Kent Steffes," *People,* May 8, 1995, p. 151.

3. Newt Gingrich, speech to Republican National Convention, San Diego, August 13, 1996.

4. Murray Kempton, "GOP Managers Steal Party's Soul," *Newsday,* August 16, 1996, p. A-40.

5. Walter Shapiro, "Only Bounce Here Is Beach Volleyball," *USA Today,* August 15, 1996, p. 2A.

6. Bill Boyarsky and Amy Wallace, "GOP Convention.'96," August 16, 1996, p. A-18; "The San Diego Republicans," *The Weekly Standard,* August 26, 1996, p. 13.

7. See, for example, William Kristol and David Brooks. "What Ails Conservatism," *The Wall Street Journal,* September 15, 1997, p. A-22; David Brooks, "A Return to National Greatness," *The Weekly Standard,* March 3, 1997, pp. 16–21; David Brooks, "Bully for America," *The Weekly Standard,* June 23, 1997, pp. 14–23.

8. Daniel Bell, *The Cultural Contradictions of Capitalism* (New York: Basic Books, 1976), p. 70.

9. Christopher Lasch, *The Culture of Narcissism: American Life in an Age of Diminishing Expectations* (New York: Norton, 1979), p. 102, 123.

10. Kirkpatrick Sale, *Rebels Against the Future* (Reading, Mass.: Addison-Wesley, 1995), pp. 274–275.

11. Friedrich A. Hayek, *The Constitution of Liberty* (Chicago: University of Chicago Press, 1960), p. 41.

12. Johan Huizinga, *Homo Ludens: A Study of the Play Element in Culture* (Boston: Beacon Press, 1950), p. 28. This translation is based on Huizinga's 1944 German edition and an English translation he did shortly before his death in 1945; although its foreword is dated 1938, the book includes references to events at least as late as September 1939. Interestingly, Hayek recommends *Homo Ludens* as a "masterly and revealing analysis . . . insufficiently appreciated by students of human order." F. A. Hayek, *The Fatal Conceit: The Errors of Socialism,* ed. W. W. Bartley III (Chicago: University of Chicago Press, 1988), p. 154.

13. Huizinga, *Homo Ludens,* pp. 46, 7–8, 10.

14. Ibid., p. 211.

15. Ibid., p. 180.

16. Bell, *The Cultural Contradictions of Capitalism,* p. 13.

17. William Shakespeare, *Macbeth,* Act II, scene ii, lines 36–39.

18. Margaret A. Boden, *The Creative Mind: Myths and Mechanisms* (New York: Basic Books, 1991), pp. 178–179.

19. Sylvan Barnet, ed., *The Complete Signet Classic Shakespeare* (New York: Harcourt Brace Jovanovich, 1972), p. 27.

20. Boden, *The Creative Mind,* p. 49. On the subject of domains, see also Mihaly Csikszentmihalyi, *Creativity: Flow and the Psychology of Discovery and Invention* (New York: HarperCollins, 1996) pp. 36–50.

21. Bell, *The Cultural Contradictions of Capitalism,* p. 33.

22. David Cohen, *The Development of Play* (New York: New York University

Press, 1987), rp. 106–109. Cohen finds that such "role incongruities" are often a source of children's laughter. One of his own son's favorite games as a baby was to have his mother put his pacifier in her mouth, which was funny because it was inappropriate. The little boy also laughed when his older brother, then about five years old, played at being an adult by typing on Cohen's typewriter.

23. Jerome S. Bruner, "Nature and Uses of Immaturity," from *American Psychologist* (August 1972), reprinted in Jerome S. Bruner, Alison Jolly, and Kathy Sylva, eds., *Play: Its Role in Development and Evolution* (New York: Basic Books, 1976), p. 79.

24. Johan Huizinga, *Homo Ludens*, p. 8.

25. W. H. Auden, "Freedom and Necessity in Poetry," in *The Place of Value in a World of Facts: Proceedings of the Fourteenth Nobel Symposium,* ed. Arne Tiselius and Sam Nilsson (New York: Wiley Interscience Division, 1970), p. 135.

26. Cohen, *The Development of Play,* pp. 160–161.

27. Douglas Rushkoff, *Playing the Future: How Kids' Culture Can Teach Us to Thrive in an Age of Chaos* (New York: HarperCollins, 1996), pp. 127–128.

28. Huizinga, *Homo Ludens*, p. 3.

29. Bell, *The Cultural Contradictions of Capitalism,* pp. 12–13.

30. Dan Lynch, e-mail to the author, January 11, 1996 and September 16, 1997.

31. Dan Lynch, interview with the author, December 21, 1995.

32. Jerry Yang (interview), "Turn On, Type In and Drop Out," *Forbes ASAP,* December 1, 1997, p. 51.

33. Tom Henry, interview with the author, May 22, 1997.

34. Elizabeth Wayland Barber, *Women's Work: The First 20,000 Years: Women, Cloth, and Society in Early Times* (New York: Norton, 1994), pp. 89–94.

35. Daniel Bell, *The Cultural Contradictions of Capitalism,* 20th anniversary ed. (New York: Basic Books, 1996), p. 294. In his 1996 afterword, Bell grows quite fanatical on the evils of adornment, particularly cosmetics, which he sees as signs of decadence and illusion.

36. Cyril Stanley Smith, "On Art, Invention, and Technology," *Technology Review* (May 1976): 36–41.

37. Cyril Stanley Smith, "Art, Technology, and Science: Notes on Their Historical Interaction," in Duane H. D. Roller, ed., *Perspectives in the History of Science and Technology* (Norman, Okla.: University of Oklahoma Press, 1971), p. 134. See also: Cyril Stanley Smith, *Metallurgy as a Human Experience* (Metals Park, Ohio: American Society for Metals, 1977). *From Art to Science: Seventy-Two Objects Illustrating the Nature of Discovery* (Cambridge: MIT Press, 1980). "Reflections on Technology and the Decorative Arts in the Nineteenth Century," in Ian M. G. Quimby and Polly Anne Earl, eds. *Technological Innovation and the Decorative Arts Winterthur Conference Report 1973,* (Charlottesville: University Press of Virginia, 1974) pp. 1–64. "Matter versus Materials: A Historical View," *Science,* November 8, 1968, pp. 637–644. "A Highly Personal View of Science and Its History," *Annals of Science* (January 1977): 49–56.

38. Bruce Ames, interview with the author, September 16, 1997.

39. Mihaly Csikszentmihalyi, *Flow: The Psychology of Optimal Experience* (New

York: HarperCollins, 1990), p. 126.

40. This consistency is emphasized in Csikszentmihalyi's early study, *Beyond Boredom and Anxiety*, because it runs counter to previous theories: "Perhaps the most striking agreement is about the creative and problem-solving dimensions, which were marked high by all groups except basketball players. Rock climbing is supposed to provide the experience of vertigo, dance that of mimicry; yet both groups ranked 'designing or discovering something new' as a closer experience to their activity than anything related to vertigo or mimicry. 'Exploring a strange place' and 'solving a mathematical problem' also were ranked high in similarity by most of these groups. The underlying similarity that cuts across these autotelic activities, regardless of their formal differences, is that they all give participants a sense of discovery, exploration, problem solution—in other words, a feeling of novelty and challenge." Mihaly Csikszentmihalyi, *Beyond Boredom and Anxiety: The Experience of Play in Work and Games* (San Francisco: Jossey-Bass, 1975), pp. 28–30.

41. Csikszentmihalyi, *Flow*, pp. 39–40.

42. Bell, *The Cultural Contradictions of Capitalism*, p. 17.

43. "A drone" was the contemptuous response of T. J. Rodgers, the CEO of Cypress Semiconductor, when I read him this quote in an interview. This response is particularly interesting because Rodgers is no playful hippie but a hyperrational manager who emphasizes tight controls and expresses macho contempt for all touchy-feely business philosophies. He is, however, a fierce competitor who is completely absorbed in his work and wants Cypress employees to be similarly obsessed. Play is, in its many forms, the core culture of Silicon Valley. T. J. Rodgers, interview with the author, December 21, 1995.

44. Tom Peters, interview with the author, May 19, 1997. Published as "The Peters Principles," *Reason* (October 1997): 48.

45. For a good overview of this transformation, see Brink Lindsey, "Big Mistake," *Reason* (February 1996): 20–28.

46. David Brooks, "The Cosmic Capitalists," *The Weekly Standard*, July 14, 1997, p. 23.

47. Ibid., p. 21.

48. Konrad Lorenz, "Psychology and Phylogeny," from *Studies in Animal and Human Behavior*, trans. Robert Martin, in Bruner, Jolly, and Sylva, ed., *Play*, pp. 90-91; Peter C. Reynolds, "Play, Language and Human Evolution" (excerpts from a paper presented at the Annual Meeting of the American Association for the Advancement of Science, Washington, D.C., December 1972) in Bruner, Jolly, and Silva, *Play*, pp. 627–628; M. J. Ellis, *Why People Play* (Englewood Cliffs, N.J.: Prentice-Hall, 1973); Jane Goodall, *The Chimpanzees of Gombe: Patterns of Behavior* (Cambridge, Mass.: Belknap Press of Harvard University Press, 1986), pp. 369–372, 562–564; David Post, e-mail to the author, May 7, 1998.

49. M. J. Ellis, *Why People Play* (Englewood Cliffs, N.J.: Prentice Hall, 1973), pp. 115–116.

50. Mihaly Csikszentmihalyi, *Creativity: Flow and the Psychology of Discovery and Invention* (New York: HarperCollins, 1996), p. 108.

51. Tom Henry, interview with the author, May 22, 1997.

52. Paul Krugman, "The Accidental Theorist," *Slate,* January 30, 1997, pp. 32–34, www.slate.com/dismal/97-01-23/dismal.asp. The article is aimed at William Greider's *One World, Ready or Not:* "I suspect that Greider is the victim of his own earnestness. He clearly takes his subject (and himself) too seriously to play intellectual games. To test-drive an idea with seemingly trivial thought experiments, with hypothetical stories about simplified economies producing hot dogs and buns, would be beneath his dignity. And it is precisely because he is so serious that his ideas are so foolish."

53. Margaret A. Boden, *The Creative Mind: Myths and Mechanisms* (New York: Basic Books, 1991), pp. 13–18, 49–59.

54. Bruce Ames, interview with the author, September 16, 1997. Also, John Tierney, "Not to Worry," *Hippocrates* (January–February 1988): 29–38.

55. Tierney, "Not to Worry," p. 30.

56. Ronald Coase, remarks at the Inaugural Conference for the International Society for New Institutional Economics, Washington University, St. Louis, Missouri, September 20, 1997.

57. Daniel J. Boorstin, "The Fertile Verge: Creativity in the United States" (address at the Carnegie Symposium on Creativity, Inaugural Meeting of the Council of Scholars of the Library of Congress, November 19–20, 1980), p. 3.

CHAPTER EIGHT
ON THE VERGE

1. Tobias Smollett, *The Expedition of Humphry Clinker,* ed. Lewis M. Knapp (London: Oxford University Press, 1966), p. 88. The word for which *heels* has been substituted was *kibes,* an allusion to a line in the gravedigger scene in *Hamlet:* "The age is grown so picked that the toe of the peasant comes so near the heel of the courtier he galls his kibe," *Hamlet,* Act V, scene I, lines 142–144.

2. Typescript headed "Explanatory note. June, 1939," by "TC" in file for General Correspondence, 1891, Telamon Cuyler Collection, University of Georgia. The typescript contains a woman's comments reflecting on her youth in Atlanta and specifically discussing three photos, with the general theme "of how utterly mixed-up was the social life" in the 1890s.

3. Sir James Goldsmith, *The Trap* (New York: Carroll & Graf Publishers, 1994), p. 104.

4. E. F. Schumacher, *Small Is Beautiful: Economics As If People Mattered* (New York: Harper & Row, 1973), p. 68.

5. John Gray, *Beyond the New Right: Markets, Government and the Common Environment* (London: Routledge, 1993), p. 159.

6. John Brewer, *The Pleasures of the Imagination: English Culture in the Eighteenth Century* (New York: Farrar Straus Giroux, 1997), p. 31.

7. Daniel J. Boorstin, "The Fertile Verge: Creativity in the United States" (address to the Carnegie Symposium on Creativity, Inaugural Meeting of the Council of Scholars of the Library of Congress, November 19–20, 1980), pp. 3–4.

8. Ibid., p. 14.

9. Thomas Schatz, *The Genius of the System: Hollywood Filmmaking in the Studio Era* (New York: Henry Holt, 1988), preface by Steven Bach (1996). In his discussions of Irving Thalberg's mastery of the business, Schatz often uses the language of verges: "It was during those screening sessions that Thalberg began to reckon the complex equation of filmmaking, with its curious melding of art and commerce, craft and technology, story and spectacle. . . . Thalberg was not the most powerful man at Loew's/MGM, nor was he the most artistic individual at the studio. But he occupied a critical position in the system—poised, in effect, between New York and L.A., between capitalization and production, between conception and execution. He developed a system that kept those forces in equilibrium, and he carved out his own role as studio production chief in the process. It was a role that Thalberg virtually created and defined, and by the late 1920s, it was the most important role in the Hollywood studio system" (pp. 16, 47).

10. Edward L. Ayers, *The Promise of the New South: Life After Reconstruction* (New York: Oxford University Press, 1992), pp. 405–408: "As their early histories make clear, these churches were profound acts of creation, of invention. They did not grow by default, in isolation from the main currents of American life. In virtually every case, the Holiness and Pentecostal churches grew out of an interaction between movements from outside of the South and indigenous leaders who had already begun to strive toward a new vision. Whites and blacks, men and women, worked together and argued with one another to bring the new churches into being; Southerners clashed and cooperated with Northerners, Midwesterners, and Westerners." In the early decades of the twentieth century, Pentecostal churches were concentrated in rapidly growing and industrializing southern cities. Today, recapitulating their historical association with urbanization, these churches flourish among Latino immigrants, many from rural villages, in such U.S. cities as Los Angeles, as well as among rural migrants to the rapidly expanding cities of Latin America. Ruben Martinez, "An Evangelical Revival," *Los Angeles Times,* March 29, 1998, pp. M1, M3; John Marcom, Jr., "The Fire Down South," *Forbes,* October 15, 1990, pp. 56–71. Marcom focuses on the *favelas,* or shantytowns, of Brazilian cities.

11. Boorstin, "The Fertile Verge," p. 16.

12. Benjamin R. Barber, *Jihad vs. McWorld: How Globalism and Tribalism Are Reshaping the World* (New York: Times Books, 1996).

13. Alan Lomax, *Folk Song Style and Culture* (Washington, D.C.: American Association for the Advancement of Science, 1968), p. 4: "To a folklorist the uprooting and destruction of traditional cultures and the consequent grey-out or disappearance of the human variety presents as serious a threat to the future happiness of mankind as poverty, overpopulation, and even war. Soon there will be nowhere to go and nothing worth staying at home for. . . . Everywhere the pitchmen and the preachers persuade the innocent of the earth to laugh at or to forget the unified folkways of their forefathers, in exchange for broken speech, plastic saints, and novel vices. Meantime Telstar [the communications satellite] rises balefully on the western horizon."

14. Orlando Patterson, "Ecumenical America: Global Culture and the American

Cosmos," *World Policy Journal* (Summer 1994): 104–105.

15. Ibid., pp. 106–108.
16. Scott Kraft, "After *le Brainstorming*, French Start War on Words," *Los Angeles Times*, June 28, 1994, World Report section, p. 1. Also, Scott Kraft, "Jacques Toubon," interview, *Los Angeles Times*, July 10, 1994, p. M3.
17. Frederick Turner, *Tempest, Flute, and Oz: Essays on the Future* (New York: Persea Books, 1991), pp. 23–24. Turner is no relation to Frederick Jackson Turner, of the frontier hypothesis.
18. Ibid., p. 31.
19. Barber, *Jihad vs. McWorld*, p. 242.
20. Ibid., 274. "Casting aside" attributes to these young migrants far more volition than Barber allows; he describes them as passive victims "stripped" of culture by McWorld. Barber quotes the shopping mall line from Dirk Johnson, "It's Not Hip to Stay, Say Small-Town Youth," *The New York Times*, September 5, 1994, p. A-1.
21. Joel Garreau, *The Nine Nations of North America* (New York: Avon, 1981), pp. 155–160.
22. Kevin Heubusch, "Small Is Beautiful," *American Demographics* (January 1998): 42–49. Heubusch defines a "micropolitan" as at least one central city and its surrounding county, which are not part of an official Metropolitan Statistical Area (MSA). The city must have at least fifteen thousand residents and the county at least forty thousand, including the city population. By Heubusch's definition, many fast-growing micropolitans, such as Rocky Mount, North Carolina, have recently become MSAs in their own right, while others, such as Fredericksburg, Virginia, have stretched to become the outer suburbs of existing MSAs.
23. Garreau, *The Nine Nations of North America*, p. 160.
24. Joel Garreau, speech at Reason Weekend, Palm Desert, California, March 8, 1997. Mall-hating social critics inevitably hail from large, long-ago-developed metropolitan areas, usually in the Northeast. A better-informed portrayal of the role malls have played in the rest of the country comes from comedian Brett Butler, describing her home town on the far fringes of Atlanta: "Cumberland Mall's a very big mall there. It used to have 109 stores. When people who had only been to shopping strips their whole lives saw Cumberland Mall, it was like watching Neil Armstrong walk on the moon! You had to blink, there were so many stores!" Malls brought variety, not homogeneity—and in many cases, actually established a town center where none existed. Mark Seal, "The Bell of the South," *American Way*, September 1, 1995, pp. 46–51.
25. See, for instance, Christopher Lasch, *The Revolt of the Elites: And the Betrayal of Democracy* (New York: Norton, 1995), pp. 117–128. The term *third place* comes from Ray Oldenburg, *The Great Good Place: Cafés, Coffee Shops, Community Centers, Beauty Parlors, General Stores, Bars, Hangouts, and How They Get You Through the Day* (New York: Paragon House, 1981).
26. Howard Schultz and Dori Jones Yang, *Pour Your Heart into It: How Starbucks Built a Company One Cup at a Time* (New York: Hyperion, 1997), pp. 118–122.
27. The Greek word for *fish* is formed of the first letters of the words in that lan-

guage for Jesus Christ, Son of God, Savior. As a Christian symbol, a line drawing of a fish predates the cross.

28. Richard Rodriguez, *Days of Obligation: An Argument with My Mexican Father* (New York: Viking, 1992), pp. 197–198.

29. Schultz and Yang. *Pour Your Heart into It,* p. 117.

30. Lily Dizon, "Five Korean Churches May Have to Move," *Los Angeles Times,* June 19, 1997, Orange County edition, p. B-1.

31. Jodi Wilgoren, "Troubled House of Worship," *Los Angeles Times,* July 9, 1997, p. B-1.

32. David W. Chen, "When Churches Want to Grow and Towns Say No," *The New York Times,* October 20, 1996, Section 13NJ, p. 6.

33. Barry Shlachter, "Gay Church Sues City After Zoning Rejection," *The Fort Worth Star-Telegram,* April 26, 1997, p. 21; Nita Thurman, "Cross-Town Conflict," *The Dallas Morning News,* April 10, 1997, p. 23A.

34. Maria Alicia Gaura, "Sikh Temple Plans Run Afoul of Neighbors," *San Francisco Chronicle,* December 25, 1997, p. A21.

35. Paul Rogers, "Hundreds Fight Plan to Build Synagogue," *The Record,* August 12, 1997, p. L-1; Paul Rogers, "Urban Flight: Second Temple Wants to Leave Paterson for Franklin Lakes," *The Record,* December, 18, 1997, p. L-1; Gerald Jacobs, "West Hartford Synagogue Plan Rejected," *The Hartford Courant,* May 7, 1996, p. B1. In most cases, the synagogues have buildings in either cities or older suburbs and want to follow younger families to growing areas. In the West Hartford case, however, the proposed move was to accommodate a dwindling, older congregation whose members could no longer walk across a busy street to services.

36. Chen, "When Churches Want to Grow and Towns Say No."

37. Carol Eisenberg, "Rift over Plans for Synagogue," *Newsday,* October 1, 1980, North Hempstead edition, p. 1.

38. Gaura, "Sikh Temple Plans Run Afoul of Neighbors," p. A21.

39. Henry Allen, "Thanks, Folks. See Ya," *The Washington Post,* February 15, 1996, p. C-1.

40. Joseph Nocera, "Fatal Litigation," *Fortune,* October 16, 1995, pp. 60–82. Nocera reported the net worth of John O'Quinn, a Texas attorney who had at that time earned some $40 million from breast-implant cases, at a half billion dollars. Peter Brimelow and Leslie Spencer, "The Plaintiff Attorneys' Great Honey Rush," *Forbes,* October 16, 1989, pp. 197–203; Deirdre Fanning, "How Lawyers Get Rich," *Forbes,* October 16, 1989, pp. 212–219. Brimelow and Spencer quote Ned Good, a plaintiff attorney making an estimated $3.5 million a year: "We all consider ourselves social engineers. . . . We are crusaders of good. None of us do it for the money, what we are paid is coincidental." Social engineering is, of course, the classic technocratic activity—an attempt to mold the future to one's own idea of perfection.

41. Joel Mokyr, "Progress and Inertia in Technological Change," in John A. James and Mark Thomas, eds., *Capitalism in Context: Essays on Economic Development and Cultural Change in Honor of R. M. Hartwell* (Chicago: University of Chicago Press, 1994), pp. 234–235. See also Joel Mokyr, "Man vs. Machine,"

Reason (January 1996): pp 59–62, a review of Kirkpatrick Sale's *Rebels Against the Future*. In this context, Mokyr includes as "technology" not just physical inventions but organizational forms.

42. Joel Mokyr, "Creative Forces," *Reason* (May 1993): p 65.
43. David Post, interview with the author, March 16, 1998.
44. Mokyr, "Creative Forces," p. 66.
45. David S. Landes, *Revolution in Time: Clocks and the Making of the Modern World* (Cambridge, Mass.: Harvard University Press, 1983), p. 27. Joseph Needham, *Science in Traditional China* (Cambridge, Mass.: Harvard University Press, 1981), pp. 73–76. Needham notes that during the T'ang dynasty (618–906), "foreign people and things were all the rage [and] there was hardly a city in China unfamiliar with the *hu* [Arab and Persian] merchants."
46. Joel Mokyr, *The Lever of Riches: Technological Creativity and Economic Progress* (New York: Oxford University Press, 1990), pp. 209–238; Needham, *Science in Traditional China*.
47. Joseph Needham, Wang Ling, and Lu Gwei-Djen, *Science and Civilization in China*, vol. 4, part III (Cambridge: Cambridge University Press, 1971), pp. 524–528.
48. Landes, *Revolution in Time*, p. 33.
49. Ibid.
50. Wen-yuan Qian, *The Great Inertia: Scientific Stagnation in Traditional China* (London: Croom Helm, 1985), p. 30.
51. Mokyr, *The Lever of Riches*, p. 237.
52. Hillary Rodham Clinton, speech at the Annual Meeting of the World Economic Forum, Davos, Switzerland, February 2, 1998. Aside from the flaws in Bell's own argument, discussed in Chapter 7—and the utter lack of empirical evidence that capitalism is languishing—there is something unseemly about a wealthy and powerful woman (and former Wal-Mart director) lecturing a selection of the world's wealthiest people on the evils of consumer aspirations. Intellectuals easily accept such ideas because they tend not to count their own pleasures, such as travel, books, art, gourmet food, or tax-deductible conferences in Switzerland, as "consumerist" indulgences. And for those motivated primarily by power or fame, of course, consumer products are trivial pleasures.
53. See, for instance, Irving Kristol, "Capitalism, Socialism, and Nihilism," in *Two Cheers for Capitalism* (New York: Mentor, 1978), pp. 51–65.
54. Mancur Olson, *The Rise and Decline of Nations: Economic Growth, Stagflation, and Social Rigidities* (New Haven: Yale University Press, 1982).
55. Joseph A. Schumpeter, *Capitalism, Socialism and Democracy*, introduction by Tom Bottomore (New York: Harper Torchbooks, 1976), pp. 143–155. Schumpeter's book was originally published in 1942.
56. In March 1995, Representatives Charles Schumer (D-N.Y.) and Sam Gejdenson (D-Conn.) held a press conference and released a report denouncing breakfast cereal companies for high prices. They demanded an antitrust investigation. Nothing much came of their demands, but they did attract considerable media attention. Laura B. Benko, "Lawmakers Call Cereal Prices

Unfair," *Los Angeles Times,* March 8, 1995, p. D-2; Marian Burros, "U.S. Is Urged to Investigate Cereal Prices," *The New York Times,* March 8, 1995, p. C-8. As reporters noted at the time, prices fluctuate and all major cereal makers were experimenting with different strategies, including reducing cents-off coupons and cutting prices, reducing coupons but spending the savings on more advertising, and offering low-price generic cereals packaged in plastic bags. Burros also did a price and taste comparison of name-brand and store-brand cereals, concluding that in most cases store brands were just as good and much cheaper. Marian Burros, "Eating Well; Crackle, Pop, Compare," *The New York Times,* March 15, 1995, p. C-1. The dynamic analysis of the news reporters was in sharp contrast to the politicians' crisis rhetoric.

57. Larry Mantle, *Air Talk,* KPCC-FM, February 9, 1998.
58. Jonathan Rauch, *Kindly Inquisitors: The New Attacks on Free Thought* (Chicago: University of Chicago Press, 1993), p. 154.
59. Martha Bayles, "Censorship, Politics, and the Culture of Transgression," lecture for the Gould Center's Fall 1997 series, Claremont McKenna College, Claremont, California, December 4, 1997.
60. Oliver Morton, "Overcoming Yuk," *Wired* (January 1998): 44.
61. James Howard Kunstler, "The War on Cars," Dialogue with James Q. Wilson, Message 4, February 5, 1998, *Slate,* www.slate.com/Code/DDD/DDD.asp?file=Cars&iMsg=4.
62. Fareed Zakaria, "Paris Is Burning," *The New Republic,* January 22, 1996, pp. 28–29.
63. Brink Lindsey, interview with the author, April 12, 1996.
64. The argument about Mars has been made, in varying forms, by such diverse dynamists as poet Frederick Turner, astrophysicist and science-fiction writer Gregory Benford, and economist Julian Simon.
65. Friedrich A. Hayek, *The Constitution of Liberty* (Chicago: University of Chicago Press, 1960), p. 41.

INDEX